the
Ultimate
Omega-3
Diet

the Ultimate Omega-3 Diet

**Maximize the Power of Omega-3s to
Supercharge Your Health, Battle Inflammation,
and Keep Your Mind Sharp**

EVELYN TRIBOLE, M.S., RD

New York Chicago San Francisco Lisbon London Madrid Mexico City
Milan New Delhi San Juan Seoul Singapore Sydney Toronto

Library of Congress Cataloging-in-Publication Data

Tribole, Evelyn, 1959–
    The ultimate omega-3 diet : maximize the power of omega-3s to supercharge your health,
  battle inflammation, and keep your mind sharp / Evelyn Tribole. — 1st ed.
      p.   cm.
  Includes bibliographical references and index.
  ISBN-13: 978-0-07-146986-9 (alk. paper)
  ISBN-10:   0-07-146986-9
  1. Omega-3 fatty acids—Health aspects.   2. Essential fatty acids in human nutrition.
3. Nutrition.   4. Diet.   5. Self-care, Health.   I. Title.

QP752.O44T7555   2007
612.3'97—dc22   2006103345

1 2 3 4 5 6 7 8 9 10 11 12 13 14 15 16 17 18 19 20 21 22 23 24   FGR/FGR   0 9 8 7

ISBN-13: 978-0-07-146986-9
ISBN-10:   0-07-146986-9

Interior design by Monica Baziuk

McGraw-Hill books are available at special quantity discounts to use as premiums and sales
promotions, or for use in corporate training programs. For more information, please write to the
Director of Special Sales, Professional Publishing, McGraw-Hill, Two Penn Plaza, New York, NY
10121-2298. Or contact your local bookstore.

The information contained in this book is intended to provide helpful and informative material
on the subject addressed. It is not intended to serve as a replacement for professional medical
advice. A health-care professional should be consulted regarding your specific situation.

This book is printed on acid-free paper.

To my mother, Dolores Grimm;
your unconditional love dances in my heart.

Contents

Acknowledgments

I AM ESPECIALLY GRATEFUL to the scientists from around the world who provided answers on this complex topic, offering lengthy discussions and thoughtful correspondence. Never have I witnessed such a passionate group of researchers so enthusiastic about their research on omega-3 fatty acids (not that they all agree—far from it). A special thank-you to these scholars for reviewing my manuscript and sharing their valuable suggestions:

- Penny Kris-Etherton, Ph.D., RD, Department of Nutritional Sciences, Pennsylvania State University
- Sonja L. Connor, M.S., RD, Departments of Medicine and Pediatrics, Oregon Health Sciences University
- Scott Kahan, M.D., Director, Institute for Evidence-Based Nutrition, Johns Hopkins University
- William E. M. Lands, Ph.D., omega-3 fat pioneer and biochemist extraordinaire

To the scientists attending the 2006 conference of the International Society for the Study of Fatty Acids and Lipids (ISSFAL) in Australia, thank you for taking the time to answer my questions, regardless of the venue (including elevators), particularly Stephen Cunnane, Ph.D.; Joseph Hibbeln, M.D.; Joyce Nettleton, D.Sc., RD;

Wendy Oddy, Ph.D., M.P.H.; Robert Pawlosky, Ph.D.; Stanley Rapport, M.D.; and Jay Whelan, Ph.D., M.P.H. Also, I appreciated the e-mail and phone discussions from Gérard Ailhaud, Ph.D., and his research team: Sebastian Cianci; Les Cleland, Ph.D., FRAC; William S. Harris, Ph.D.; Ray Rice, Ph.D.; Norman Salem Jr., Ph.D.; David Trott, doctoral candidate; and Lauren Bartell Weiss, M.S.

My deepest gratitude to my trusty, bleary-eyed reviewers and sounding board, who read multiple revisions of my manuscript and listened to my "omega on my mind" rants: Sharon Bear, Ph.D.; Diane Keddy, M.S., RD; Dale Kiken, Esq.; and Elaine Roberts. Also, I am indebted to my assistant and future dietitian, Tram Tran, who worked without complaint; no task was too small. A special thank-you to my family and dearest friends for their patience and understanding while I was sequestered away to research and complete this project.

Lastly, I am indebted to my longtime agent, David Hale Smith, who championed my book from inception to completion. And thank you to Deborah Brody, my editor, for keeping with the vision.

the
Ultimate
Omega-3
Diet

PART 1

The **Basics** of Omega Fats: A Mini Primer

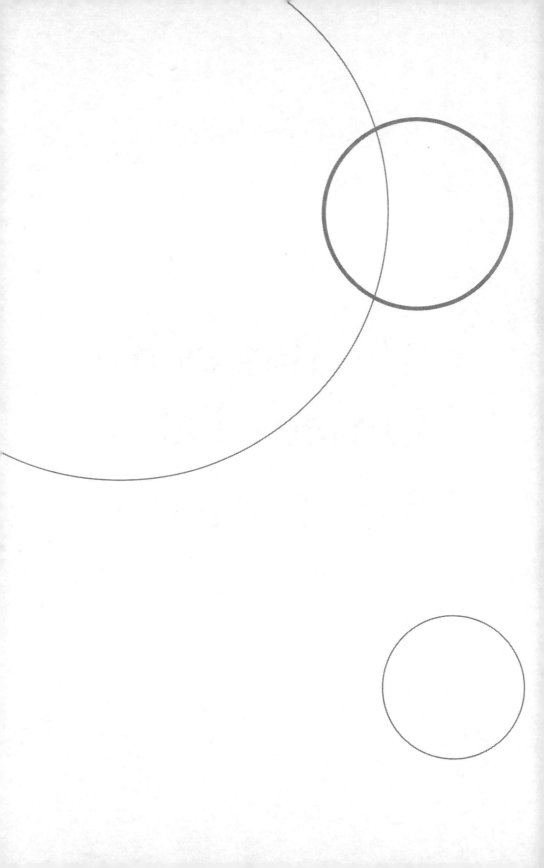

Omega-3 and Omega-6 Fats

U NLESS YOU LIVE in an isolated bubble, you have likely seen the bounty of headline-grabbing studies on omega-3 fats, with their far-reaching benefits from preventing cancer and heart attacks to treating depression and arthritis. Indeed, short of describing these fats as a panacea, the research is quite astounding.

How can one type of fat affect so many different parts of your body (such as your brain and heart) and ultimately influence your health and well-being? There are two key reasons. First, omega-3 fats are really like vitamins (originally called vitamin F when discovered). Unfortunately, the vast majority of Americans are deficient in vitamin F or omega-3 fats.

Second, although few people know it, we have a striking fat imbalance in our diet. The typical American diet dramatically antagonizes the benefits of omega-3 fats in the body. *Even if you consider yourself health-conscious, you are not likely free of this problem!* The problem of this dietary fat imbalance affects you whether you eat heart-healthy, are a strict vegetarian, have become an Atkins carnivore, or something in between. We eat too much of the so-called heart-healthy fats, which, ironically, interfere with the benefits of omega-3 fats in our bodies. These supposedly healthful fats are the omega-6 fats, which have flooded our food supply in the forms of margarine, soybean oil, corn oil, safflower oil, cottonseed oil, and sunflower oil.

In short, we have two key problems. We don't eat enough (and the right kinds) of omega-3 fats; call this problem *omega-3 fat deficiency*. And we eat too much of the so-called healthy fats that hamper omega-3 fat's benefits, causing what some researchers call *omega-6 fat syndrome*. Let's take a closer look.

Omega-3 Fat Is a Vitamin

In the 1920s, one of the several omega-3 fats was discovered. The researchers determined that it is essential for health and met the scientific criteria to be called a vitamin. Appropriately, this fat was named "vitamin F." Yet you probably haven't heard of vitamin F.

Why not? You can rule out omega-3's fatty nature as the reason it lacks "vitamin status," because there are other fat-based vitamins: vitamins A, D, E, and K. Instead, chalk it up to a bit of politics and bad timing. At the time of the vitamin F discovery, vitamin E also had just been discovered. Because of the scientific excitement over the newly discovered vitamin E, vitamin F was ignored and disappeared into oblivion (until the last decade). Although research on omega-3 fats has exploded, the name *vitamin F* never resurfaced.

It's too bad that the *vitamin F* nomenclature didn't stick. That term alone would emphasize how essential these fats are to our body. As with vitamins, our body can't make these fats (or enough of them), so they are required in our diet. Also, a step up to "vitamin status" could have spurred earlier research on the vital roles that omega-3 fats play in human health and disease prevention.

After the discovery of omega-3 fats, 50 years passed until the first human case of omega-3 fat deficiency was identified. A child too sick to eat was fed intravenously with a mixture that contained no omega-3 fats. Instead of getting better, the child got unexpectedly worse and displayed symptoms of numbness, tingling, weakness, inability to walk, leg pain, psychological disturbances, and blurred vision. Ralph

T. Holman, an expert in omega-3 fats, identified the cause of the child's problem as a deficiency of omega-3 fatty acids. His discovery put omega-3 fats on the map, beyond an esoteric research interest.

The incredible research into omega-3 fats *within the context of their role as an essential vitamin* helps to explain omega-3's sweeping effects on health and disease. A new picture emerges of a nutrient deficiency that wreaks havoc in many different parts of the body, from the inner workings of the brain to the battlegrounds of immunity and inflammation. A vast majority of Americans do not get enough omega-3 fats in their diet.

Different Omega-3 Fats Affect Your Body in Different Ways

Just as there is more than one type of B vitamin (vitamins B_1, B_2, B_{12}, and so forth), there is more than one type of omega-3 fatty acid. Each of these omega-3 fatty acids affects your body in different ways. The types of omega-3 fatty acids found in plant foods are very different from those found in fish. So if you are tanking up on plant sources of omega-3 fat, such as flax meal or flaxseed oil, you still could be deficient in the other omega-3 fats that are found primarily in fish. For example, many of the foods that boast of their omega-3 fat content are fortified with the plant form of omega-3 fat, not the types found in fish. This is not necessarily bad, but some consumers might be under the wrong impression that they are getting enough omega-3 fats when they are actually still deficient in certain types.

Structural Sentries

Omega-3 fats are involved in nearly every key function in the body and are an important structural part of *every* cell in your body. They are not the kind of fat that sits around for a rainy-day famine, waiting to be utilized. Let's look briefly at some of these vital roles:

- **Biological fence.** Omega-3 fats are the gatekeepers of cells. They make up the key architecture of the membrane, the biological fence that surrounds each cell. This affects the fluidity of the cells, which in turn influences a number of activities in your body.

Notably, the composition and fluidity of cell membranes depend to a great extent on what you eat.

- **Brain's building blocks.** Omega-3 fats are the key building blocks of the brain and eyes. They are to your brain as calcium is to your bones. In fact, the majority of the brain (60 percent) is composed of fat—the second highest concentration of fat in the body.

Essential Activities

Omega-3 fats are industrious worker bees throughout your body. Here's a glimpse at their far-reaching impact on your health:

- **Cellular communication.** The cells in your body use wireless communication, and omega-3 fats help them stay in touch. It's a lot like cell phone reception. If you don't have enough omega-3 fats, your cell-to-cell communication can be "out of range." This is especially significant to brain function, which affects mood, learning, concentration, and memory.

- **Turning genes on and off.** Throughout your life, your genes are constantly being regulated, or turned on or off like a light switch. Amazingly, according to a new and dynamic area of research called nutrigenomics, what we eat influences our genes. Omega-3 fats regulate genes in our brain and other parts of our body.

- **Potent power brokers.** Omega-3 fats help create highly potent substances called *eicosanoids*. Eicosanoids have an impact on a wide range of functions, including fertility, digestion, kidney function, breathing, blood flow, heart health, and immunity.

- **Fighting inflammation.** Like the nutritional equivalent of aspirin, omega-3 fats help fight inflammation and infection. This has many implications for autoimmune and inflammation disorders, including asthma, arthritis, lupus, inflammatory bowel disorders, psoriasis, cancer, allergies, and migraines.

Specific Roles in Your Body

As if these activities were not impressive enough, omega-3 fats play key roles in maintaining the health of your organs. Recall the symptoms of the sick child who contracted omega-3 fatty-acid deficiency: numbness, tingling, weakness, inability to walk, leg pain, psychological disturbances, and blurred vision. These symptoms illustrate the many different body functions affected by omega-3 fats:

- **Brain.** Omega-3s help make and regulate key chemicals in the brain that affect your mood. These fats are required for growth and development of the brain, not to mention brain cell communication, which can affect learning and IQ. This role of omega-3s has many implications for mood and learning disorders, dementia, stress, and hostility.

- **Vision.** Omega-3 fats are critical for vision throughout the life cycle, from eyesight development in the womb to prevention of vision problems in the twilight years. This role has many implications for vision disorders and learning.

- **Blood.** While blood is supposed to be thicker than water, blood thickness (viscosity) can be hazardous to your health. Omega fats keep your blood flowing smoothly, which allows your heart to pump blood with less effort. Omega-3 fats also protect your arteries by keeping them elastic and flexible. This role has many implications for heart disease and stroke.

- **Heart's natural pacemaker.** Omega-3 fats help the heart maintain a steady and slower beat. This may help prevent sudden cardiac death, which is a frequent consequence of cardiac arrhythmia.

- **Sturdy bones.** Omega-3 fats help increase calcium absorption and bone formation, and they prevent destruction of cartilage, thus playing a role in preventing and treating osteoporosis.

It's not too hard to imagine that inadequate intakes of omega-3 will have some effect on every part of the body, including the brain. Clearly, omega-3s are required for a sound body and mind!

Omega-6 Fat Syndrome

The last reason that omega-3 fats affect so many different aspects of your body and, ultimately, your health involves their interaction with another key group of fats, omega-6 fats. We consume omega-6s in soybean oil, cottonseed oil, safflower oil, corn oil, sunflower oil, margarines, and salad dressings.

When I was researching this book, I contacted a prominent omega-3 fat researcher at the National Institutes of Health (NIH). He began the interview by asking me a rhetorical question: "Do you know why omega-3 fats affect so many parts of our body and so many diseases?" He continued, "It's because too much omega-6 fats in our diet prevent omega-3 fats from doing their normal course of work in our body." Then he proceeded to describe how he balanced the fat in his own diet by cutting out omega-6 fats, food by food. Wow.

If you have never heard of omega-6 fat, you are not alone. When people hear the term *omega*, they often assume omega-6s are beneficial and related to omega-3 fats. While both groups of fats work together very closely, they have opposite effects in the body, like a seesaw. And as with children on a seesaw, the actions of one affect the other. If these fats are not balanced in your diet, they can dramatically affect your health. That's the problem. The American diet is bombarded with unhealthful levels of omega-6 fats, which impede the benefits of omega-3 fats.

Omega-6 Fats Promote Disease

The problem with eating too much omega-6 fats is that they are disease promoting. In fact, the NIH's Essential Fats Education program makes a profound declaration on its website: excessive omega-6 fats in the diet trigger a rise in health problems, including heart attacks, blood clots, arthritis, asthma, menstrual cramps, headaches, and tumor metastases.

Eating too much omega-6 fat is a predicament affecting most Westernized countries, not just the United States. This quandary has been documented in many cultures and is referred to as a health paradox or *omega-6 fat syndrome.*

Most Omega-6 Fats Are Found in "Healthy" Oils

The paradox is that omega-6 fats have been indiscriminately promoted as "heart-healthy fats." Many well-meaning health organizations touted "heart-healthy" oils (including corn oil, soybean oil, and margarine) to lower blood cholesterol and reduce the risk of heart disease. Consumers were (and are) urged to replace artery-clogging saturated fats in their diet with heart-smart polyunsaturated oils, *which consist primarily of omega-6 fats.*

Unwittingly, this health advice triggered people to eat more of the fats that work *against* the omega-3s. The so-called heart-healthy omega-6 oils displaced other fats in many people's diets. Grocery store shelves overflowed (and still do) with foods containing "heart-smart" oils. But it turns out that the idea of eating polyunsaturated fats to prevent heart disease was based on an incomplete picture; emerging studies have shown otherwise. (This is discussed in depth in Chapter 5.)

Countries including Israel embraced heart-healthy eating by eating more polyunsaturated oils (omega-6 fats). Israel is especially notable because it consequently has one of the world's greatest intakes of omega-6 fats. But with the increase of omega-6 fats came an increase in Western diseases such as cancer and diabetes.

Researchers used the term *omega-6 fat syndrome* to describe the cause of chronic illness plaguing an unusually healthy group of people in Okinawa, a region of Japan. The scientists discovered that Okinawans were eating too much omega-6 fat at the expense of omega-3 fat, and this imbalance was at the root of their new chronic health problems.

We Eat Fat That Did Not Exist 100 Years Ago

Today, we eat fats that didn't exist a century ago, including cotton-seed oil. Check the ingredients list on some of your favorite foods. More often than not, it will be listed, as it's among the top four oils consumed in the United States. Our foods are now filled with omega-6 fats because of technology and pressure to eat more heart-smart fats.

Farming Practices Increase Omega-6 Fats in Meats and Plant Foods

Lastly, agricultural practices have dramatically altered the content of omega-6 and omega-3 fats in our diet. Plant foods used to have higher omega-3 fat levels, which had a positive trickle-down effect on the rest of our diet. In the bygone days of cattle grazing, cows used to nibble on plants containing omega-3s. And in the you-are-what-you-eat manner, these cows incorporated omega-3 fat into their own body. Voilà: the cows yielded milk and meat containing omega-3 fats, which in turn would be eaten by consumers. Today the amount of omega-3 fat in commercial beef is virtually undetectable. Instead, feedlot animals eat a grain-based diet, which offers little in the way of omega-3 but is higher in omega-6. Consequently, their meats are also higher in omega-6 fat.

We Need to Fix the Omega Fat Imbalance

Indeed, the typical Western diet delivers a double whammy: insufficient omega-3 fats and too many omega-6 fats. The consequence is many chronic diseases, from osteoporosis to inflammation disorders, which we can't cure simply by reaching for a fish oil supplement. *If you have too much omega-6 fat in the diet, it interferes with the benefits of omega-3 fats!* A healthy balance of omega-6 fats and omega-3 fats in our diet is a key health factor that has been ignored for too long. Whereas our ancestors ate equal proportions of these fats, today the omega-6 fats in the American diet outnumber omega-3 fats by 10- to 20-fold!

Vegetarians are not off the hook, because studies show that they eat even more omega-6 fat in their diets than the typical person who eats meat. At the other extreme, those indulging in bacon and cream cheese in the name of weight loss, dieting Atkins style, also have a problem. These fats—saturated fats—also compete against the omega-3s.

I wrote *The Ultimate Omega-3 Diet* to help solve our fat imbalance and its ensuing health problems. I want to be clear, however, that I use the term *diet* to describe a pattern of eating, not a method for weight loss. I am strongly against weight-loss diets because of the impact on mind and body.[1]

The Ultimate Omega-3 Diet is divided into four parts. The first part of the book is a mini primer on omega-3 and omega-6 fats, including how these fats work in tandem and what happens to your health when they are out of balance in your diet. The second part of the book explains the truly astounding benefits of omega-3 fats. (Each chapter stands alone. If you want the scientific info, it's in Part 2. If you just want to know what and how to eat, you can skip this section entirely.) The research is quite stunning, showing that omega-3 fats play a key role in preventing many illnesses and conditions:

- Inflammation
- Stroke
- Allergies
- Cancer
- Alzheimer's disease

They may also be effective in treating:

- Depression
- Attention deficit disorder
- Dyslexia

---

1. For more information, see E. Tribole and E. Resch, *Intuitive Eating* 2nd Ed. New York: St. Martin's Griffin, 2003.

- Cystic fibrosis
- Asthma
- Arthritis

Lastly, omega-3s have been shown to play a key role in:

- Brain development and function
- Learning and IQ

The key how-to advice in this book comes in Part 3, "How to Omega-Optimize Your Diet." This section describes how you can get the most benefit out of your omega-3 fats, in four key steps, each delineated in a separate chapter. Chapters 10 and 11 tell you how to eat enough of two categories of omega-3 fats: short-chain and long-chain omega-3s. Chapter 12 offers advice on omega-3 supplements. And Chapter 13 addresses the other side of the fat equation: how to cut your intake of omega-6 foods.

The last part of the book, "The Ultimate Omega-3 Lifestyle," provides makeovers, menus, and recipes balanced in their omega-3 and omega-6 fat content. The makeover section shows how to implement the steps to maximize your omega-3 fats, regardless of your lifestyle. I created menus with different themes to help with your particular eating style, from eating out to "I hate fish." There are also nearly 40 recipes, each of which describes the omega-optimize technique, so you can apply these strategies to get the most out of omega-3s in your own favorite recipes.

Throughout the chapters, charts and tables will help you find foods that are high in omega-3 fats and low in omega-6 fats. Appendix A is a handy listing of specific foods' omega-3 and omega-6 fat content, including the ratio of the two fats. Appendix B offers metric conversions you can apply to the recipes if you prefer to use the metric system. I've also included an in-depth references section, which includes the key studies and sources for the information presented in this book.

Omega Fats Are Not Created Equal

"I THOUGHT ALL OMEGA fats are healthy." I can't tell you how often I hear people saying this.

While many people imagine that the term *omega* is synonymous with omega-3 fats, that impression is far from correct. It's easy to get confused, because the fats and their names can be a bewildering tower of Babel, especially for the uninitiated. There are different omega fat families, which have completely different effects on health and disease. Even within the category of omega-3 fats, you'll find more than one type. Then there are saturated and unsaturated fats (with the latter no longer universally viewed as *the* healthy class of fats).

How do you keep it all straight? Before we delve into the specifics of omega-3 fats and how to get them to work best for you (let alone get enough of them), let's get familiar with the various types of fat. Figure 2.1 provides a general overview of how the different fats we eat are interrelated.

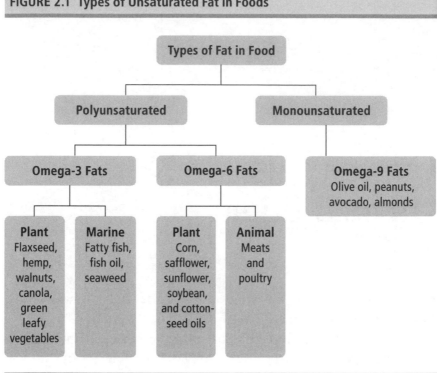

FIGURE 2.1　Types of Unsaturated Fat in Foods

Meet the Omega Families

Omega actually refers to the system of how the fatty-acid atoms are counted and named (see sidebar). Each fat family is very different from the other, as in a neighborhood, where families reside on the same street but each at a different address, which signifies a completely different household. (You don't expect the family living on 33 Main Street to be the same family living on 66 Main Street.) We will focus primarily on the omega-3 and omega-6 families, but you might like to know that olive oil comes from the omega-9 fat family, which is considered healthful.

Each omega family has individual members called fatty acids, each with a different name. Each omega-3 and omega-6 fat family has a parent fatty acid, from which the other individual fats can

What Is "Omega"?

The term *omega* refers to how the various fat families are named, based on a counting system. Fat molecules are long; the typical fat molecule found in food is between 12 and 22 carbon atoms long. Think of each carbon atom as a link in a bracelet. We would represent a 22-carbon "bracelet" this way:

C-C-C-C-C-C-C-C-C-C-C-C-C-C-C-C-C-C-C-C-C-C

That's a lot of carbons to count. To save time, scientists count from the end of the chain, where the first unsaturated pair of carbons is located (known as a double-bond arrangement). So that everyone remembers this counting system, the beginning of the chain is designated as the *alpha* side, named after the first letter in the Greek alphabet. The end of the chain is the *omega* side, named after the last letter in the Greek alphabet.

C-C-C-C-C-C-C-C-C-C-C-C-C-C-C-C-C-C-C-C-C-C
Alpha   Omega

In the case of the omega-3 family, the double-bond arrangement is located three carbons from the end (the omega side):

C-C-C-C-C-C-C-C-C-C-C-C-C-C-C=C-C-C

Similarly, in the case of the omega-6 family, the double bond is six carbons from the end:

C-C-C-C-C-C-C-C-C-C-C=C-C-C-C-C-C

This difference may seem inconsequential, but it's huge. It's like the impact the location of a decimal point has on a number (especially money!). For example, would you rather have $1.500000 or $1500.000? Both quantities have the same digits, but the values

Continued

of these amounts differ considerably, just because of where the decimal is placed. The one dollar and fifty cents is like the omega-6 fats; the decimal point is six digits from the end. Likewise, the fifteen hundred dollars is like the omega-3 fats; the decimal point is three digits from the end. Just as a decimal point can make numbers far different, the location of the initial omega bond on a fat molecule makes a huge biological difference to the body.

originate. Notably, each of these parents is considered an *essential fat*, meaning the body cannot make it and it needs to be supplied by the diet. Table 2.1 identifies dietary sources of the major types of omega-3 and omega-6 fatty acids.

The individual fatty acids differ in significant ways. The omega-3 fat found in plants is very different from the omega-3 fatty acids found in seafood. *It's possible to eat plenty of plant-based omega-3 fats but still be deficient in the other omega-3 fatty acids found in marine foods.* This is a big source of confusion for consumers. Here's a brief description of the key omega-3 fatty acids:

TABLE 2.1 Omega-6 and Omega-3 Fats at a Glance

	Omega-3 Family	Omega-6 Family
Omega parent (essential fatty acid)	*Alpha-linolenic acid (ALA)*: flax oil, canola oil, hemp, green leafy vegetables like spinach, walnuts	*Linoleic acid (LA)*: soybean oil, corn oil, safflower oil, sunflower oil, cottonseed oil
Omega potent kids (biological power brokers)	*Eicosapentaenoic acid (EPA)* and *docosahexaenoic acid (DHA)*: fatty fish and their oils, some seaweeds, enriched foods	*Arachidonic acid (AA)*: meats and poultry

- **Alpha-linolenic acid (ALA).** The parent of all the fatty acids in the omega-3 family is known as alpha-linolenic acid (ALA). Technically, all the omega-3 fatty acids can be made or originate from ALA, but research shows that this is rarely the case. ALA is one of the shortest among the omega-3 fats, making it a short-chain fatty acid (see Table 2.2). ALA is found in plants, green leafy vegetables, flax oil, canola oil, and hemp.

- **Eicosapentaenoic acid (EPA) and docosahexaenoic acid (DHA).** EPA and DHA are known collectively as long-chain fats and are found primarily in fish and fish oil. Stories about the marvelous benefits of omega-3 fats usually involve one (or both) of these powerful fatty acids.

Here's the problem. Although laboratory tests showed that ALA can be made into EPA and eventually DHA, recent studies on humans indicate that this is not what the human body actually does. Therefore, you cannot assume that if you eat the parent form of omega-3 fats, ALA, it will indeed create EPA and DHA. If you take flaxseed oil supplements or eat a lot of flax foods as your primary source of omega-3 fats, they provide ALA, but you could still be deficient in EPA and DHA. In fact, the latest research shows that less than 1 percent of ALA gets made into EPA, and seldom (if ever) does it make DHA. That's why many researchers believe that all three of these omega-3 fats are essential.

TABLE 2.2 The Key Omega-3 Fats

Fatty Acid	Category	Size	Main Sources
Alpha-linolenic acid (ALA)	Polyunsaturate	Short-chain	Plants
Eicosapentaenoic acid (EPA)	Polyunsaturate	Long-chain	Fish
Docosahexaenoic acid (DHA)	Polyunsaturate	Long-chain	Fish

Meet the Omega-6 Fat Family

Omega-6 fats, when eaten in excess, can cause a variety of health problems. The omega-6 fat problem is a bit like Americans' excess consumption of salt (sodium). Sodium is a nutrient that is very easy to get in the diet without ever lifting a saltshaker. Similarly, omega-6 fats are in nearly every food we eat, so we really don't need to make an extra effort to eat them. Here's a brief description of the key omega-6 fatty acids:

- **Linoleic acid (LA).** The omega-6 parent, linoleic acid (LA), accounts for the majority of polyunsaturated fats in the American diet and is considered an essential fat. (Yes, you are reading this name correctly; it is remarkably similar to the omega-3 fat parent, alpha-linolenic acid.)

- **Arachidonic acid (AA).** Arachidonic acid can be found in animal products but is readily made from the parent omega-6 fat, LA. (This is unlike omega-3 fats, where there is limited conversion of the parent to its potent "kids.") Too much of this fat in the body can trigger inflammation and cause blood clotting. AA is also known as the long-chain omega-6 fatty acid.

Fat Family Rivalry: Omega-6 Versus Omega-3 Fats

Both omega-3 and omega-6 fats make powerful substances in your body that play key roles in the structure and function of *every* cell and ultimately your health and well-being. But they are chemically distinct families with opposite effects on your body. For example, a diet high in omega-6 fats promotes blood clotting, while omega-3 fats prevent the blood cells from clumping. Omega-6 fats act to raise blood pressure, while omega-3 fats work to lower blood pressure.

   Once you eat these fats and they enter your body, they are in direct competition with each other. Like rival gangs, both of these fat families compete for the same limited resources (enzymes) to make their subsequent potent compounds. The bigger family will "win" the resources that ultimately shift your body toward health or disease.

Saturated Versus Unsaturated Fat: A Big Difference to Your Health

No fat that you eat, whether oil or butter, is made up of just one particular type of fatty acid. For example, butter is known as a saturated fat (and indeed has a high level of this fat), but as shown in Table 2.3, it still has a bit of polyunsaturated and monounsaturated fats. Olive oil is known as a monounsaturated fat but contains some saturated and polyunsaturated fat. And canola oil is 7 percent saturated fat, 59 percent monounsaturated fat, and 30 percent polyunsaturated fat. Its polyunsaturated fat consists of 69 percent omega-6 fat and 31 percent omega-3 fat.

Fats commonly thought of as healthful are not necessarily so. Researchers realize that it is no longer adequate to assume that all fats within a class behave the same way in our bodies. This is especially true for polyunsaturated fats, including omega-3 and omega-6 fat families. But let's begin with the saturated fats, as little has changed—they are still widely considered a health problem.

TABLE 2.3 Comparison of Dietary Fats in Common Oils and Butter

Oil	Saturated %	Monoun-saturated %	Polyunsaturated Fat		
			% Total	%Omega-6	%Omega-3
Butter	51	21	3	90	0.3
Canola oil	7	59	30	69	31
Corn oil	13	28	55	98	2
Flaxseed oil	9	20	66	19	81
Olive oil	14	73	11	93	7
Soybean oil	14	23	58	88	12

Saturated Fats

The saturated fats are the infamous artery-clogging fats that raise blood cholesterol. They are called "saturated" because of how their carbon atoms are connected. (Technically, they are 100 percent *saturated* with *hydrogen* atoms.) These fats are found in animal products, including meats, poultry, dairy products, eggs, and butter, and in some plant foods, including palm oil, palm kernel oil, and hydrogenated vegetable oil. Our bodies have no need for saturated fat. Saturated fats interfere with the beneficial effects of omega-3 fats in the body.

Unsaturated Fats

Unsaturated fats may be monounsaturated or polyunsaturated. *Monounsaturated fats* have one pair of carbon atoms that are not saturated with hydrogen atoms (hence the term *mono*). They include

Hydrogenation: How Food Manufacturers Turn Polyunsaturated Fat into Saturated Fat

When food manufacturers add hydrogen to PUFA oil, it becomes *hydrogenated* oil. This chemical process converts oil into a saturated fat (saturated with hydrogen), which makes the oil hard or solid. These fats have typically been used in foods where a firmer texture is preferred, such as stick margarine.

During hydrogenation, *trans fats* are created. These nefarious fats are created when oil is partially hydrogenated. The oil's chemical architecture is twisted into a "trans" configuration, which is like taking the two wheels on a bicycle and contorting them. As a result, you still have a bike with two wheels, but the ride is bumpy and potentially dangerous. These fats trigger double trouble for the heart: they raise LDL (bad) cholesterol and lower HDL (good) cholesterol. Trans fats also compete and interfere with omega-3 fats in the body.

olive oil, which is the dominant type of this fat in the diet. Canola oil also is high in monounsaturated fat. Monounsaturated fats are generally recognized as healthful types of fats.

Polyunsaturated fatty acids (PUFAs) have at least two pairs of carbons that are not saturated with hydrogen. Polyunsaturated fats come in different lengths, known either as short or long chain, based on the number of carbons.

A polyunsaturated fatty acid with at least 20 carbon atoms is a *long-chain polyunsaturated fatty acid*. For example, the plant source of omega-3 fat, ALA, has 18 carbons and is considered a short-chain PUFA, while EPA has 20 carbons and is considered a long-chain PUFA (DHA has 22 carbons). Omega-3 and omega-6 fats are both polyunsaturated; EPA and DHA are long-chain omega-3 fats, and arachidonic acid (AA) is the long-chain omega-6 fat.

For a quick summary of these categories and their effects on health, see Table 2.4.

TABLE 2.4 How the Different Fats Affect Health and Omega-3 Function

Type of Fat	General Health Effect	Effect on Omega-3 Function in the Body	Food Sources
Saturated fat	Negative	Negative	Full-fat dairy (such as butter, ice cream), meats, palm oil, poultry fat (skin)
Monounsaturated fat	Positive	Neutral	Olive oil, canola oil
Polyunsaturated fat: omega-3	Positive	Positive	Fatty fish, walnuts, flax, hemp, green leafy vegetables
Polyunsaturated fat: omega-6	Negative when in excess (main contributor to inflammation); lowers cholesterol	Negative	Corn oil, safflower oil, sunflower oil, soybean oil, cottonseed oil, traditionally raised meats and poultry
Trans fat	Negative	Negative	Fried foods, shortening

In the next chapter we will take a closer look at why the balance between the omega-6 and omega-3 fats is so important to your health.

Summary of Chapter 2

• •

There are three classes of dietary fats that are found in foods we eat.

■ Saturated fats are found primarily in animal foods and tropical oils; they are considered unhealthy.
■ Monounsaturated fats are found primarily in olive oil and are considered healthy.
■ Polyunsaturated fats are found in many plant foods and seafood.
■ No fat or oil we eat is made up of just one of class of fats.

Polyunsaturated fats are made up of two distinct fat families:

■ Omega-3 and omega-6 fats are polyunsaturated fats, which have opposite effects in the body.
■ Each omega "family" is "headed" by an essential fatty acid, fats that our body cannot make.

There are three key fatty acids that make up the omega-3 fat family.

■ The essential fat or parent fat is alpha-linolenic acid (ALA), which is a short-chain omega-3 fat found in flax, walnuts, hemp, green leafy vegetables, and canola oil.
■ The long-chain omega-3 fats are EPA and DHA and are the most potent and beneficial omega-3 fats. These fats are found mainly in seafood.

- ALA eventually gets made into EPA and DHA (ALA⇒EPA⇒ DHA).
- Omega-3 fats have a positive effect on health.

There are two key fatty acids that make up the omega-6 fat family:

- Linoleic acid (LA) is an essential fatty acid and the parent of the omega-6 fats. It is found in nearly every food but especially soybean oil, corn oil, safflower oil, margarines, salad dressings, sunflower oil, and cottonseed oil.
- Arachidonic acid (AA) is the potent long-chain omega-6 fat. Our body easily makes it from LA (LA⇒AA). AA is also found in animal foods.

Omega-6 Fat Syndrome
Why You Need to Balance the Fats

IT'S NOT ENOUGH to supplement your diet with fish oils or to eat enough omega-3 fats in your diet—it's merely a good start. The health benefits of omega-3 fats depend on the balance of omega-6 fats in your diet. But that's a big problem in the United States and many other Western nations.

We eat too much of the so-called heart-healthy omega-6 fats, which compete with and even destroy the benefits of omega-3 fats. To make matters worse, we don't eat enough omega-3 fats. Consequently, most of us have a major fat imbalance in the diet.

In this chapter you will discover why the balance of omega-6 and omega-3 fats really matters to your health. You'll learn why just about every food you eat is inundated with omega-6 fats, and you'll discover the impact of eating excess omega-6 fats, including increased risk for Alzheimer's disease, asthma, cancer, heart disease, vision disorders, inflammation disorders, learning disorders, rheumatoid arthritis, sleep disorders, and stress.

Mega Omega Problem in Our Food Supply

Today we eat fats that did not exist 100 years ago, including margarine, shortening, and cottonseed oil. As a result, we eat 10 to 20 times the amount of omega-6 fats that our forebears did. How did our fat balance get so out of whack?

It would be easy to point fingers at the food-processing industry, but we can't only blame this easy scapegoat (although it certainly contributed). A multitude of factors, including industrialization, agribusiness, food manufacturing, and the promotion of "heart-healthy" oils, contributed to fewer omega-3 fats and too many omega-6 fats in our food supply.

Even if you reach for a food that you think contains omega-3 fats, unfortunately it may not. For example, soybean oil is stripped of its naturally occurring omega-3 fats when it is hydrogenated. Farmed salmon has a higher amount of omega-6 fats than wild salmon. Yet how could you know this, since this information is not disclosed on food packaging?

Let's take a closer look at these factors, so you'll have a better idea how almost every food you eat has been penetrated with more omega-6 and shortchanged of its omega-3 fats.

The Case of the Fatted Calf

Before 1850, virtually all cattle in the United States spent four to five years grazing on grass, which naturally contains omega-3 fats, before slaughter. But today feedlot operations get a steer to slaughter in just about one year. As a result, cows have much less omega-3 in their meat today than they used to. A recent study from Ireland underscores this point; it found that the longer the cattle grazed, the higher their DHA content. Dining in the pasture also improved their fat profile, with lower levels of omega-6 fats in their meat.

Feedlot Cuisine. Today, 99 percent of cows in the United States dine in feedlots, exclusively on a corn-grain diet, which is rich in omega-6 fats and practically devoid of omega-3 fats. Consequently modern beef is fatter and has an entirely different fatty-acid profile: lower in omega-3 fatty acids, higher in omega-6 fatty acids, and higher in saturated fat. Wild animals and free-range or pasture-fed cattle do not display this unhealthy fat profile.

Commercially raised chickens, lamb, fish, and pigs also have a much lower omega-3 content in their meat and fat (think bacon here). Reports as early as 1968 showed that range-fed animals have higher amounts of omega-3 fatty acids. Foraging on grass rather than grains increases omega-3 fat accumulation in animals, as shown in Table 3.1.

The Meat (and Dairy Foods) We Eat Reflect the Diet of the Cow. The typical cow fattened on grain has 14 times more omega-6 than omega-3 fatty acids in its meat, far more than the grass-fed cow. This has a trickle-down effect in the food chain. The commercial meat and dairy products we eat also lack omega-3 fats while yielding a much higher load of omega-6 fats. This significance is aptly illustrated when you look at cheeses made from grazing cows versus feedlot-fed cows (see sidebar).

TABLE 3.1 Omega-3 Content (Percentage) in Meats: Grass- v. Grain-Fed Animals

Animal Food	Omega-3 Fat as Percent of Total Fat	
	Feedlot	Free Range/ Pastured/Wild
Beef	0.60	2.90
Bison	1.50	5.40
Chicken eggs	.03	9.00
Elk	—	5.00
Pork	0.02	5.90
Salmon	17.00	20.00

SOURCE: For details, see References under Koizumi, Rule, Simopoulos ("Evolutionary Aspects . . ."), and USDA.

The Alpine Paradox

• •

The Swiss and the French eat a lot of cheese yet have a low death rate from heart disease. As detailed in Table 3.2, researchers found that regional Swiss cheese is significantly higher in omega-3 fatty acids and lower in omega-6 fats, because the cows graze in the grassy Alps. In contrast, commercial Swiss cheese from the United States not only is devoid of EPA but also has the highest ratio of omega-6 to omega-3 fats of the cheeses listed.

TABLE 3.2 Swiss Cheese Cuisine: The Difference Grazing Makes

	Type of Cheese			
Omega-3 Fatty Acid	Alpine, 100% Grass Fed	Alpine, Partially Grass Fed	Swiss, Omega-3 Enriched	U.S. Swiss Conventional
MILLIGRAMS/100 GRAMS OF CHEESE				
ALA (short chain)	495	305	245	352
EPA (long chain)	39	24	23	0
Total omega-3 fatty acids	1,600	1,500	1,300	352
RATIO OF OMEGA-6 TO OMEGA-3 FATTY ACIDS				
	1:1	1:2	1:4	2:1

SOURCE: Hauswirth et al., 2004; U.S. Department of Agriculture Nutrient Database, nal.usda .gov/fnic/foodcomp/search.

Why Too Many Omega-6 Fats in Our Diet?

A convergence of well-meaning health advice, food processing, and industrialization resulted in a wide variety of foods overflowing with omega-6 fats, from frankfurters to granola. Many of those fats come from vegetable oils. Today only four oils—cottonseed oil, corn oil, soybean oil, and canola oil—account for 96 percent of the vegetable

TABLE 3.3 Top Four Fats and Oils Used in Food in the U.S.

Oil	Millions of Pounds per Year		Ratio of Omega-6 to Omega-3 Fats
	1970–1971	2001–2002	
Cottonseed oil	805	539	258:1
Corn oil	403	950	46:1
Soybean oil	5,780	17,818	8:1
Canola oil	319*	904	2:1

*Data for 1995, when canola oil was first tracked.

SOURCE: Economic Research Service, USDA, ers.usda.gov/data.

oil consumed in the United States (see Table 3.3). With the exception of canola oil, these oils are particularly high in omega-6 fats and low in omega-3 fats. These oils are used to make margarine, shortening, and salad dressings—which amplify your omega-6 fat intake.

Industrial RevOILution

Advances in technology increased worldwide vegetable oil production and introduced new edible oils, such as cottonseed oil. The large-scale addition of newfangled oils to our food supply significantly altered both quantitative and qualitative aspects of fat in our diet, causing our consumption of omega-6 fats to skyrocket. Vegetable oil is inherently higher in omega-6 fats, while being low in omega-3 fats. As our consumption of vegetable oil has grown, it has become our main source of polyunsaturated fatty acids. (Keep in mind that polyunsaturated fats are synonymous with omega-6 fats.) Figure 3.1 shows that in 1909 only 32 percent of our polyunsaturated fats came from oils; by 2000 that share had more than doubled. So if you eat vegetable oil (whether by using it for cooking or eating it in salad dressings, margarine, and mayonnaise), you will almost always increase your omega-6 fat intake. With the exception of olive oil and canola oil, vegetable oil is synonymous with omega-6 fats.

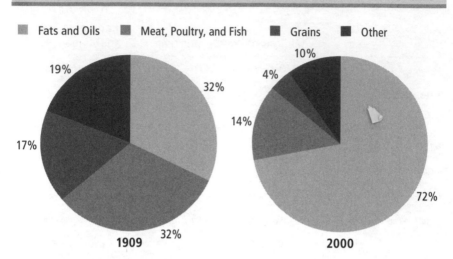

FIGURE 3.1 Sources of Polyunsaturated Fatty Acids in the U.S. Food Supply

Fats and Oils   Meat, Poultry, and Fish   Grains   Other

1909

2000

SOURCE: Gerrior, S., L. Bente, and H. Hiza. *Nutrient Content of the U.S. Food Supply, 1909–2000, Home Economics Research Report No. 56*. Washington, DC: U.S. Department of Agriculture, Center for Nutrition Policy and Promotion, November 2004. Accessed at cnpp.usda.gov/publications/foodsupply/foodsupply1909-2000.pdf.

New Foods Created: Margarine and Shortening

In 1897 the invention of hydrogenation (adding hydrogen to oil) allowed vegetable oils to become solid. Voilà—shortening and margarine were born. The timing was just right, too. The escalating prices and scarcity of butter during World War I paved the way for lower-cost alternatives. Toss in the medical community's recommendation to replace butter with modern vegetable fats, and margarine's place at the kitchen table was assured. In the last century, U.S. consumption of shortening quadrupled. The typical American ate about one pound of margarine per year in 1909 and now eats more than 6 pounds per year. Hydrogenated oils also helped extend the shelf life of convenience foods, which became popular for saving time in the kitchen, especially as more women entered the workforce.

Heart-Healthy Oils

The "heart-healthy" polyunsaturated fats have a distinguished history. Since the 1950s, the cholesterol-lowering effects of these fats dominated research. And for good reason: early studies showed that when polyunsaturated fats replaced the saturated fats, blood cholesterol was lowered. Thanks to the well-meaning "war on saturated fat" to reduce heart disease, polyunsaturated fats were heralded as *the* lifesaving fat and were indiscriminately promoted. Meanwhile, an important group of polyunsaturated fats—omega-3 fats—were simply ignored.

Foods with "heart-healthy" oils proliferated, and omega-6-rich fats increased in the American diet. Manufacturers jumped on the heart-health bandwagon, and foods were marketed as being cholesterol free and low in saturated fat. But this was achieved by using omega-6-rich oils, many of which were hydrogenated.

Ironically, hydrogenated oils *appeared* to be the more healthful alternative to saturated fats at that time. Even fast-food restaurants replaced the beef fat in the fryers with partially hydrogenated oils (shortening).

You are probably aware that hydrogenation introduced its own set of health hazards. Not only does this process create the infamous trans-fatty acids, which increase the "bad" LDL cholesterol, but hydrogenation also destroys omega-3 fats. For example, when soybean oil (which has 920 milligrams of omega-3 fats per tablespoon) is hydrogenated, its omega-3 fat content drops to 30 milligrams per tablespoon.

Now there is a new twist. In an effort to mitigate the problem of trans fat, food manufacturers are using new strains of soybeans to make more stable oil that contains negligible amounts of the omega-3 fats and higher levels of omega-6 fats! This is significant because soybean oil is the number-one oil used in the United States.

In December 2005, Kellogg, the world's largest cereal maker, made headlines when it announced its commitment to using low-linolenic soybean oil (soybean oil that is low in omega-3 fat) to replace trans fat that had been used in its foods. That decision has helped fuel a tremendous demand for low-linolenic soybean oil. About 80 million pounds of low-linolenic soybean oil were produced in 2005, with five times that output (400 million pounds) estimated for 2006, according to the Institute of Shortening and Edible Oils. But this trend is double trouble. This oil has an even higher omega-6 fat content than regular soybean oil (see Table 3.4).

TABLE 3.4 *Trans*-Formation of Soybean Oil: Disappearing Omega-3 Fat

Type of Soybean Oil	Milligrams per Tablespoon		Ratio of Omega-6 to Omega-3
	Omega-6	Omega-3	
Basic soybean oil (salad or cooking oil)	6,940	920	8:1
Mayonnaise, soybean oil	5,200	690	8:1
Spread, 70% vegetable oil (soybean and *hydrogenated* soybean oils)	2,060	220	9:1
Margarine, hard stick, *hydrogenated* soybean oil	2,740	210	13:1
Low-linolenic (1%) soybean oil	7,620	136	56:1
Partially hydrogenated, industrial, all-purpose soybean oil	1,170	30	39:1
Shortening, frying, heavy-duty, *hydrogenated* <1% linoleic	30	10	3:1

SOURCE: ESHA food processor SQL software; Iowa State University.

Meanwhile, manufacturers of cottonseed oil jockey for their market share by offering their product as a more healthful replacement for trans fat in processed food. But it has a much worse omega-6 profile. In cottonseed oil, omega-6 fats outnumber its omega-3 content by 234 to 1! Of all the fats ranked in Table 3.5, cottonseed oil is the worst in terms of its ratio of omega-6 to omega-3 fats.

Why the Balance of Omega-6 and Omega-3 Fats Affects Your Health

The balance of omega-6 and omega-3 fats affects whether your cells promote health or disease. If you eat too little omega-3 fat and/or too much omega-6 fat, you are setting the stage for health problems, as you will see in the remainder of this chapter.

TABLE 3.5 Proportion of Omega-6 to Omega-3 Fats in Oils

Fat or Oil	Ratio of Omega-6 to Omega-3 Fats
Cottonseed oil	234:1
Sunflower oil	180:1
Safflower oil	77:1
Evening primrose oil	75:1
Low-linolenic (1%) soybean oil	56:1
Corn oil	46:1
Partially hydrogenated soybean oil	39:1
Palm oil	30:1
Chicken fat	19:1
Olive oil	13:1
Lard	10:1
Butter	9:1
Margarine, hard stick, hydrogenated soybean oil	9:1
Basic soybean oil (salad or cooking oil)	8:1
Mayonnaise made with soybean oil	8:1
Walnut oil	5:1
Beef fat	2:1
Canola oil	2:1
Flaxseed oil	0.3:1.0
Perilla oil	0.3:1.0

When it comes to fat, you are what you eat. Unlike carbohydrates and protein, fat is the only macronutrient that does not get broken down into smaller units when you eat and digest it. These intact fats have a tremendous impact on the function of your body. If you eat chiefly omega-6 fats, that's what you will find in your body: primarily omega-6 fats in your cells. (The same thing happens to the meat of animals raised on feedlot diets of grains rich in omega-6.) Conversely, if you eat a lot of omega-3 fats such as fish, that intake, too, will be reflected proportionately in your cellular makeup—if (and this is a big *if*) you don't have too many omega-6 fats in your diet as well.

The Type of Fat You Eat Shifts Your Body's Biological State

The preponderance and type of fat in your cells dramatically affects the biological actions in your body. That's because both omega-3 and omega-6 fats make powerful, hormone-like chemicals that shift the landscape of your body toward promoting either disease or health. The proportion of these fats eaten ultimately influences the inner workings of your cells, becoming a predictable biomarker of both your diet and disease. Simply put, show me the amount of omega-6 and omega-3 fats in your diet, and I'll show you your body's biological state: pro-disease or pro-health.

The omega-3 and omega-6 fats work like a seesaw moving up and down, trying to achieve a healthy equilibrium for your body. This balance works at keeping your blood pressure normal, maintaining a regular heartbeat, healing wounds, and keeping your mood flowing smoothly. When the amounts of these fats eaten are in balance, this tandem relationship works well.

One of the key reasons omega-6 fats have such sway over omega-3 fats is that these fat families need the same enzymes to make their potent biological compounds in the body. Those indiscriminate enzymes are in limited supply, like taxis on rainy day in New York. It's harder to get a taxi during inclement weather because so many more people use them (a case of competitive supply and demand). Once the taxis are saturated with people, no cabs are left for others, no matter how great their need.

Doesn't it seem odd that there would be such an antagonist metabolic environment? Remember, it wasn't always that way. For thousands of years, our ancient ancestors chomped on a diet that provided equal amounts of omega-6 and omega-3 fats. Therefore, the body had no problem with fats sharing enzymes.

A Diet Rich in Omega-3 Fat Protects Health

The omega-3 fats that make their way from your dinner plate down to your tiny cells can shift the biological state of your body. They do so by making compounds that fight inflammation, prevent blood clots, and reduce stress chemicals, all of which help to prevent chronic diseases, including heart disease and cancer. This biological shift is so profound that heart disease scientists created the "Omega-3 Index" blood test, which reflects the content of omega-3 fats in your heart cells. Some researchers believe that the omega-3 index may be one of the best predictors of heart disease.

A Diet High in Omega-6 Fat Promotes Disease

Omega-6 fats have distinct and opposite effects in your body. They are in direct competition with omega-3 fats to make their powerful and often opposing biological compounds. When omega-6 fats greatly outnumber the omega-3 fats, they behave like a dietary bully, dominating your body's cellular playground.

A diet rich in omega-6 fats shifts the biological state in your body to one that sets up the conditions to promote diseases: inflammation, blood clotting, and increased stress chemicals. The omega-6 fats create damaging compounds associated with arthritis, Alzheimer's disease, heart disease, stress, mood disorders, and cancer, to name a few. In fact, death from heart disease is predicted linearly from the amount of omega-6 fat in the body.

A brief point needs to be made about the key omega-6 fats, linoleic and arachidonic acids: They are essential fatty acids, too. Yes, they are nutrients—yet archrivals, if you will, of the omega-3 fats. Omega-6 fats are not unlike other essential nutrients, such as vitamins A and D. They are required for your body to function, but when taken in high levels, they can pose dangerous health problems.

The Paradox of Excess: Omega-6 Fat Syndrome

The impact of the fat imbalance gets clearer when you explore different regions of the world. We'll take a brief look at what happened when Okinawans, Israelis, and urban Indians shifted their diets to high levels of omega-6 fats. Their experiences shed light on the ways that too much omega-6 fat affects your health. The "omega-6 syndrome" documented in Okinawa is particularly telling.

Omega-6 Syndrome and the Okinawa Paradox

The residents of the Japanese island of Okinawa held the bragging rights for the longest life expectancy in the world—until their diet dramatically changed after World War II. Following the war, they ate less fish at meals and ate meat instead. This occurred in part because of exposure to Westernized eating, as Okinawa was under U.S. jurisdiction until 1972. A well-publicized problem of mercury contamination also spurred eating less fish. Consequently, consumption of omega-3 fat dropped. During U.S. rule, there was also a rapid shift to cooking with vegetable oils instead of animal fats because they were considered superior for health. Consequently, Okinawans more than tripled their omega-6 fat content by 1990.

These changes were followed by a dramatic rise in Okinawans' health problems, including Western-type cancers, allergic reactions, and heart and blood circulation diseases. Notably, the abrupt rise in health problems paralleled the Okinawans' increased use of omega-6 fats. When Okinawa lost its longevity status, a scientific investigation began.

Researchers attributed the cause of Okinawans' health problems to their Westernized diet, which was too low in omega-3 fats and too high in omega-6 fats. Their shift to a diet high in omega-6 fats with the concomitant rise in chronic diseases was strikingly similar to what occurred in the Westernized world.

To solve the panoply of health problems, researchers recommended eating less omega-6 fats and more omega-3 fats, with a balanced ratio of 2 to 1. That ratio means that a person who ate two grams of omega-3 fats should limit intake of omega-6 fats to just four grams for the day—the amount of omega-6 fat found in one granola bar or one tablespoon of mayonnaise. Notably, the scientists emphasized that eating less omega-6 fat without eating enough omega-3 fat is ineffective at lowering the health-damaging compounds made from omega-6 fats.

Keep in mind that the typical American eats an average of 13 grams of omega-6 fats per day. That's more than four times the quantity of omega-6 fats consumed by a typical Okinawan.

India and Israel: Diets High in Omega-6 Fats and More Chronic Diseases

Israel also made the switch to the so-called healthier oils, resulting in one of the greatest omega-6 fat intakes in the world. Israelis' average dietary omega-6 fats outnumber omega-3 fats by 22 to 1.

In spite of Israel's exemplary heart-healthy eating (a diet low in artery-clogging saturated fat, high in polyunsaturated fats, and low in total calories), Israelis have a high prevalence of heart disease, not to mention high blood pressure and diabetes. Now they have a *higher* cancer rate than in Western countries. Researchers say this is a consequence of eating too many omega-6 fats.

The prevalence of heart disease is also high in the residents of urban areas in India, despite their low-fat diet in which 15 to 27 percent of calories come from fat. Researchers attribute the higher rate of heart disease to eating too many omega-6 fats. Interestingly, the rural dwellers have a much lower incidence of heart disease, not to mention lower rates of other related chronic illnesses. Why? They dine on "poor man's food" consisting of mustard oil and grains. Consequently, the rural residents have a diet much lower in omega-6 fat than their urban counterparts.

Omega-6 Fats Increase Risk for Specific Diseases

High levels of dietary omega-6 fat increase the risk for many different diseases and conditions. Here's a quick look at some of the problems, which will be discussed in more depth throughout this book:

- **Increased risk for cancer.** A study of 854 veterans showed over the course of eight years that those following the corn oil diet (which substituted corn oil for the saturated fats in their diet) had twice the fatal cancer rate of those eating a standard diet.

- **Greater fat storage.** Studies indicate that omega-6 fats have a remarkable ability to trigger fat storage in the body. Several studies show that when animals are fed diets high in omega-6 fats, they become fatter than animals fed diets with identical calories. While more research is clearly needed in this area, it adds one more compelling reason to balance the fats.

- **Clogged arteries in susceptible people.** High levels of omega-6 fats increased damage to the arteries when given to people who have high fat levels (triglycerides) in their blood or who make too much of a compound called LOX, which promotes inflammation.

- **Poorer recoveries by sick patients.** When standard soybean oil was fed to patients intravenously, they had more complications and more detrimental inflammation compounds in their blood than those infused with less omega-6 fat. Notably, the higher the omega-6 fat from the intravenous feeding, the longer the patients remained in the hospital.

- **Worsened brain function and mood.** The rise in diagnosed psychiatric disorders parallels the rise in omega-6 fat consumption. Some experts believe that the skewed high ratio of omega-6 to omega-3 fat accounts for the decade-by-decade rise in depressive disorders.

- **Increased vision problems associated with age.** A high intake of linoleic acid (the parent omega-6 fat) increases the risk for age-related macular degeneration, a serious problem that causes decreased vision. Conversely, a diet rich in omega-3 fats and fish appears to decrease the risk, if the diet is low in omega-6 fat.

The Most Powerful (and Damaging) Omega-6 Fat: Arachidonic Acid

Arachidonic acid (AA) is the epicenter of all that is problematic with excess omega-6 fat in our diets and ultimately with our health. AA is *the* fatty acid that creates the compounds that cause inflammation and blood clotting, among many other problems. In fact, many medications (including aspirin, Motrin, naproxen, Depakote, and Singulair) work by blocking the effects of AA. Researchers have just started to scratch the surface of AA's impact, but here are some striking findings:

- **Turned-on cancer genes.** Scientists from San Francisco discovered that AA turns on a dozen genes involved in cancer. When they added AA to human prostate tumor cells, the cells grew twice as fast. Notably, over the past 60 years, the rate of prostate cancer in the United States has increased steadily along with the dietary intake of omega-6 fats.

- **More heart attacks.** In separate studies from different regions of the world, researchers found that people with more AA in their body had a higher risk of getting a heart attack.

- **Mood disorders.** Researchers recently figured out why many mood-stabilizing medications are effective for treating mood disorders. They work by lowering the level of arachidonic acid in the brain.

Balanced Omega-6 Fat Matters for Health and Disease Prevention

From petri dishes to human studies, vast and diverse research overwhelmingly demonstrates the need to balance the fat families. A high proportion of omega-6 to omega-3 fat paves the way for many health problems, including mental illness, cancer, cognitive impairment, inflammation, arthritis, asthma, allergies, immunity disorders, heart disease, diabetes, Alzheimer's disease, and vision and bone health problems, to name just a few examples.

The more omega-6 fat you eat, the higher your risk for disease. Research highlights are summarized in Table 3.6. When the term *ratio* is used in this table, it refers to the proportion of omega-6 to omega-3 fats.

TABLE 3.6 Impact of Ratio of Omega-6 to Omega-3 Fats on Health and Disease

Health Condition	Ratio of Omega-6 to Omega-3 Fat	Comment
Alzheimer's disease	4:1	A fat balance of 4:1 improved the quality of life for Alzheimer's patients, whereas higher ratios had no benefit.
Asthma	5:1	Twice the ratio (10:1) had adverse consequences on asthma.
Bone health	—	A high ratio is associated with lower bone density, regardless of hormone replacement status.
Brain function	4:1	A dose-dependent study indicated that optimal learning occurred at this ratio.
Breast cancer	1:1–2.5:1	A study on French breast cancer patients showed that the balance between omega-6 to omega-3 fats, rather than the individual amount of fats, had the greatest impact on breast cancer prevention. A study on five countries reported similar findings.
Cancer prevention	1:1–2:1	A review published in the *American Journal of Clinical Nutrition* concluded that we need to eat a diet with a lower ratio of omega-6 to omega-3 fats (1:1 or 2:1) to lower the risk of getting cancer.
Cardiovascular health	4:1	A ratio of 4:1 has been associated with a 70% decrease in death rates.

Health Condition	Ratio of Omega-6 to Omega-3 Fat	Comment
Colon cancer	1:1–2.5:1	Fish oil supplements were beneficial *only* with a low ratio of 2.5:1.0.
Dry-eye syndrome	Lower ratio protective	A high ratio is associated with more than double the prevalence of dry-eye syndrome relative to those with a low ratio.
Healing	<1:1	The ratio influences a critical step in healing, collagen production. When the ratio was less than 1:1, collagen formation increased in a dose-dependent manner.
Inflammation	1:1	Ratios of 1:1 (or less) decrease inflammation. When patients were supplemented with fish oil, a ratio of 3.5:1.0 had no benefit.
Insulin resistance	2:1	Diets high in omega-6 fats trigger insulin resistance, which is implicated in diabetes, obesity, and heart disease. Animal studies show that a ratio of 2:1 may prevent this problem.
Pregnancy complication	—	A lower ratio was associated with a 46% reduction in risk for preeclampsia, a condition that can progress to a life-threatening situation for both Mother and Baby.
Rheumatoid arthritis	2:1–3:1	A lower ratio suppresses the harmful effects of inflammation.
Sleep	4:1	Two studies on students showed significant improvement in sleep at this lower ratio.
Stress	4:1	A lower ratio reduces the production of stress chemicals.

SOURCES: For details, see References under Simopoulos and Cleland, Weiss, Larson, Chajes, Oddy, Davis, and Ghafoorunissa.

The Benefits of Balanced Diets Low in Omega-6 Fat

The significance of less omega-6 fat in the diet has been overshadowed (and even discounted) by the excitement over the benefits of omega-3 fats. However, two landmark studies—the Greenland Eskimo study and the Lyon Diet Heart Study—indicate its importance.

The Greenland Eskimos

In the 1980s, the Greenland Eskimos were discovered to have an unusually low rate of heart disease compared with Danes, although both groups had similar blood cholesterol levels. In fact, the Eskimos ate twice as much cholesterol as the Danes, which puzzled the researchers. The healthy difference turned out to be the amount of fish eaten by the Eskimos. Soon the world was buzzing about the benefits of eating fish and omega-3 fats.

In all of the excitement, an important finding was lost. The Eskimo fish diet was also much lower in omega-6 fat than the Danes' diet (see Table 3.7). The omega-6 dietary factor is quite telling when comparing the diets from Japan, Okinawa, the United States, Denmark, and Greenland. Note how much higher omega-6 fat levels are in the American diet. This was reflected in their blood, too. Lower levels of omega-6 fats in the body meant more health protection. But excitement over the omega-3 fat discovery eclipsed the significance of the low levels of omega-6 fats in the Eskimo diet.

TABLE 3.7 Comparison of Omega-6 and Omega-3 Fat Consumption by Country/Region

	All of Japan		Okinawa	United States	Denmark	Greenland Eskimo
	1955	1985	1986–90	1985–89	1970	1970
Omega-6 fat grams	2.6	6.4	6.7	28.0	4.2	1.9
Omega-3 fat grams	0.9	1.6	1.1	2.7	1.2	5.3
Ratio of omega-6 to omega-3 fats	3:1	4:1	6:1	11:1	3:1	0.4:1.0

SOURCE: For details, see References under Okuyama ("Dietary Fatty Acids . . .") and USDA. Note: The numbers in this chart are rounded.

The Mediterranean Diet: It's Not Just the Olive Oil

This oversight happened again in 1994, with the Lyon Diet Heart Study, which popularized the Mediterranean-style diet for its health benefits. A significant feature of the Mediterranean diet is that it is low in omega-6 fat levels, yet that aspect receives little if any mention, even when leading researchers demonstrate its importance.

In the Lyon Heart Diet Study, French researchers led by Michel de Lorgeril used the key dietary components of the Mediterranean diet and applied them to residents of the city of Lyon. The results of the study, which was supposed to last five years, were so striking that it was halted midway by an ethics committee. Remarkably, there was a complete prevention of cardiac sudden death in participants eating a Mediterranean-style diet; the control group, which followed the classic heart-health diet (which does not distinguish between the types of polyunsaturated fat) had no such benefit.

A subsequent follow-up of Lyon Diet Heart Study participants was even more remarkable—an unprecedented lower death rate from *all* causes, especially cancer. This was an unexpected finding. The stunning results were published in the American Heart Association's scientific journal, *Circulation*, in 1999, accompanied by an editorial, which emphasized that only the diet with the lower omega-6 fat and higher omega-3 fat successfully lowered the death rate from all causes, including cardiac. The classic cardiac diet—which does not distinguish between the types of polyunsaturated fat, therefore mostly omega-6 fat—failed to improve the overall prognosis.

Michel de Lorgeril continues to write extensively on the need to lower dietary omega-6 fat, as it is one of the hallmarks of his famous study. Yet that advice seems to have had little impact. At least he is not alone. In 2000, an international group of scientists that specialize in omega-3 fats issued guidelines to cap omega-6 consumption toward a balanced level. Two years later, Japan issued similar public health recommendations to limit the amount of omega-6 fat in the diet. In Australia, patients participating in the Early Arthritis Clinic are advised to reduce their omega-6 fats to keep inflammation at bay. Keep in mind that no health agency or omega-3 fat expert is recommending we get rid of omega-6 entirely—only that we bring it back into balance.

Benefits of Balancing the Omega-6/Omega-3 Ratio

A clever study from Harvard Medical School showed dramatic results when a gene spliced into worms gave them the ability to make their own omega-3 fats. The worms began automatically producing a balanced fat ratio of 1-to-1 in their cells, with incredible benefits:

- Heart cells decreased susceptibility to irregular heartbeats.
- Cancer cells were naturally destroyed (a natural process known as apoptosis).
- Inflammation was reduced in cells that line and protect the entire circulatory system.
- Brain cells were protected from premature death.

In 1993 researchers from Israel tested the optimal balance of omega-6 and omega-3 fats for brain performance, using incremental fat ratios, ranging from 3-to-1 to 6-to-1. They found the ratio of 4-to-1 was the most effective for improved learning, sleep, and pain threshold. Other studies have demonstrated similar results. This same research team also used this ratio on Alzheimer's disease patients, who experienced significant improvement in quality of life.

Less Omega-6 Fat Dramatically Reduces Artery Clogging

Researchers looked at the impact of balancing fats on preventing atherosclerosis in a particular strain of mice susceptible to clogged arteries. The mice were fed diets with the identical quantity of fat, but the proportions of omega-6 to omega-3 fats varied. The researchers found a dose-dependent effect on the development of heart disease: the lower the ratio, the better the outcome. Notably, the low-ratio group had the best HDL (good cholesterol), lowest blood clotting, and least clogged arteries.

Balanced Ratio in Early Life Prevents Childhood Asthma

The Australian Childhood Asthma Prevention Study (CAPS) found that high-risk kids placed on a balanced omega diet since birth (modest omega-3 supplement with diet low in omega-6 fats) had significant reduction of a type of cough that is a strong predictor of asthma.

Arthritis Improves with Lowering Omega-6 Fat in Diets

Researchers put one group of rheumatoid arthritis patients on a diet low in arachidonic acid (the most potent omega-6 fat) and supplemented them with fish oil. The other two groups of patients either were given fish oil and a regular diet or served as the control, with a regular diet and placebo supplement. The group following the low-AA diet had the most improvement (less pain, less tenderness and swelling of joints). Notably, those on the regular diet with fish oil had improvements, too, but that treatment was less effective than the low-AA diet. Researchers also found that the more AA eaten, the higher the disease activity.

Omega-3 Supplements Do Little Without Balanced Omega-6 Fat Levels

As indicated in the arthritis study, for you to get the most benefit from fish oil supplements, you have to lower the level of omega-6 fat in your diet. Here are more examples:

Volunteers were given 4.4 grams of fish oil daily. It effectively suppressed the growth of cells that occur in colorectal cancer, but only if the ratio of dietary omega-6 to omega-3 fat was limited to 2.5-to-1.0. When the ratio was increased to 4-to-1, there was no such benefit.

Australian patients with rheumatoid arthritis were put on a diet containing less than 10 grams of omega-6 fats and were given a fish oil supplement. They had superior improvement in symptoms relative to members of the control groups.

Asthmatic adults took fish oil while eating a typical American diet high in omega-6 fats (ratio of 10-to-1), but they still had diminished breathing capacity. However, when the omega-6 fats were lowered to a ratio of 2-to-1, they experienced improved breathing and decreased asthma-triggering compounds.

Why It's Not Enough to Rely on the Ratio

An optimal balance between omega-6 and omega-3 fats has yet to be determined. Many experts believe that a dietary fat ratio in the range of 1-to-1 to 4-to-1 is optimal, but it can differ based on the health condition. Ultimately the quantities of each type of fat do matter, but it's not that simple or straightforward. Some scientists talk about diet ratios, while others talk about tissue ratios (the proportions of the fats in cells of the body); these ratios are related but very different. Some health organizations have different research agendas, such as heart health, while overlooking cancer prevention. See the sidebar for some recommendations that have been made.

International Ratio Recommendations and How Countries Stack Up

• •

Several countries and international organizations have issued guidelines for balancing the omega-6 and omega-3 fats. While these ratios vary, they are markedly improved from the typical Western diet.

Country/Organization	Recommended Ratio of Omega-6 to Omega-3
International Society for the Study of Fatty Acids and Lipids	1:1–2:1*
Japan	2:1
Sweden	5:1
United States	4:1–16:1*
World Health Organization (WHO)	2.5:1–8:1

*This is the resulting ratio if you eat according to their guidelines.

When a Number Is Not What It Seems

Many researchers don't like using a "ratio" to describe the fat requirements needed for health, because it is not accurate. There are several reasons why ratios can be misleading.

Decreasing Omega-6 Fat Won't Fix a Deficiency of Omega-3 Fat. If your diet is deficient in omega-3 fats and you only decrease your intake of omega-6 fats without increasing your intake of omega-3 fats, you still have a problem. Even though your ratio of omega-6 fats to omega-3 fats would be lower, that won't do you a whole lot of good without enough omega-3s. Remember, the average American does not eat enough omega-3 fats, let alone enough of the right *kinds* of omega-3 fats.

The Ratio Can Be Misleading When You're Trying to Balance Dietary Fats. If you rely on the ratio to select foods low in omega-6 fats, it can lead you into the opposite result! For example, olive oil has an apparently high ratio of 13-to-1. This is misleading, however; ounce for ounce, olive oil has one of the lowest contents of omega-6 fat for an oil, with 1,320 milligrams per tablespoon.

In contrast, walnut oil has a much lower ratio of 5-to-1. At first glance, it would seem the better choice. But compared with olive oil, walnut oil has more than five times the amount of omega-6 fats per tablespoon: 7,190 milligrams.

Why the disparity? The ratio doesn't consider the other fats present in the food (such as monounsaturated and saturated fats). Olive oil is made up of mostly monounsaturated fats, so the net amount of omega-6 and omega-3 fats is relatively low. Walnut oil, however, is made up of mostly polyunsaturated fats (omega-6 and omega-3 fats), so its ratio packs more of a wallop.

Also, just a small percentage increase in the calories from the most common omega-6 fatty acid in our food supply (linoleic acid) halts omega-3 fat metabolism by 50 percent. A ratio would not indicate that significance, which is quite substantial. *The more omega-6 fats you eat, the greater your requirement for omega-3 fats can become.* In essence, the goal for omega-3 fat intake can be a moving target, enough to make your head spin.

Lastly, the ratio is incomplete because it does not distinguish between the different types of omega-3 fats, each of which has markedly different effects in the body. Recall that there are several key omega-3 fatty acids, just as there are several types of B vitamins. ALA is the parent omega-3 fat, found in plant foods, while EPA and DHA are the biological power brokers, found in fish and fish oil.

Alternatives to Ratios. A more accurate way to balance the omega-6 and omega-3 fats, rather than using ratios, is to target specific amounts. I use the guidelines published in 2000 by the International Society for the Study of Fatty Acids and Lipids (ISSFAL). This group includes scientists from academia, government, industry, and health agencies from around the world.

It's not as if Americans have been cautioned about their fat imbalance—far from it. There are no policy or scientific guidelines for a balanced omega-3 and omega-6 fat diet in the United States (explained further), yet they exist in other countries, including Japan.

The American Paradox: Institute of Medicine's 2005 Recommendations

The Institute of Medicine (IOM), an American-based nonprofit organization that is part of the National Academy of Sciences, issues scientific recommendations on the amount of nutrients we should eat. The IOM's most recent report, 2005's *Dietary Reference Intakes*, did not suggest any guidelines to balance our omega-6 and omega-3 fats. The report has been criticized for recommending a diet too high in omega-6 fats and far too low in omega-3 fats, especially the long-chain omega-3s, EPA and DHA.

To make matters worse, the amount of omega-3 fat deemed to be "adequate" for Americans was determined by using the *median* omega-3 fat consumed in the U.S. diet. That's like taking the median exercise level of the typical American and saying that it's a healthy amount of activity, even though a majority of Americans are couch potatoes! It is especially unsettling given the abundant research demonstrating the need for more omega-3 fats in our diet. In essence, the report really advocates for the status quo, because the recommendations are based on Americans' current median consumption of both omega-3 and omega-6 fats. Let's take a closer look at that diet:

- **Not enough omega-3 fat.** According to the IOM, the average American needs only 130 to 260 milligrams per day of long-chain omega-3 fats (EPA and DHA). That's a huge gap with international recommendations, which call for five times as much, or 650 milligrams per day.

- **Too much omega-6 fat.** The IOM did not recommend a ceiling for omega-6 fat consumption, which is especially frightening, given its dominance in our diet. Instead, the IOM recommends nearly four times the amount of the omega-6 fat linoleic acid (up to 16 grams per day) as in the international guidelines. The range is set so high that you could be eating a whopping 17-to-1 ratio of omega-6 to omega-3 fats—quite lopsided and far from "adequate."

The IOM 2005 guidelines don't come close to reflecting the international recommendations, in spite of the bounty of research and scientists supporting the need for balancing the omegas (see Table 3.8). International guidelines were published in 2000, by a respected group of fatty-acid experts, from a meeting organized by the ISSFAL. They include scientists from academia, government, industry, and health agencies from around the world.[1] Ironically, some of the United States' best scientists attended the ISSFAL workshop (which

---

1. Simopoulos, A. P., et al. "Workshop Statement on the Essentiality of and Recommended Dietary Intakes for Omega-6 and Omega-3 Fatty Acids." *PLEFA* 63(3) (2000): 119–21.

took place in Washington, D.C.) to formulate global recommendations. Yet, even when measured up to the IOM's lax 2005 guidelines, the American diet falls short in omega-3 fats, as you can see in the right column of Table 3.8.

Here's the clincher: In 2006 a group of U.S. scientists concluded that Americans currently eat so much omega-6 fat that they need to boost their long-chain omega-3 fat intake to about 3,700 milligrams a day in order to prevent diseases and stay healthy. (That amount is what you find in six capsules' worth of high-potency fish oil). Clearly, it's time for a change. The remaining chapters will show you why and how to omega-optimize your diet.

TABLE 3.8 International Versus U.S. 2005 IOM Recommendation and the American Diet

	Recommended Amount (milligrams per day)		Amount Americans Eat (milligrams per day)
	International	United States	
OMEGA-6 FAT			
Adequate intake of linoleic acid	4,400	11,000–16,000	13,000
Upper limit for linoleic acid	6,670	No upper limit	
OMEGA-3 FAT			
ALA (plant-based)	2,200	1,100–1,600	1,300
DHA + EPA (long-chain)	650	130–260	85
DHA minimum	220*	No minimum	57
EPA minimum	220	No minimum	28

*For women who are pregnant or breastfeeding, the minimum recommended DHA level is 300 milligrams.

SOURCE: For details, see References under Simopoulos and IOM.

Summary of Chapter 3

• •

Americans are eating more omega-6 fats at the expense of omega-3 fats because:

■ Heart-health advocates indiscriminately recommend eating polyunsaturated fats, which are mostly omega-6 fats.
■ Industrialization brought us new foods high in omega-6 fat, including margarine, shortening, salad dressing, and cottonseed oil.
■ Livestock are no longer grazing on the range on wild grass. Instead, 99 percent of livestock eat a feedlot diet of grains, which results in high omega-6 fat in their meat and fatter cows.

The number-one source of omega-6 fat in the American diet is soybean oil.

■ Between 2001 and 2002, Americans ate more than 17 million pounds of soybean oil.
■ Soybean oil has eight times the amount of omega-6 fat to omega-3 fat and is the dominant oil in mayonnaise, salad dressings, and margarine.

The fat you eat shifts the biological state of your body toward health or disease promotion.

■ High omega-6 fat diets increase inflammation, blood clotting, and insulin resistance.
■ Omega-3 fats fight inflammation, prevent blood clotting, and lower stress chemicals.

Continued

Omega-6 fat syndrome: health problems increase as this fat rises in the diet.

- Chronic diseases skyrocketed when Okinawans ate more omega-6 fat.
- Israel has the highest omega-6 fat consumption in the world, with higher disease rates.
- The Lyon Diet Heart Study researched a low omega-6 fat diet that improved overall mortality.

Omega-6 fats need to be limited and omega-3 fats need to increase.

- High levels of omega-6 fats can be harmful (like other nutrients, such as vitamin D at high levels).
- Omega-3 supplements do little good when there is too much omega-6 fat in the diet.
- When dietary omega-6 fats increase by a small amount, it cuts omega-3 fats' effectiveness.

PART 2

Omega-3 Fats and the Prevention of Diseases

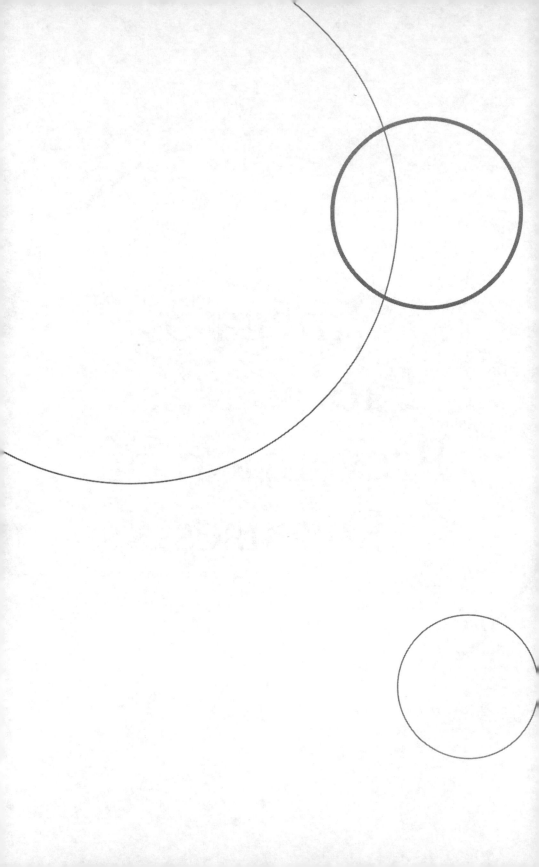

Dousing Inflammation
The Hotbed of Chronic Diseases

WHAT DO ARTHRITIS, heart attacks, cancer, asthma, and depression have in common? Inflammation! Yes, the same process that occurs when you stub your toe—swelling, pain, redness, and heat—is at the root of many of today's chronic health problems.

In this chapter we'll look at some of the basics of inflammation and how what you eat helps or worsens the process.

Inflammation 101

Your body's inner 911 is known as the inflammation response. Without it, a little injury such as a cut on your foot could be life threatening. Your body's arsenal, from tiny cells to special chemicals, responds in a number of ways—such as forming blood clots to prevent blood loss or raising the temperature of your body—in an effort to destroy bacteria that may have entered your wound.

This type of inflammatory response is essential for healing, but another kind of chronic low-grade inflammation promotes disease. Consequently, the healing blood clots that prevent bleeding to death can trigger a heart attack or stroke.

How Your Body's Inner First-Aid Kit Became a Slow Weapon of Death

Your body's inner first-aid kit depends on a wide array of tools that include a powerful class of chemicals called *eicosanoids* (pronounced *eye-CO-suh-noids*). These potentially healing compounds are made from fat. Eicosanoids made from omega-6 fats promote inflammation. Omega-3-based eicosanoids have the opposite effect: dousing inflammation. It is a complicated contradiction—but in a way, no different from the opposing tools used for repairing a house. You might need a demolition ball to tear out a rotten wall and then a crane to deliver wood for building a new wall. Or you might need a scraper to remove paint and a thin, wispy brush to apply paint in delicate corners. Similarly, the inflammation process uses eicosanoids that constrict or dilate blood vessels, prevent blood clots or trigger blood clots, and so forth. These seemingly opposite actions are necessary for maintaining your health.

Imagine, however, that while repairing your house, you received mainly tools for demolition. In a simplified manner, that is the dilemma that takes place in our bodies. Today, via the inflammation response from the food we eat, we have a preponderance of the tools that are destruction-oriented toward our bodies. If you eat too many omega-6 fats, your body makes too many pro-inflammation tools. This problem is amplified when you don't eat enough of the counterbalancing omega-3 fats.

The proportion of omega-6 and omega-3 fats eaten will determine the type of fats holstered in your cells, which in turn determines the type of eicosanoids created and ultimately your inflammation status. Nearly 15 years ago, one researcher concluded that the typical American diet sets the biological stage for a near maximal inflammation response from eating a chronic excess of omega-6 fats and too few of the omega-3 fats (see Figure 4.1).

Today inflammatory responses from excess omega-6 eicosanoids are at the root of many diseases, including diabetes, heart disease, arthritis, asthma, cancer, and Alzheimer's disease. People are pop-

FIGURE 4.1 Powerful Eicosanoids and Omegas

Eicosanoids are potent chemicals that affect inflammation. They are made from omega-6 and omega-3 fats, with the help of COX and LOX enzymes. Many pain medications work by blocking these enzymes. The three eicosanoid groups are thromboxanes, prostaglandins, and leukotrienes.

Short-chain omega-6 fat *Linoleic acid (LA)* Soybean oil, corn oil, cottonseed oil, margarines, salad dressing, safflower oil, mayonnaise, sunflower oil	**Short-chain omega-3 fat** *Alpha-Linolenic Acid (ALA)* Flax, walnuts, hemp, green leafy vegetables, canola oil

↓ *Shared enzymes to make long chain fats* ↓

Long-chain omega-6 fat *Arachidonic acid (AA)* Mostly made from LA (above)	**Long-chain omega-3 fat** *EPA and DHA* Seafood and fish oil

↓ *Shared enzymes (COX and LOX) make eicosanoids* ↓

Eicosanoids Too many omega-6 fats in the diet create excess omega-6 eicosanoids in your body, which promotes inflammation.

↓   ↓   ↓

Thromboxanes	**Prostaglandins**	**Leukotrienes**
Are important for: blood clotting, constricting blood vessels, white blood cells In excess associated with: stroke, heart disease, inflammation, deadly blood clots	Are important for: birth and brain function, kidney and GI function, preventing blood clots and infection, lung and bone health In excess associated with: cancer, osteoporosis, Alzheimer's, pain, fever and inflammation, stroke, migraine, arthritis	Are important for: lung function, brain function, inflammation, bone health In excess associated with: asthma, clogged arteries, cancer, lung diseases

ping a record number of anti-inflammatory medications to block the problems caused by eating too many omega-6 fats.

Anti-Inflammatory Drugs and Omega-3 Fats Work by Blocking Omega-6 Fat

When you have a headache, do you reach for aspirin, ibuprofen (Motrin), or naproxen (Aleve)? These over-the-counter medications are known as nonsteroidal anti-inflammatory drugs (NSAIDs). They work by blocking the effects of the omega-6 fat arachidonic acid, which creates eicosanoids that trigger pain, fever, swelling, and cramping.

Sometimes, these over-the-counter drugs aren't enough to combat inflammation, so your doctor might prescribe something stronger, such as Celebrex, which also works by preventing omega-6 fats from making eicosanoids. Omega-3 fats work in a similar manner and can even outperform some medications without their side effects.

COX Inhibitors Halt Omega-6 Fat (Arachidonic Acid)

Anti-inflammatory drugs work by blocking enzymes called *cyclooxygenase* (COX). When this enzyme is blocked, arachidonic acid (the most potent omega-6 fat) is unable to make its inflammatory compounds.

Arachidonic acid is like an unlit match. The COX enzymes "light" arachidonic acid, which then creates compounds that trigger inflammation and blood clotting. Anti-inflammatory medications act like water; they prevent arachidonic acid from being lit. Aspirin and other COX inhibitors work by blocking excess omega-6 fats from creating powerful eicosanoids. Ironically, if you take Motrin for a headache and eat foods that are high in omega-6 fats (like corn oil margarine on your toast), you may worsen inflammation. It's like throwing shredded paper on an inferno that the fire department is trying to extinguish. Omega-6 fats are fuel for the COX enzymes. More fuel leads to more inflammation.

COX-2 Inhibitors Block Omega-6 Fat, Too

For decades, aspirin has been touted as the wonder drug, but chronic use causes problems. Approximately one-third of patients taking aspirin and other NSAIDs develop ulcers, and over 100,000 patients are hospitalized each year for GI complications.

To alleviate pain and the side effects from aspirin, pharmaceutical companies developed a new class of drugs, called COX-2 inhibitors, which selectively block COX enzymes. These drugs, including Vioxx and Celebrex, became popular for managing a variety of conditions, including arthritis, menstrual cramps, and headaches.

Unfortunately, a deadly side effect was discovered: heart problems. Unlike aspirin, COX-2 inhibitor medications allow the formation of blood clots, a key risk factor in heart disease.

LOX: The Smoking Gun from Asthma to Atherosclerosis

Another enzyme, called LOX, converts omega-6 fat into even more potent inflammatory compounds, called leukotrienes. The leukotrienes include a potent asthma-triggering chemical, which is also linked to clogged arteries.

Aspirin and similar anti-inflammatory medications do not affect the LOX enzyme. But omega-3 fats are able to block the LOX enzyme, as do asthma medications (such as Singulair and Zyflo), which prevent leukotriene formation from omega-6 fat.

Omega-3 fats also work like corticosteroid medications, which block the release of the "holstered" arachidonic acid from the cells. Less AA means the LOX can't make leukotrienes.

Fish oil not only blocks both COX and LOX enzymes without the side effects of medications, it also confers health benefits. The EPA (one of the omega-3s) in fish oil competes with the powerful omega-6 fat arachidonic acid and lessens its ability to make the inflammatory eicosanoids. When AA is knocked out of the picture, EPA steps in and uses the same enzymes to generate inflammation-blunting compounds. In particular, DHA (the other omega-3 in fish oil) uses LOX to make a compound that protects the brain.

Beyond Medication: Omega-3s Turn Off Inflammation Genes and More

There's more to inflammation than the myriad of eicosanoids. Genes must be switched on and off in order to make proteins that play pivotal roles in inflammation and immunity. Omega-3 fats also influence these players in the orchestration of inflammation:

- DHA switches off the genes that make enzymes that trigger inflammation.
- EPA inhibits cytokines, which destroy bone cartilage. In contrast, NSAIDs *increase* this destructive response.

While medications have their role in managing diseases, fish oil does not have the side effects such as bleeding ulcers from aspirin or adverse cardiac events from COX-2 inhibitors. Fish oil helps reduce blood pressure, whereas many of these medications increase it.

Table 4.1 compares the effects of medications with those of fish oil. However, while fish oil can reduce the need for medication, it takes about 12 weeks for its benefits to kick in.

TABLE 4.1 Effects of Anti-Inflammatory Medications Versus Omega-3 Fats from Fish Oil

Fish oil works like many of the medications used to fight pain and inflammation, without the side effects. Moreover, fish oil offers health benefits. Medications (and fish oil) that inhibit the COX and LOX enzymes halt the inflammation process.

	Medication or Nutrient				
Chemical or Process Affected	Aspirin and NSAIDs (Naproxen, Ibuprofen)	COX-2 Inhibitors (Vioxx, Celebrex)	Asthma Medications (Zyflo, Accolate, Singulair)	Cortico-steroids	Fish Oil
COX-1 enzyme (inflammation)	Inhibit	—	—	—	Inhibits

	Medication or Nutrient				
Chemical or Process Affected	Aspirin and NSAIDs (Naproxen, Ibuprofen)	COX-2 Inhibitors (Vioxx, Celebrex)	Asthma Medications (Zyflo, Accolate, Singulair)	Cortico-steroids	Fish Oil
COX-2 enzyme (inflammation)	Inhibit	Inhibit	—	—	Inhibits
LOX enzyme (inflammation)	No effect	No effect	Inhibit	—	Inhibits
Omega-6 release (from cell membrane)	—	—	—	Inhibit	Inhibits
Cartilage destruction (cytokines)	Increase	—	—		Inhibits
Blood pressure	Increase	Increase	—	Increase	Decreases
Blood clotting	Inhibit	Increase	—	—	Inhibits
Genes (inflammation)	—	—	—	—	Turns off
Toxicity	Gastric ulcers and bleeding, kidney failure, anemia, liver failure, asthma, and dizziness	Heart problems	Nausea; stomachache	Weight gain diabetes, slowed healing, osteoporosis, cataracts, acne, weak muscles, infection risk, and stomach ulcers	—
Collateral health benefits	Benefits to the heart (for aspirin only)	Decrease in colon cancer	—	—	Benefits to heart, mood, cancer, and more

Powerful Synergy: When Fish Oil and Aspirin Unite

Scientists recently discovered that the combination of aspirin and omega-3 fats creates novel healing compounds. These compounds, resolvins and neuroprotectins, are potent anti-inflammatory chemicals. The research is in its infancy but is quite promising. The resolvins (made from EPA) dramatically prevented the formation of inflammatory bowel disease in genetically prone mice. When applied topically, the resolvins stopped the destruction of gum and bones in rabbit periodontitis (which is similar to human periodontitis, or gum disease). Neuroprotectins (from DHA) protect the survival of stressed-out brain cells and may help prevent Alzheimer's disease.

Omega-3 Fats Shorten Hospital Stays and Reduce Complications

Given the vast healing properties of omega-3 fats, researchers have turned their attention to patients who require intravenous feeding, also known as total parenteral nutrition (TPN). Up until the 1980s, a person who was unable to eat could die from malnutrition. But during that decade, scientists developed solutions that could be delivered through a tube into the patient's vein to provide nutrition. The source of fat in these solutions is typically soybean oil. But a recent critical review of the fats used in TPN indicated that soybean oil might hamper patient recovery because it contains a high level of omega-6 fat.

During Hospitalization

When soybean oil is replaced with fish oil, the effects are striking. Studies showed that omega-3 fats improved outcome in very sick patients by lowering the magnitude of the inflammatory response:

- The infection rate was lower, so there was less need for antibiotics.
- Complications, including the need to go back into surgery, were less frequent.

- The length of stay in intensive-care units declined by nearly half, from nine to just five days.
- There was a decreased need for mechanical breathing.

In contrast, the standard soybean oil infusion *increased* the inflammation compounds in the blood and the amount of days spent in the hospital.

Omega-3s: Prevention and Treatment of Inflammatory Diseases

Omega-3 fats are effective in the management of inflammatory diseases and offer the added benefit of less need for medication.

Cooling Pain and Stiffness in Rheumatoid Arthritis

Greenland Eskimos and indigenous Japanese have lower rates of rheumatoid arthritis than people in Western countries, which is significant because they have a genetic propensity to this disorder. Researchers attribute their lower disease rates to their diet, which is high in omega-3 fat and low in omega-6 fat.

To date, researchers have reported 15 well-designed fish oil studies on the treatment of rheumatoid arthritis patients with marked effectiveness. Benefits of using fish oil included reduced pain and morning stiffness and decreased use of pain medication by nearly 50 percent. A standard therapeutic dose of EPA and DHA is 2.7 grams combined.

Asthma and Respiratory Problems: Omega-3 Fats Help You Breathe

Globally, asthma affects about 300 million people of all ages and ethnicities. While progress has been made in the treatment of asthma, its prevalence is rising, which researchers attribute, in part, to the stellar rise of dietary omega-6 fats.

University of Wyoming researchers gave two groups of people fish oil and a diet that was either high in omega-6 fat (a level similar to the typical Western diet) or low in omega-6 fat. Those on the diet that was high in omega-6 fat had diminished respiratory capacity. But the group whose diet was low in omega-6 fat had a marked improvement in breathing, as well as a decrease in the asthma-triggering leukotrienes. Notably, fish oil was not effective for those eating a diet high in omega-6 fat.

Eating a diet rich in omega-3 fats is associated with fewer asthmatic problems. One study found that children who eat fish more than once a week are one-third as likely to develop asthma, compared with those who do not eat fish.

Exercise is a powerful trigger of asthma symptoms. Promising research shows that fish oil supplementation significantly ameliorates the severity of exercise-induced airway narrowing in both elite athletes and asthmatics, with a 30 percent reduction in inhaler use. Researchers are hopeful that using omega-3 fats could result in less medication use.

Omega-3s and Chronic Obstructive Pulmonary Disease (COPD)

Chronic obstructive pulmonary disease (COPD) is the fifth leading cause of death worldwide and is characterized by chronic inflammation in the lungs. Sadly, no medication can slow the progression of this disease. But researchers from Japan gave COPD patients an omega-3 supplement for two years, resulting in improved exercise tolerance and less inflammation (less leukotrienes) compared with the placebo group. The improved exercise tolerance is significant because it improves survival in these patients.

Fish Oil Fights Inflammatory Bowel Diseases

The inflammatory bowel diseases Crohn's disease and ulcerative colitis are chronic and incurable diseases of the gastrointestinal tract. Fish oil is promising, as studies show it can lessen medication use and increase remission. An encouraging double-blind study on children with Crohn's disease found that adding fish oil prevented relapse for eight months. In contrast, 95 percent of the kids in the standard treatment group relapsed by the first month of medical treatment.

Cancer: Wounds That Do Not Heal

Many cancers are associated with inflammation, reflected by elevated COX and LOX enzymes. Many of the drugs used for pain relief and inflammation also suppress cancer formation. The COX inhibitors have a strong preventive effect on colon cancer. Most recently, a Celebrex drug study dramatically prevented the recurrence of adenoma cancer. But there's a huge catch: there was an increased risk of heart disease.

Omega-3 fats, which inhibit both COX and LOX enzymes, have been shown to block cancer in many studies. Some of the compounds made from omega-6 fat enhance the tumor-making process while suppressing the body's natural ability to get rid of cancerous cells. Many studies indicate that the ratio of dietary omega-6 to omega-3 fats is associated with the risk of cancer.

The Brain Hardwired for Inflammation

The immune system is integrally connected to the brain. Psychological stress triggers the production of inflammatory compounds, which can trigger anxiety. Notably, the type and levels of fat in the blood predict the inflammation response to psychological stress. Major depression has an acute phase response in which inflammation is increased. The imbalance of omega-6 and omega-3 fats found in major depression may be related to the increased production of inflammatory eicosanoids.

Bone Health: Beyond Calcium

Omega-6 fat makes compounds that trigger bone loss and prevent bone formation. While most of the studies to date have been on animals, the limited human studies are compelling:

- Diets high in omega-6 fats are associated with lighter bones, which increase the risk of fracture.

- Lower bone density is associated with higher proportions of dietary omega-6 to omega-3 fats, regardless of hormone replacement status.

Individuals using NSAIDs to relieve pain have higher bone densities and fewer fractures. These medications inhibit the COX enzymes that make the bone-eroding compounds. There's no doubt that omega-3 fats, also COX inhibitors, will play a role in maintaining our bone health.

Heart Disease and Inflammation

It is widely accepted that inflammation is at the root of heart disease. It may be the reason why patients with inflammation conditions (including rheumatoid arthritis, asthma, allergy disorders, lupus, and depression) have a higher risk of heart disease. In the next chapter, you'll find out more about how omega-3s protect the heart.

Summary of Chapter 4

• •

nflammation is at the root of many chronic diseases, which is influenced by diet and eicosanoids.

- Eicosanoids are powerful chemicals in the body made by omega-6 and omega-3 fats.
- Omega-6 fats make the eicosanoid compounds that trigger inflammation.
- Omega-3 fats make the eicosanoids that have the net effect of anti-inflammation.
- The rise in inflammatory diseases parallels the rise in dietary omega-6 fats.

The dominating fats in your cells ultimately determine the inflammation status of your body.

- High omega-6 fat diets shift your body to a near maximal inflammation response.
- High dietary omega-3 fats help fight inflammation, if omega-6 fats are kept in balance.

Many medications work by blocking the effects of omega-6 fat.

- NSAIDs, including aspirin, naproxen, and ibuprofen, work by blocking the COX enzymes that turn omega-6 fat into inflammatory and blood-clotting compounds.
- COX-2 inhibitors, such as Celebrex and Vioxx, work by preventing omega-6 fats from making damaging eicosanoids.
- The asthma medications Singulair, Accolate, and Zyflo prevent omega-6 fats from making the lung-constricting leukotrienes; they inhibit the LOX enzyme.
- Corticosteroids used in inflammation disorders such as inflammatory bowel disorders prevent omega-6 fats from being released from the cells.
- Omega-3 fats are natural COX, LOX, and omega-6 fat inhibitors.

Omega-3 fats counteract inflammation in other ways that drugs do not:

- Omega-3 fats turn off the genes that trigger inflammation.
- Omega-3s displace omega-6 fat and prevents it from making its omega-6 eicosanoids.
- Omega-3 fats decrease other inflammatory compounds, such as cytokines.
- Omega-3 fats create novel potent healing compounds when used with aspirin.

Heart Health
Nutrition 911 for Your Heart

Omega-3 fats are such powerful heart protectors that the American Heart Association recommends eating fish twice a week—and taking daily fish oil supplements if you already have heart disease.

In this chapter you will see the compelling ways omega-3 fats keep your heart healthy: by steadying heartbeat, maintaining flexible arteries, lowering fats in the blood, smoothing blood flow, and even preventing sudden death. You will learn how eating too much omega-6 fat (such as margarine) can create problems for your heart.

American Heart Association Recommendations

- All adults should eat fatty fish at least two times a week.
- Patients with documented heart disease should take one gram of EPA + DHA combined per day.
- Patients with high triglycerides should take two to four grams of EPA + DHA combined per day.

Omega-3 Fats and Healthy Blood Vessels: Go with the Flow

Omega-3 fats profoundly benefit your arteries and blood system, including blood pressure and blood clotting.

Flexible and Wide Arteries

Your arteries are like freeways, serving as a transportation corridor for blood cells. Have you ever driven on a freeway in which the lanes narrow to just one? As the cars funnel into one lane, they create a traffic jam. That's similar to what happens to your blood cells when your arteries constrict. It's harder for them to travel smoothly. Under stress, your body produces a chemical (norepinephrine) that starts a chain reaction leading to narrower arteries. Omega-3 fats counteract this problem by widening the arteries. This yin and yang of artery widening and narrowing is triggered by eicosanoids, made from omega-6 and omega-3 fats.

Your arteries work best when they are elastic and supple. Stiff arteries diminish blood flow to the heart and increase your risk of heart disease. A recent study showed that fish oil supplements, when taken daily for seven weeks, increased the elasticity of arteries.

Under Pressure: Omega-3 Fats

High blood pressure (hypertension) is the most preventable cause of stroke and a major risk factor for heart disease. Hypertension damages your arteries and makes them stiff. Here's how hypertension damages your blood vessels:

- **Sheer stress.** Even diamonds can be cut with water if the pressure is high enough. Similarly, blood flowing at higher pressure erodes the artery, causing injury, which triggers inflammation. Lesions develop in these areas, especially at points of high wear and tear, where arteries branch out or at curvatures. Notably, these lesions will trigger plaque formation, which clogs arteries.

- **Overstretching it.** Hypertension stretches out the blood vessel, which makes arteries more permeable. Consequently, inflammation compounds, including the "bad" cholesterol, LDL, easily get enmeshed in the arterial wall.

- **Bursting your bubble.** If you fill a balloon with too much air, it can burst. Similarly, your blood vessels can burst from high blood pressure. Blood vessels in the eyes can burst or bleed, which may cause vision changes resulting in blindness.

Shaving even a few points off your blood pressure can help your arteries. More than 60 studies found that fish oil has a modest but significant effect on lowering blood pressure.

Omega-3 Fats Keep Blood Flowing Smoothly

Omega-3 fats help blood flow efficiently and prevent blood clots. They do so by preventing blood cells, specifically platelets, from clustering together, which would hamper blood flow. This is like drivers slowing down to gawk at an accident; the clustered cars amplify traffic snarls. This type of traffic jam in the blood is known as *platelet aggregation*. Omega-3 fats also help break down fibrin, a mesh-like compound that forms a blood clot.

Fish oil also helps keep blood flowing smoothly by lowering a category of fats called triglycerides, which in high levels are a risk factor for heart disease. More than 70 studies clearly show fish oil has a potent ability to lower these fats. Consuming just two to four grams of fish oil lowers triglycerides by 20 to 50 percent.

What About Cholesterol?

You probably know that elevated blood cholesterol is a risk factor for heart disease. Yet half of the people with heart disease have *normal* blood cholesterol levels. Despite changes in lifestyle and the use of medications to lower blood cholesterol, the death rate from heart attacks in the United States is among the worst in the world. The explanation? Inflammation, not cholesterol itself, has the most profound impact on heart disease.

Your Arteries: The Super Inflammation Highway

Heart disease or atherosclerosis is often described as "clogged arteries," but this is a misnomer. It is an inflammatory disorder, which is much more than the accumulation of plaque in the arteries.

Inflammation as the Cause of Heart Disease: An Old Idea, Newly Embraced

While the notion of inflammation as *the* cause of heart disease still grabs headlines, the idea is hardly new: it originated nearly 200 years ago! The inflammation theory went in and out of vogue depending on the medical opinion leaders of the time.

In 1815 surgeon Joseph Hodgson published *Treatise on the Diseases of Arteries and Veins*, which identified inflammation as the cause of artery damage. But he wasn't popular, so neither was his theory. About 40 years later, pathologist Rudolf von Virchow resurrected the inflammation theory. But another prominent doctor disagreed. It would take more than a century for scientists to settle this issue.

Old-School Lipid Theory. In the 1900s, scientists created clogged arteries in rabbits by adding cholesterol to their food, which gave rise to the theory that dominated most of the 20th century. According to this theory, plaque builds up in the arteries, limiting blood flow, resulting in a heart attack. This sounds logical, but there is actually more to the processes causing heart attacks.

New-School Inflammation Theory. Thanks to technology, it became clear that blood clots (which are caused by inflammation) play a pivotal role in heart attacks. Inflammation was widely accepted as the culprit of heart disease in 1999, when Russell Ross published his landmark paper, "Atherosclerosis: A Chronic Inflammatory Disease," in the *New England Journal of Medicine*.

What about clogged arteries? Plaque buildup in the arteries is certainly a problem, but it is akin to loading a bullet into a gun—it's dangerous but not lethal in and of itself. The chronic inflammation process ultimately pulls the trigger by causing plaque to accrue and then rupture, spewing a blood clot and inflammatory compounds into the blood. Let's take a closer look.

Inflammation of Arterial Highway 101

Inflammation is triggered by a microscopic injury to the artery, which can be caused by high blood pressure, smoking, and *oxidized* LDL, a more toxic form of cholesterol.

Attempting to self-heal, the injured artery releases a chemical SOS, which initiates the inflammation cascade, resulting in plaque formation. The core region of the plaque consists of fat and immune cells, surrounded by a tough cap (like a scab). The inflammation process ensues, causing the cap to weaken. Consequently, the plaque ruptures like a lethal volcano, spilling its toxic contents into the blood. Your arteries become the inflammation highway, circulating these compounds, one of which is the omega-6 fat arachidonic acid.

Omega-3 Fats Keep the Pace and Rhythm of the Heart

The heart is an "excitable" tissue, meaning the heart cells generate electric currents, which trigger the heart to beat regularly. Fatal rhythms occur when the electrical signals get chaotic, which disables the heart's ability to beat and pump blood. One of the ways omega-3 fats benefit the heart is by stabilizing their electrical action.

Omega-3 Fats Improve Heart Rate Variability

Heart rate variability reflects your heart's autonomic function, which allows your heart to beat automatically, without you thinking about it. Omega-3 fats, especially DHA, improve this heart function.

EPA and DHA Are Comparable to Anti-Arrhythmia Medication

A Harvard research team evaluated the effects of the long-chain omega-3 fats, EPA and DHA, on heart rhythm. In every instance, the omega-3 fats stopped violent fibrillation (deadly heart beat rhythm) and helped the heart cells resume a normal beat.

Omega-3 Fats Slow the Pace of Beating Hearts

Lowering your heart rate a few beats may appear trivial, but it may help prevent sudden death, as shown in a French study that followed nearly 8,000 healthy men for 23 years. The men who remained healthy had a slower heart rate by four beats per minute.

A review of 30 studies indicates that omega-3 fats lower heart rate by nearly two beats per minute. This effect occurs after 12 weeks of fish oil supplementation, which is how long it takes omega-3 fats to get holstered into your heart cells.

Clearly, omega-3 fats help maintain a healthy heartbeat, which is why scientists believe they are protective against sudden cardiac death.

Omega-3 Fats: Your Inner Defibrillator

More than half of all sudden cardiac deaths occur in people without any history of heart disease. One of the main causes of sudden death is a sustained abnormal heartbeat called ventricular arrhythmia. (That's why defibrillators save lives: they jolt the heart into normal rhythm.)

Alexander Leaf of Harvard University led the landmark study demonstrating omega-3 fats' ability to prevent sudden death. His lab gave arrhythmia-prone dogs fish oil just before they performed a treadmill stress test. The results showed that fish oil prevented sudden death in the dogs.

These remarkable results prompted studies to see if similar benefits could be achieved in people. Hints already existed, as eating fish one to two times weekly was associated with a nearly 50 percent reduction in sudden death.

Fish or Fish Oil Decreases Sudden Death

A study called the Diet and Reinfarction Trial told heart attack patients to eat two fish servings per week. The study's results indicated a 29 percent reduction in death. Another study, the GISSI-Prevenzione Trial, involved over 11,000 heart attack patients. In that study, men given 850 milligrams of long-chain omega-3 fats had a 45 percent reduction in sudden cardiac death compared with the unsupplemented group. The U.S. Physician's Health Study added a vital piece of evidence: omega-3 fats reduce the risk of sudden death even among men without a history of heart disease.

Omega-3 Fats Prevent Arrhythmia in Heart Surgery Patients

A dangerous heart rhythm, atrial fibrillation, is one of the main complications after open-heart surgery. Italian researchers randomly gave fish oil supplements to 80 of 160 patients scheduled for heart surgery. The supplemented group had a marked reduction in atrial fibrillation and spent fewer days in the hospital. The fish oil's effectiveness was comparable to that of the heart-stabilizing medications sotalol and amiodarone—but without their serious side effects, including assorted problems in the liver, lungs, and heart.

Omega-3 Fats May Prevent Arrhythmia in High-Risk Patients

Researchers are hopeful that omega-3 fats will provide an alternative to anti-arrhythmia drugs for patients with implanted defibrillators. But studies on these patients show conflicting results, so the jury is still out.

Omega-6 Increases the Odds of Developing Heart Disease

Excess omega-6 fats trigger blood clotting, clustering of blood cells, and tightening of blood vessels—a compelling bit of information. When you consider the role of omega-6 fats as a contributor to heart disease, the information is chilling.

The William Lands Theory:
Excess Omega-6 Fat Creates Chronic Diseases

• •

B iochemist William Lands has championed the notion that our dietary omega-6 fat imbalance is slowly killing us. He has written two scholarly books on the subject, including the recent *Fish, Omega-3 and Human Health*,[1] and has published hundreds of studies. Yet today there is not a single health agency that recommends balancing the omega-6 fats.

In the early 1980s, Lands showed that omega-3 fat supplements prevented heart attacks in animals by competing with the actions of omega-6 fats.

Lands created a scientific formula that reliably predicts how much of the omega-6 and omega-3 fats eaten will actually end up in the cells of your body. He demonstrated how the intake of one greatly influences the effects of the other. But he said, "Sadly, I don't think many people read those papers, and I don't think anyone used the equation."[2]

While Lands has a few vocal peers who view the omega-6 fat issue as inconsequential, he remains undeterred. He developed a free software program that predicts your risk for heart disease based on your consumption of omega-6 and omega-3 fats (see page 180). In 2006, the International Society for the Study of Fatty Acids and Lipids honored Dr. Lands for his scientific contributions.

1. Lands, W. E. M. *Fish, Omega-3 and Human Health*, 2nd ed. Champaign, IL: AOCS Press, 2005.

2. Lands, W. E. M. "Dietary Fat and Health: The Evidence and the Politics of Prevention." *Annals of the New York Academy of Sciences* 1,055 (2005): 179–92.

In the 1970s, there were clues that excess omega-6 fat hurts the heart. Scientists infused animals with the omega-6 fat arachidonic acid, and it caused sudden death within minutes. The cause of death was thrombosis (blood clots).[3] This lethal effect did not occur after using the *same amount* of other fats.

Furthermore, all the eicosanoids made from arachidonic acid, except for one, have been found to be potent *arrhythmogenic agents* (causes of arrhythmia), according to Alexander Leaf's research. Based on these and other findings, Leaf in a 2001 scientific editorial urged a lowering of dietary omega-6 fats in order to promote heart health.

Notably, the higher the level of arachidonic acid in your body, the greater your risk of death from heart disease. Let's take a closer look.

Phospholipids

Oil and water don't mix, so fats need a shuttle to move throughout your blood, which is mainly water. One of these "shuttles" is a *phospholipid*, which holds one pair of fatty acids. Phospholipids are a major component of all cells, including heart cells, blood cells, and brain cells.

Each phospholipid is like a hanger in which there are two clamps to hold a long pair of pants (but instead of pants, they are fatty acids). One of the clamps, called position 2, is reserved for long-chain fats. Typically, the coveted position goes to one of three fats: the omega-6 fat arachidonic acid or the omega-3 fats EPA or DHA. Which gets in? Whichever fat is in most abundant supply. The supply is based on the proportion of omega-6 to omega-3 fats in the diet. In the case of the American diet, omega-6 fat wins a great majority of the space in the phospholipids, which is why about 75 percent of the long-chain fats in the American body are omega-6 fats.

---

3. Silver, M. J., et al. "Arachidonic Acid Causes Sudden Death in Rabbits." *Science* 183 (129) (1974): 1085–87.

A new blood test, called the *Omega-3 Index*, measures the phospholipid content of omega-3 fats. The higher your omega-3 index, the more protection your heart will have. Researchers believe this test might be one of the best indicators for risk of death from heart disease.

LDL Cholesterol: Special-Delivery Taxi for Omega-6 Fat. The last *L* in LDL stands for lipoprotein, which is a protein that serves as a taxi for fat. In its center region is the fat payload, including cholesterol and phospholipids, which it delivers into the artery wall.

LDL carries an enzyme[4] that serves as the release pin for the arachidonic acid tethered to the phospholipid. Once freed, the arachidonic acid can make potent omega-6 eicosanoids that trigger blood clotting, inflammation, and arrhythmias—obviously not good for the heart. An elevated blood level of this enzyme is an independent risk factor for heart disease and indicates the *extent* of artery damage.

Diets High in Omega-6 Fats Promote Atherosclerosis

Diets that are high in omega-6 fats may be especially harmful to people with a genetic disposition to heart disease (who are just being identified, thanks to robust research from the human genome project). The potent omega-6 eicosanoid made from the LOX enzyme (a known trigger of asthma) is powerfully linked to atherosclerosis, especially in people who are genetically wired to make higher levels of this enzyme.

A profound study published in the *New England Journal of Medicine* found that eating a diet high in omega-6 fat (typical levels in a Western diet) caused an increase in the production of the damaging LOX-based compounds, leading to atherosclerosis. Both omega-6 fats, linoleic acid and arachidonic acid, were significantly associated with increased severity of artery damage.

In another study, Tufts University researchers reported in the May 2006 issue of *Circulation* that people who have a variation of a

---

4. The enzyme is called lipoprotein-associated phospholipid lipase A-2.

gene called apolipoprotein A5 have a higher risk for heart disease, especially if they eat a diet high in omega-6 fats.

Diets Low in Omega-6 Fats Reduce Death from Heart Disease

The Lyon Diet Heart Trial was a large study designed to see if eating a Mediterranean-style diet would protect against the recurrence of a heart attack, compared with the standard diet recommended by the American Heart Association. The omega-6 fats in the diet were limited to seven grams a day, about what you find in just one tablespoon of corn or soybean oil. The results surprised even the researchers. After four years on this diet, participants experienced a reduction in *all* causes of death, including heart disease. The impact of this diet was also reflected in blood phospholipids, with a lower ratio of omega-6 to omega-3 fats.

In spite of the compelling evidence of omega-3 fat's detriment to heart health, there is not much "buy-in" from the medical community. Since the late 1980s, respected scientists from around the world[5] have brought attention to the omega-6 fat problem in eloquent editorials and studies, only to seemingly fall on deaf ears.

Instead, many health organizations indiscriminately promote the use of polyunsaturated fats to replace artery-clogging saturated fat. Since omega-6 fats are the dominant fat found in *polyunsaturated* oils (soybean oil, cottonseed oil, sunflower oil, safflower oil, corn oil)—if you seek them out, you will overwhelmingly increase your dietary load of omega-6 fats, which is counterproductive to health.

Fortunately there are ripples of change. In 2005, Joint British Societies issued guidelines to prevent cardiovascular diseases, which not only recommended regular fish consumption, they urged replacing saturated fat with *monounsaturated* fats (like olive oil). This is significant, because this is the first health association that does not

---

5. The prestigious scientists include Alexander Leaf, M.D., of Harvard; the principal investigator of the Lyon Diet Heart Trial, Michel de Lorgeril from France; noted biochemist W. E. M. Lands, Ph.D., from the United States; Artemis Simopoulos, M.D.; Les Cleland, M.D., from Australia.

indiscriminately recommend increasing *polyunsaturated* fats for saturated fats.

To keep your heart healthy, it's a great start to eat more omega-3 fats, whether from fish or supplements. But it is not enough. Dietary omega-6 fats need to be lowered to a healthier balance. This balance is also important for the developing brain, which is discussed in the next chapter.

Summary of Chapter 5

Omega-3 fats keep blood vessels healthy by:

- Decreasing blood pressure and triglycerides
- Keeping arteries flexible and wide for smooth blood flow
- Decreasing clotting and clumping of blood cells

Chronic inflammation is at the root of heart disease, which involves:

- The body's attempt to heal blood vessel injury, resulting in plaque formation
- Ruptured plaque releasing blood clots and inflammatory agents into the blood

Omega-3 fats act like an inner defibrillator.

- Omega-3 fats significantly reduce the risk of sudden cardiac death.
- Omega-3s prevent deadly heart rhythms—atrial fibrillation and ventricular arrhythmia.
- Omega-3 fats improve heart rate variability and also slow heart rate.
- Fish oil rivals some medications for preventing complications from heart surgery.

Excess omega-6 fats worsen inflammation and heart disease.

- Every omega-6 eicosanoid, except for one, is pro-arrhythmic.
- LDL, or "bad," cholesterol delivers omega-6 fat into the arteries.
- The Lyon Diet Heart Trial showed reduced death from all causes in participants eating a diet low in omega-6 fat.
- Diets high in omega-6 fats increase artery damage in susceptible individuals.
- No health organization has addressed the omega-6 fat issue, in spite of urging from scientists.

The Developing Brain
From Womb to High Chair
(Even Rocking Chair)

O MEGA-3 FATS (particularly DHA) are vital for development, especially creating the architecture of a baby's brain. Omega-3s have both immediate and long-term consequences that can affect a baby's health for the rest of his or her life.

Virtually all brain cells or neurons (nerve cells) in the brain are formed before birth. During the last 12 weeks of pregnancy, omega-3 fat content increases in the baby's brain three to five times. Therefore, what an expectant mother eats has a significant impact on the baby's brain, from influencing IQ to determining which genes get turned on. In this chapter, we will explore how omega-3s shape a baby's development with implications throughout the lifespan.

(A special word to mothers: No guilt allowed if your diet during pregnancy wasn't ideal. Freud did enough in the guilt department for generations of mothers. It's best to operate under the assumption that you do the best you can until you learn otherwise. Many diseases and health conditions arise from a variety of factors, and once a child is born, how she or he lives can have a significant impact on overall health. So, please, no blaming the mother here.)

Pregnancy: You Are What Your Momma Ate

Before, during, and after pregnancy, omega-3s play a critical role for both mom and baby. Therefore, it's crucial for mom to build and maintain adequate DHA stores. It's similar to keeping your checking account in the black by making regular deposits. If your funds are insufficient, your checks will bounce, and you'll pay a penalty. But it's a little more complicated with your "DHA checking account": you don't get statements indicating your omega-3 balance, and withdrawals can be compounded by many factors, some of which are not obvious.

Before birth, all of the omega-3 fats accumulated by the developing baby must come from the mother via the ultimate maternal straw, the umbilical cord, where nutrients are transferred to the baby. DHA withdrawals are taken from the mother's stores to supply the critical building blocks for the baby's developing brain.

Each pregnancy drains maternal stores of omega-3 fat, and unless they are replenished, the stores get lower with each birth. They continue to drain if a mother breastfeeds her baby. Researchers believe that depleted maternal stores of omega-3 fat are a contributing factor to postpartum depression.

Benefits to Mom During Pregnancy

Omega-3s play a role in a healthy pregnancy, which naturally benefits the baby. They create the powerful cascade of eicosanoids, which activate labor, so they influence the length of the gestation period.

Omega-3s may prolong gestation by blunting one of the compounds that start labor. In 2002 scientists in Denmark found that the risk of premature birth is greatly reduced if mothers eat oily fish during pregnancy. Their research, published in the *British Medical Journal*, showed that the average birth weight and length of pregnancy appeared to increase in direct relation to the amount of fish eaten. Low consumption of seafood was a strong risk factor for preterm delivery and low birth weight.

In another study, researchers gave high-risk pregnant women either fish oil or a placebo. The fish oil group had a significant reduction in preterm delivery.

Benefits to Baby During Pregnancy

Nearly all of the baby's brain cells are formed in the womb, although they mature after birth. Each brain cell requires DHA to ensure proper brain development. Several studies indicate that if the mother is not eating enough DHA, less DHA is present in the baby's brain. Consequently, the baby's emotional and intellectual development can be greatly affected.

Mature Brain Development. The young brain cell is like a sapling that grows into a tree. Brain cells mature by getting longer and branching out. DHA is critical to this process. Pregnant women who eat more DHA give their babies a better chance of mature brain development, according to a first-of-its-kind study reported in the September 2002 issue of the *American Journal of Clinical Nutrition*. Researchers evaluated sleep patterns of babies because those patterns reflect the brain's maturity. Mothers with higher DHA blood levels had babies with heartier sleep patterns in the first 48 hours after delivery. Babies born to women with low DHA levels had less advanced sleeping patterns (less brain maturity). Furthermore, the balance of omega-6 to omega-3 fats in the prenatal diet had a significant impact; diets that were higher in omega-6 fats resulted in babies having less advanced sleeping patterns.

Impact on Language and Learning. Pregnant women who ate fish regularly had toddlers with better language and communication skills, according to research on 7,421 children born in 1991 and 1992. Scientists tested each child's cognitive development at ages 15 and 18 months. Overall, eating fish during pregnancy was consistently linked to children's higher test scores. (Keep in mind that it is important to choose low-mercury fish, as described in Chapter 11.)

The largest effect was seen in the children's ability to understand words at the age of 15 months. Children whose mothers ate fish at least once a week recognized 7 percent more words than those whose mothers never ate fish. A similar pattern was seen in another study that evaluated social activity and language development.

Boost to Babies' Intelligence. Researchers at the University of Oslo found that children whose mothers took cod-liver oil during pregnancy scored higher on intelligence and achievement tests at four years of age. This study is notable because it was randomized and double-blind (the gold standard of a well-designed study).

Better Metabolism of Chemicals Promoting Attention and Memory. DHA plays a big role in creating and storing chemicals involved in mood, memory, and concentration. A decrease of DHA in the developing brain alters the metabolism of the neurochemical dopamine, which is vital to attention, motivation, and child development.

Influence on Genes (Now and Later). Omega-3 fats turn on and off many genes in the brain. Genes are like factories that have the recipe to make proteins. When genes are turned on, the assembly line begins, churning out specific proteins such as a blood cell. Conversely, when genes are turned off, the assembly halts.

Recently, researchers explored whether eating omega-3 fats during the perinatal period could influence brain gene expression later in life. (The perinatal period is generally considered to start at the 20th to 28th week of gestation and ends one to four weeks after birth.) Among 1,600 genes examined in rats, omega-3 deficiency altered the expression of several important genes in the offspring. (Clearly, it's not ethical to do this sort of experiment on a human.)

Genes: Fate and Fat

As the embryo grows into billions of cells and differentiates into organs, nutritional adequacy is crucial. More biological milestones are passed before birth than after, and once a critical developmental phase is passed in the womb, you can't start over. Some of these milestones won't be evident at birth. For example, you won't know if a newborn's adolescent parts are working until children reach their preteen years. And so it goes with diseases that can take decades to develop, such as cancer.

Scientists believe that when the fetus is nutritionally deprived, nutrients have to be allocated. The developing brain gets priority. This leaves important organs like the kidney and heart vulnerable to not developing properly, possibly increasing the risk of diseases related to those organs. Here are some provocative examples.

Protection of Daughters from Breast Cancer

A headline-grabbing study was presented at the 2005 annual meeting of the American Association for Cancer Research. The results indicated that mothers who eat foods rich in omega-3 fats during pregnancy and breastfeeding and continue to feed their babies such a diet (after weaning) may reduce their daughter's risk of developing breast cancer later in life.

It's been known that maternal diets high in omega-6 fats increase maternal estrogen levels, which in turn are linked to increased breast cancer among female children. In a study involving rats predisposed to cancer, Elaine Hardman of Louisiana State University gave them a diet high in either omega-3 or omega-6 fats while they were pregnant, breastfeeding, and weaning. All of the offspring exposed to the maternal omega-6 diet developed breast tumors. But the omega-3 offspring had a lower tumor incidence rate of 13 percent. While this study is far from definitive, the results are provocative.

Prevention of Asthma

Children whose asthmatic mothers ate oily fish during pregnancy were 71 percent less likely to develop asthma, according to research presented at the 2004 international conference of the American Thoracic Society. In contrast, the researchers also found that children whose mothers ate fish sticks during pregnancy were twice as likely to develop asthma. What gives? Fish sticks are deep-fried and contain omega-6 fatty acids, which are pro-inflammatory.

Why Do Study Results Conflict?

• •

Omega-3 fat studies can yield different results for several reasons. First, researchers still don't know which omega-3 fat is responsible for a particular action in the body, let alone the right dose! For example, although women with low DHA stores are at higher risk for postpartum depression, EPA is the omega-3 fat that helps mood regulation. When a woman eats fish, she is getting both EPA and DHA.

To confound the problem, there is no standard supplement. Different fish oil brands contain different amounts of EPA and DHA. Sometimes researchers will use pure EPA or pure DHA, rather than fish oil. Sometimes the dose of omega-3 fats given is too low to produce a benefit. There are so many variables just from the dose and type of omega-3 fats that you can easily get different results.

There is also the issue of the background diet. Quite often the level of omega-6 fats is not taken into account, even though omega-6 levels can influence the results of a study (as you saw in the first chapters of this book).

Also, when it comes to babies, the effects of diet may show up much later in life. Benefits may not be detected because the tools available for assessing brain function are less sensitive early in life. For example, it is well known that iron deficiency during infancy causes significant problems in the brain, yet the problems do not appear until the baby reaches 12 years of age. Similarly, cocaine use while pregnant can harm the baby, but the damage is not observed until the baby reaches 24 months. If the baby is evaluated at 6 months of age, no harm is demonstrated.

Likewise, the effects of omega-3s in the infant's diet may not be apparent until later in life. Until we have more sensitive tests and longer studies that follow the developmental milestones beyond infancy, we are bound to see conflicting results.

Prevention of Allergies

Australian researchers examined the effect of fish oil supplementation in 40 mothers-to-be on the immune response in their infants. The women all had a history of hay fever or asthma, making their children at increased risk of developing allergies. At one year of age, the children of mothers who took fish oil were 3 times less likely be sensitized to egg allergen and 10 times less likely to have severe atopic (allergic) disease.

Blood Pressure

While hypertension is unusual during childhood, studies have shown that blood pressure tracks from early childhood (and now the womb) into adulthood. In a recent animal study, omega-3 deficiency during pregnancy caused high blood pressure later in life, *even if the offspring were subsequently rehabilitated* with omega-3s. Early omega-3 deficiency, regardless of subsequent supply, resulted in hypertension.

A compelling study on children showed that blood pressure at age six was lower in those who as infants had been fed with a formula supplemented with omega-3s than in children fed formula without omega-3s.

Diabetes

If expectant moms eat enough omega-3 fats, it may prevent their babies from getting diabetes. The Norwegian Childhood Diabetes Study Group found that babies fed cod-liver oil during the first year of life had a 25 percent lower risk of type 1 diabetes. The researchers believe that omega-3 fats influence the genes that cause diabetes.

Breastfeeding and Nutrition in the First Year of Life

Breastfeeding offers many health benefits, and some of these involve the role of omega-3 fats. In addition to containing nutrients that the baby needs, breast milk has disease-fighting substances that are not found in formulas.

Disease Prevention

Breastfed infants have a decreased incidence of many health conditions, including obesity, insulin resistance, hypertension, diabetes, cardiovascular disease, and asthma. Notably, many studies show that omega-3 fats have benefits in all of these conditions.

Prevention of Sudden Infant Death Syndrome (SIDS)

DHA deficiency may be a link to sudden infant death syndrome (SIDS); infants who die from SIDS have much lower levels of DHA in their brains. These babies also have less mature nervous system function, in which DHA is critical. Any delay in developing mature brain cells could hamper arousal from sleep, which is believed to be an important survival mechanism likely impaired in SIDS.

Continued Brain-Boosting Benefits

As brain development continues, DHA accrues in the brain until the baby is two years old. DHA plays a key role in synapse formation. The newborn has only about 1 percent of the synapses formed in the region of the brain responsible for thought, reasoning, and memory. Synapses are points where the neurons communicate with each other. They are like electrical outlets; the more you have, the more appliances you can plug in and operate. The number of synapses influences the plasticity of the young brain, so the more, the better.

Plasticity, also known as neuroplasticity, is critical to brain development throughout life. Plasticity allows neurons to reorganize and grow based on our experiences (sensory, motor, and cognitive). Even in adulthood, our brains are capable of reorganizing in response to our experiences. Until the late 1990s, it was widely thought that from birth, our brain circuitry is wired and fixed for life. The discovery that brains continue to develop as neurons reorganize and grow is akin to learning that the earth is round, not flat.

A higher level of DHA in human milk is associated with better learning, memory, and visual and language development in breastfed infants. Here are examples:

- **Sustained attention.** Researchers at Baylor College of Medicine in Houston found that when mothers supplemented with DHA for the first four months of breastfeeding, their babies performed better on a test that measured attention.

- **Better vision and eye-hand coordination.** Breastfed infants of mothers who took DHA supplements during lactation had better eye-hand coordination and visual acuity at two and a half years than did breastfed infants of mothers without supplementation.

- **Enhanced general movements.** Omega-3s have a positive effect on the quality of general movements of healthy full-term infants. This is significant because the quality of general movements is one of the most accurate ways to assess development of the nervous system. Formula-fed babies supplemented with omega-3s for two months after birth had a significant reduction in the occurrence of mildly abnormal general movements.

The DHA and Breast Milk Problem: Diet Still Matters

While no one would question the merits of breastfeeding, there is a problem. The amount of DHA in breast milk has dramatically declined in nearly every country over the last decade (see Table 6.1). A good example of this phenomenon is in Vancouver, Canada, where the DHA in breast milk has dropped by nearly 50 percent in just 15 years. Why? In a word, diet. What a woman eats is the single most important determinant of DHA content of her breast milk and, consequently, her baby's diet.

Not Enough Omega-3s. Notably it's the fish-eating countries that have the higher levels of DHA. Breast milk differs in DHA composition depending on the quantity and type of omega-3 foods eaten, especially seafood.

Plant Versus Marine Omega-3s Make a Difference. The importance of the type of omega-3s eaten is illustrated in vegetarian moms, who

TABLE 6.1 DHA Content of Breast Milk by Country

Country	% DHA of Total Fat
China, coastal	2.8
Japan	1.1
China, rural	0.7
Europe	0.3
Africa	0.3
Canada	0.2
United States	0.1

SOURCE: Innis, S. M. "Polyunsaturated Fatty Acids in Human Milk." *Protecting Infants Through Human Milk* (August 2004): 36.

have very little DHA in their breast milk. (DHA is found mainly in fish and some animal products, which are typically excluded in vegetarian diets.) One study showed that babies breastfed by their vegetarian moms had three times *lower* DHA blood levels than babies breastfed by nonvegetarian women. Even formula-fed babies fared better, as they had nearly twice the DHA levels of vegetarian moms' babies. This is significant because breast milk DHA levels are directly correlated with the baby's DHA blood content and their nervous system development at one year of age.

While there are plant sources of omega-3 fats (alpha-linolenic acid, found in flaxseed oil), its conversion to DHA is nil. Several studies of breastfeeding women who were supplemented with alpha-linolenic acid (the parent omega-3 fat) showed no increase in their DHA levels. (But take heart, vegetarians; there is a new plant-based DHA supplement, discussed in Chapter 12.)

DHA a Nutrient. Many experts believe that DHA warrants the status of an essential nutrient, because plant-based omega-3 fat (alpha-linolenic acid) does not sufficiently create DHA, especially in early life, where it's critical for eye and brain development.

Too Much Omega-6, Trans Fat, and Saturated Fat. Eating too much omega-6 fat, saturated fat, or trans fat limits the DHA composition of breast milk. The omega-6 fat content of breast milk has substantially increased since the 1950s. Breast milk has also been found to contain manufactured trans fats, which may interfere with DHA and may hamper the baby's brain and visual development. Trans fats have been shown to blunt postnatal growth in animal studies. (In spite of these problems, there is no question that breastfeeding is superior to formula feeding. Remember, breastfed babies have lower rates of infectious diseases, sudden death, diabetes, asthma, and obesity.)

Balance of Omega-6 to Omega-3 Fats Affects the Developing Brain

Normal brain function depends on the balance between omega-3 and omega-6 fats. Without the proper balance, cognitive and behavioral changes may result, as we will explore in the next chapter.

Summary of Chapter 6

• •

Omega-3s play a role in a healthy pregnancy.

- Mom's DHA stores are affected by number and spacing of births and breastfeeding.
- Depleted stores of omega-3 fat are believed to be a contributor to postpartum depression.
- Omega-3 fats play a role in labor. Adequate dietary omega-3s may prevent complications.

Continued

Omega-3 fats, especially DHA, play a critical role in the developing brain.

- DHA is integral to the delicate architecture of the baby's brain (like calcium for bones).
- DHA builds the matrix for nerve cell communication.
- DHA influences many brain chemicals involved in mood, memory, and concentration.
- DHA plays a role in neuroplasticity (the flexible growth of and communication between brain cells).

What Mom eats during and after pregnancy (if breastfeeding) affects the amount of omega-3 fat the baby receives, which impacts:

- Baby's intelligence, attention, and development
- Genes getting turned on or off in the baby's brain, which influences risk of disease
- Strict vegetarian moms, who do not yield enough DHA in their breast milk

Omega-3 fats, especially DHA, play a key role in brain development. Low levels may:

- Decrease learning and language ability
- Increase risk of sudden infant death syndrome (SIDS)
- Decrease eye-hand coordination and vision
- Increase chronic diseases later in life: high blood pressure, diabetes, and allergies

Too much omega-6 fat in Mom's diet may:

- Lower DHA content in breast milk
- Increase risk of complications with pregnancy
- Increase risk of breast cancer in baby, if a girl
- Interfere with brain development in baby (if breastfeeding)

Why It's Good to Have a Fat Head

Omega-3s, the Brain, and Mood

I T MAY BE HARD to fathom that one nutrient can play a role that ranges from mood regulation to managing borderline personality disorder, yet that's what remarkable research shows. Promising studies on conditions ranging from depression to everyday stress show that omega-3 fats may be an effective treatment. The results have been so dramatic that sometimes just fish oil alone has been effective to regulate mood.

When you consider the pivotal role omega-3 fats play in normal brain function and development, it's not a stretch to imagine the sweeping effects of omega-3s on mood and cognition. This chapter will explore how omega-3 fats affect brain function and their role in various mood disorders, stress, learning, and cognitive decline.

The Brain Connection

The decline of omega-3 fats in the Western diet parallels a large rise in psychiatric disorders over the past century. According to experts, the epidemic rise in depression alone is not attributed to better diagnosis or a reduction in stigma. A recent review in the *American Journal of Psychiatry* compellingly points to omega-3 fat deficiency as a key contributor to mood disorders.

There is a strong connection between worldwide rates of depression and fish consumption (the major source of omega-3 fat intake). The lowest depression rate is found in the countries with the highest levels of fish consumption, such as Japan. Conversely, higher rates of depression are found in countries where fish consumption is low. An example is Germany, which has a 60 times higher rate of depression than Japan (see Figure 7.1).

Similarly, global fish consumption has been linked to protection against postpartum depression, bipolar disorder, and seasonal affec-

FIGURE 7.1 Fish-a-Day Keeps the Blues at Bay

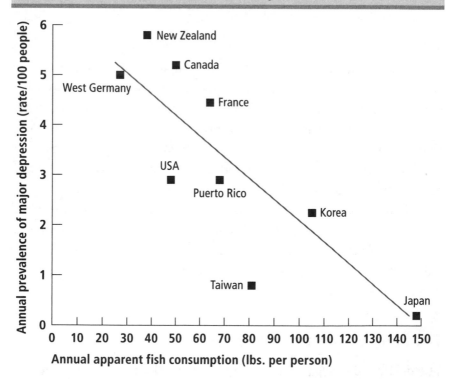

SOURCE: Reprinted with permission from Elvesier from the *Lancet*. For details see References under Hibbeln, 1998.

The Brain: Communication Central

• •

Your brain is a maze of trillions of connections capable of performing 20 million-billion calculations per second. It has three major components:

1. *Neurons:* brain cells that power the communication message
2. *Neurotransmitters:* chemicals that create the message (for example, serotonin)
3. *Receptors:* proteins that receive the message

---

tive disorder (SAD, a form of depression caused by low exposure to sunlight).

The Membrane Is the Brain

Your brain is 60 percent fat, and neurons have one of the highest concentrations of omega-3 fats. Anything that interferes with getting omega-3s into your body (inadequate diet or too much omega-6 fat) makes brain function especially vulnerable.

The human brain contains about 100 billion neurons—brain cells that carry messages through an electrochemical process. The brain cell membrane is the primary site of action for most of the brain's vital functions.

The membrane is more than just a border encircling the brain cell; it acts as an air traffic controller, switchboard operator, amplifier, receiver, and static stabilizer. The inner workings of the membrane are in continual flux; a symphony of chemical communication occurs, affecting learning, attention, and mood.

Omega-3s in the Membrane. The cell membrane looks like two parallel layers of jellyfish packed together, with their dangling tentacle toes touching each other (see Figure 7.2). The "tentacles" are actually

FIGURE 7.2   Cell Membrane with Jellyfish Omega-3 Configuration

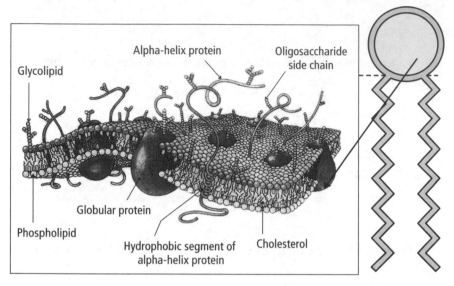

SOURCE: National Institute of Standards and Technology, NIST Center for Neutron Research (NCNR), "The Cell Membrane," NCNR website, ncnr.nist.gov/programs/reflect/rp/biology /cell_membrane.html, last modified March 18, 2003.

a pair of fatty acids, which include omega-3 fatty acids. This jellyfish-style arrangement of the membrane creates optimal fluidity, which is very important for brain cell function.

Omega-3s Enhance Fluidity. You may not feel like a walking vessel of primordial ooze, but your brain cells work best this way. The brain cell membrane needs to be at optimal fluidity for clear communication to take place, just as your blood works best when it is sludge free. Imagine having the choice to swim in water or quicksand; no doubt, the viscosity would greatly affect your performance. The same is true for brain cell function.

Optimal fluidity is required for the electric signals within the cells and for chemicals to bind. For example, the feel-good neurotransmitter, serotonin, docks on the protein ports in the harbor of the brain cell membranes. If serotonin had to sludge through viscous membranes, its soothing effects would take longer to kick in.

Your Brain Fluidity Is Affected by Your Diet

When fluidity goes awry, so does optimal brain function. The presence of omega-3s keeps the membrane fluid like a well-oiled hinge on a door. Anything that impedes omega-3s will affect the fluidity factor.

Omega-6 Fats Decrease Fluidity. If there are not enough omega-3 fats in your diet, the brain has no choice but to allow for an inferior substitution with an omega-6 fat, which does not work the same way. Therefore, the "tentacle" in the membrane that should be an omega-3 fat gets replaced with an omega-6 fat of similar size but inferior function. It's like replacing a burnt-out 100-watt lightbulb with a 25-watt bulb. You still get light, but it's a lot dimmer.

Saturated Fats Harden Brain Cells. Saturated fats are well known for hardening arteries, and they have a similar stiffening effect in our cell membranes. Therefore, their presence in the brain cell literally makes it harder to think.

Cholesterol Clogs Brain Cells. Cholesterol hardens the interior of brain cell membranes (not just arteries). Interestingly, omega-3 fats reduce the level of cholesterol in the brain cell's membrane, enhancing fluidity. While the competitor omega-6 fats, such as soybean oil, remove cholesterol from the arteries, they do *not* remove cholesterol from the interior of the cell membrane.

Factors That Impair Membrane Fluidity

- Sleep deprivation
- Aging
- Stress
- Cholesterol
- Saturated fat
- Omega-6 fats

A balance of omega-3 fat is essential for brain function. Researchers believe that many psychiatric disorders, from depression to schizophrenia, are a result of omega-3 fat deficiency. The nature and severity of symptoms are related to the magnitude of omega-3 fatty-acid deficiency (and related factors, such as too much omega-6 fat).

Mood Spectrum Disorders: Depression, Bipolar Disorder, and Schizophrenia

Mood disorders vary with the degree of symptoms, so they are best described on a continuum. Omega-3 fats are linked with each disorder. Many studies demonstrate the benefits of omega-3s in a diverse range of psychiatric disorders.

The Depression Connection

The World Health Organization (WHO) estimates that depression will become the second leading cause of disability worldwide by 2020. The incidence of depression has increased nearly 20-fold since World War II. This rise in depression parallels the Western diet's simultaneous decrease of omega-3 and increase of omega-6 fats. Notably, studies show that depressed patients have lower levels of omega-3s in their bodies. Some experts believe that the skew of too much omega-6 fat with too little omega-3s accounts for the decade-by-decade increase in major depressive disorders.

A recent study conducted over a two-year period found that both a high ratio of omega-6 to omega-3 fat and a low level of DHA in the blood predicted suicidal behavior in people with major depression.

Despite advances in medicine, a surprising number of people are not helped by antidepressant medications. The most widely prescribed class of antidepressant medication is the SSRIs (serotonin selective reuptake inhibitors), such as Prozac, Effexor, and Zoloft, but they reduce depressive symptoms by only 50 percent in less than half of patients who start them. There is clearly a need for more treatment options. But there is not much incentive for drug companies to fund research for a nonpatentable compound, such as the promising omega-3 fats. A recent review in the *British Journal of Psychiatry* found that omega-3 supplements significantly improved depression in three out of four highly controlled studies.

Researchers believe that omega-3 fats, especially EPA, can help normalize brain cell structure and function in depressed patients. When someone is depressed, the brain actually shrinks and has difficulty making new neurons. EPA may lift depression by helping to form new neurons and connections.

One notable study by Malcolm Peet and David Horrobin recruited 70 clinically depressed patients who continued to have problems in spite of taking antidepressants. They divided the patients into four groups to explore the effects of different daily doses of EPA: one gram, two grams, four grams, and zero (placebo). They found clear benefits at the lowest dose given, and three batteries of depression tests showed improvement in sleep, anxiety, depression, libido, and lassitude. The researchers noted that no drug study has shown such large improvements.

American Psychiatric Association Recommends Fish Oil for Patients

A recent American Psychiatric Association committee recommended that all patients with mood, impulse-control, or psychotic disorders should consume 1 gram of EPA + DHA per day. They also suggested that a supplemental dose ranging up to 9 grams may be beneficial (but any dose greater than 3 grams should be monitored by a physician).

Source: Freeman, et al. "Omega-3 Fatty Acids: Evidence Basis for Treatment and Future Research in Psychiatry." *Journal of Clinical Psychiatry* (67) 2006: 1954–67.

Because of the mounting evidence that links cardiovascular disease and depression, the researchers suggested that depressed patients would benefit from omega-3 supplementation for better mood and to prevent heart disease.

So far, depression studies show that the effective dose of omega-3s to improve symptoms ranges from one gram to two grams a day. DHA alone has not been shown to improve mood, while both EPA alone and fish oil (which contains *both* DHA and EPA) have shown improvement. While there is no established clinical dose of omega-3 fats for depression, the American Psychiatric Association recommends fish oil for all patients with mood disorders.

Postpartum Depression. Postpartum depression is associated with low intake of omega-3 fat, especially DHA. Both lower DHA content in breast milk and lower seafood consumption are linked with higher rates of postpartum depression in 23 different countries. Surprisingly, there are few treatment studies.

The first reported case of successful treatment was published in February 2003 in the *American Journal of Psychiatry*. A 34-year-old woman (24 weeks pregnant) had clinical depression, including suicidal thoughts. She refused antidepressant medication because of possible birth defects in her baby. As an alternative, she was given two grams of DHA with four grams of EPA, and by the fourth week of supplementation, her depression began to lift. By the sixth week, her thoughts of suicide disappeared altogether.

Kids Get Depressed, Too. An encouraging study on children ages 6 to 12 diagnosed with depression showed that omega-3 fat supplementation markedly reduced symptoms. By the end of the 16-week study, 40 percent of the kids taking the omega-3s no longer felt depressed. Not a single child in the placebo group had this relief.

Omega-3s and Bipolar Disorder

Arguably, the study that launched interest in mood and the omega-3 connection was that led by Harvard psychiatrist Andrew Stoll. In 1999 his group published stunning results in the *Archives of Gen-*

eral Psychiatry, demonstrating that omega-3 fats were effective in the treatment of patients with bipolar disorder. This was a four-month double-blind study on 30 patients with unstable bipolar disorder. They took their prescribed medication and randomly received either placebo or fish oil supplements (6.2 grams EPA and 3.4 grams DHA). In nearly every outcome measure, the fish oil group performed better than the placebo group. The results were so strong that the trial was stopped at four months.

How do omega-3 fatty acids produce this effect? One theory is that bipolar disorder symptoms are caused by an excessive amount of omega-6 fats, which wreak havoc with brain metabolism. Omega-3 fats appear to work in the same way as many of the mood-stabilizing drugs (such as lithium), which prevent interference from arachidonic acid in the brain cells and improve their ability to function. But omega-3 fats go one step further by dampening the effects of inflammation in the brain. Excess inflammation has been found in both mania and depression.

Omega-3s and Schizophrenia

Schizophrenia is one of the most severe mental illnesses, characterized by hallucinations, lack of drive, and loss of normal emotional responsiveness. As is the case with other mood disorders, schizophrenia is associated with alterations in the inflammation response. One theory (yet to be proven) is that schizophrenia may originate in the womb, when the baby is exposed to a low-grade infection. The infection is theorized to interfere with the omega-3 fats in the brain, which in turn damages neurons and triggers adult onset of schizophrenia. Notably, the gene that regulates omega-3 fat supply to the brain is located on the chromosome linked to the gene predisposing to schizophrenia.

Schizophrenic patients have higher rates of omega-3 fat destruction in their brain. Interestingly, Clozapine, the antipsychotic medication used to treat schizophrenia, appears to work in part by increasing DHA levels.

A scientific review of the effect of omega-3 supplementation and mental disorders (including depression, bipolar disorder, and schizophrenia) found that seven of eight double-blind clinical trials yielded positive results from utilizing EPA.

Omega-3s and Borderline Personality Disorder

Unstable moods are a problem in borderline personality disorder (BPD). Harvard researchers gave women with BPD either one gram of EPA per day or placebo for eight weeks. The EPA group showed marked improvement in aggression and depressive symptoms.

Omega-3 fats not only impact mood, but they also greatly affect stress, learning, and memory, which is discussed in the next chapter.

Summary of Chapter 7

• •

Omega-3 fat deficiency is linked to many neuropsychiatric disorders, including: depression, bipolar disorder, schizophrenia, personality disorders, and postpartum depression.

- Omega-3 fats keep brain cell membranes healthy and fluid, which affects mood.
- The brain is 60 percent fat and is more vulnerable to deficits of omega-3 fats.
- The brain cell membrane is the key site for vital functions involving mood and cognition.

A review of mood studies showed that omega-3 fats improved symptoms and may work by:

- Preventing brain cells from shrinking (which is common in depression)
- Improving production of key brain chemicals such as serotonin
- Stabilizing brain cells in a manner similar to mood-stabilizing medications

While there is no established dose of omega-3 fats for treating mood disorders, studies indicate:

- Doses of one to two grams per day of long-chain omega-3 fats improve depressive symptoms.
- DHA supplementation alone has no benefit.
- EPA alone, or in combination with DHA, has demonstrated efficacy for mood improvement.
- Fish oil may benefit patients with mood disorders, as recommended by the American Psychiatric Association.

Excess omega-6 fats have a negative impact on brain function:

- The excess decreases fluidity of brain cell membranes
- Excess omega-6 fats are a contributing factor in bipolar disorder.
- The rise in psychiatric disorders parallels the rise in omega-6 fat consumption.
- The skewed high ratio of omega-6 to omega-3 fat may explain the rise in depressive disorders.

The Ultimate Chill Pill

Omega-3s' Impact on Stress, Learning, and Memory

E VERYONE EXPERIENCES STRESS, but we don't always handle it well. As this chapter explains, ongoing stress not only makes us feel bad, it can damage our health and our ability to learn and remember information. Fortunately, nature has provided us with a dietary "chill pill" in the form of—you guessed it—omega-3 fats.

The Stress Response

We may pedal along more smoothly in life and feel mighty fine while doing so, provided the right oil lubes the inner cogs of our brain. At least that's true according to intriguing studies on stress.

The stress response exerts powerful chemical effects throughout the body to help you survive danger. When you encounter a stressor, your blood pressure increases, your heart pumps quicker, you breathe faster, and you become hyper-alert, instantly ready to fight or flee the enemy. When you're stuck in traffic, you're not in imminent danger, but the body's stress response is nonetheless the same. Chemically, your body is geared up for a life-threatening fight—even if it's only battling bumper-to-bumper traffic. The stress response serves you well in an emergency, but it can lead to a host of health problems when chronically activated.

Under Pressure: Your Brain and the Stress Response

When you are stressed out, you likely do not feel your brain cells furling up and closing for business, but in essence that's what occurs. When stress chemicals remain active for too long, they injure and even kill some of your brain cells. They disrupt communication between neurons, slow the formation of new neurons, cause brain cells to age faster, and weaken the blood-brain barrier, which ordinarily prevents toxins from entering the brain.

These changes make our lives more difficult. You might recognize the stress effect on your brain in the form of learning and memory problems. For some people, the stress response can translate into hostile and aggressive behaviors, because the hyper-vigilant and aroused state triggered by the stress response makes it easier to be provoked. Let's take a closer look.

Memory and Learning. Have you ever noticed how your memory dwindles when you're feeling stressed? Too much *cortisol*, a hormone triggered by stress, can prevent the brain from storing new ideas and retrieving long-term memories, so it becomes difficult to think and remember. That's why people can get confused in a crisis. Stress also interferes with the chemicals that neurons use to communicate with each other and that enable you to think.

Cortisol damages the area of the brain critical for learning and memory—the *hippocampus*. Deterioration in this brain region is linked to cognitive decline and Alzheimer's disease.

Brain Degeneration. Studies by Robert M. Sapolsky at Stanford University demonstrated that lots of stress or exposure to cortisol accelerates the degeneration of the aging hippocampus. It's a double whammy, because this part of the brain helps turn off cortisol production. During stress, a degenerated hippocampus functions like a car zooming downhill without brakes; the accelerating production of cortisol further impairs memory and cognition.

Inflammation in the Brain. Stress increases the production of the most damaging inflammatory compound found in the brain, *interleukin-1B*, which causes cognitive problems. Consequently, this "brain-itis" results in anxiety, problems with learning and memory, an increase in the production of a protein associated with Alzheimer's disease, and perpetuation of the cycle of stress.

Omega-3s Put the Brakes on Stress

Omega-3 fats protect against the damaging effects of stress. Conversely, if your diet is low in omega-3 fats and high in omega-6 fats, cognition problems are amplified when you're stressed out:

- Cortisol impairs the formation of the omega-3 fat DHA.
- Omega-6 fats increase stress-induced inflammation.

Omega-3 Fats Act like Aspirin (COX Inhibitors). Recall from Chapter 4 that omega-3 fats inhibit production of the COX enzyme, which induces inflammation. When the COX enzyme is inhibited, it prevents the response to pain and the inflammation caused by the

Omega-3s Help You Hang On to Your Dopamine

Another chemical consequence of stress is depletion of dopamine. Dopamine is the neurotransmitter needed for healthy assertiveness, motivation, sense of readiness, fine motor coordination, and attention. Dopamine changes in the brain are associated with attention deficits and age-related cognitive decline. Depletion of dopamine results not only from stress, but also from poor sleep and inadequate intake of omega-3 fats.

onslaught of stress hormones, including brain inflammation associated with cognitive problems. COX inhibitors have shown beneficial effects on cognitive impairment in Alzheimer's and neurodegenerative diseases.

Omega-3s Lower Stress Hormones in Stressed-Out Students. Several well-designed studies on stressed-out students during peak academic time demonstrated that fish oil or DHA supplements reduce the flood of chemicals triggered by stress.

Omega-3s Lower Stress-Response Chemicals and Aid Learning. In an animal study, omega-3 fats not only reduced the stress response (by lowering cortisol), but also protected the rats in the study from cortisol's damaging effects on learning, as measured by performance on a maze test.

Omega-3s Ameliorate Stress Response Triggered by Anger and Aggression

In 1942 Dr. Hugh Sinclair persuaded the British government to supplement the diet of all children with cod-liver oil, a significant source of omega-3 fats. Sinclair speculated that poor diets could lead to antisocial behavior. His speculation has since been validated by many studies.

Researchers became interested in the hostility-aggression link because it's a component of the type A personality, a risk factor for heart disease. Some researchers believe that one of the reasons omega-3 fats prevent heart disease may be that it can lessen hostility.

Stress-related feelings, notably hostility and anger, trigger the release of stress hormones into the bloodstream, amplifying aggressive behaviors. Stress hormones constrict arteries; increase heartbeat, blood pressure, and the tendency for blood clotting; and elevate sugar and fats in your blood. The net result is an increased risk of heart disease.

The observation studies on extreme hostility are fascinating. For instance, in a 26-country study, higher rates of homicide are associated with lower rates of fish consumption. Violent men with antisocial personality were found to have lower blood levels of DHA and higher levels of omega-6 fats.

Double-blind studies on diverse groups of people, including school-age children, university students, medical students, elderly persons, and even prisoners, show that DHA supplementation markedly lowers aggression and hostility caused by stress. For example, researchers from Japan gave university students either a DHA supplement or a placebo during a stressful period. The students without DHA had a 58 percent increase in stress-induced hostility, while the DHA group had no increase in hostile behaviors.

Omega-3 Fats and Learning Disorders

Even if you are not under stress, omega-3 fats play a remarkable role in learning. Research on children and young animals shows that a deficiency in omega-3 fats triggers learning and memory impairment, which can be reversed by omega-3 supplementation. Symptoms of omega-3 deficiency parallel some of the cognition problems in learning disorders, including disturbances of perception, attention, and behavior.

What Research Tells Us About Omega-3s and Learning

A highly controlled study published in the May 2005 issue of the journal *Pediatrics* demonstrated impressive benefits of omega-3 fats on literacy skills and behavior.

ABCs and Omega-3s: Developmental Coordination Disorder (DCD)

During a three-month period, a team of University of Oxford researchers gave an omega-3 fat supplement to school-age children with developmental coordination disorder (DCD), also known as dyspraxia. The supplemented group experienced marked improvement in reading, spelling, and behavior compared with the placebo group. Notably, the children who received the omega-3 supplement made three times the expected normal gain in reading age and twice the normal gain in spelling age, bringing their average scores toward normal values.

Omega-3s and ADHD

While fatty-acid deficiency is associated with attention deficit hyperactivity disorder (ADHD), two double-blind studies showed no benefit of DHA supplementation on ADHD children. There was, however, a significant lowering of aggression in a study on ADHD using DHA-fortified foods.

As of yet, there are no supplementation studies on adults with ADHD, but a recent study found that adults with ADHD have low blood levels of omega-3 fats.

Interestingly, about 75 percent of adults with ADHD also have other disorders that are associated with a deficiency in omega-3 fats, including depression and dyslexia.

Omega-3s and Dyslexia

Dyslexia is a learning disability that causes difficulty with reading and writing despite the individual having a normal intellect. Omega-3s offer hope in this area of learning. A study on 102 dyslexic children, ages 8 to 12 years, showed that omega-3 supplementation improved reading skills relative to the placebo group.

Omega-3s and Autism

Researchers have just scratched the surface on the effects of omega-3 fats on autism. A case report published in the 2003 *Journal of Clinical Psychiatry* showed that an 11-year-old autistic boy treated with three grams of fish oil daily had notable improvement, whereas medications had failed.

A small but promising study of autistic children found that they had high blood levels of omega-6 fats and lower blood levels of omega-3 fats, particularly EPA. The autistic children were supplemented with EPA-rich fish oil (about 215 milligrams of EPA and 75 milligrams of DHA) for six months. Parents reported improvements in cognitive skills, sleep patterns, eye contact, and sociability, as well as reductions in irritability, aggression, and hyperactivity.

Omega-3s as the Cerebral Fountain of Youth

The effects of aging on brain function include a decreased ability to make DHA. And a low blood level of DHA is a significant risk factor for dementia, including Alzheimer's disease. In a remarkable study, Scottish children born in 1921 and 1936 were followed through age 64. Researchers compared their cognition at the age of 64 with mental-ability test scores from the same subjects at the age of 11 years. Omega-3 fats, especially the ratio of omega-3 to omega-6 in their blood, played a role in the retention of cognitive function in late life, independent of childhood IQ.

In 2005 the U.S. Agency for Healthcare Research and Quality (AHRQ) published a critical review of the impact of omega-3 fats on dementia. According to that report, omega-3 fat consumption, especially DHA, was associated with a significant reduction in the incidence of Alzheimer's disease.

Rusty Thinking: A High Ratio of Omega-6s to Omega-3s Impairs Cognition

Omega-6 fats are implicated as a contributing factor in age-related cognitive disturbances and Alzheimer's disease. A study comparing cognition scores over a three-year period in two groups of men, aged 69 to 89 years, found that those who ate a diet high in omega-6 fats experienced more cognitive decline. Conversely, high fish consumption was protective against impairment.

Fish: The Antidote to Rusty Thinking

The research on the benefits of omega-3 fats—including their food-rich source, fish—is remarkable:

- **Youthful state of mind.** Eating one fish meal a week is equivalent to having the brain function of a person three to four years younger, according to the Chicago Health and Aging Project.

- **Dementia prevention.** The more fish you eat, the less dementia you have. Many large studies show that eating fish provides protection against cognitive impairment and Alzheimer's disease.

- **Speedier thinking.** Higher seafood consumption is linked to faster brain processing speed. Slowed brain processing is one of the early pre-clinical signs of Alzheimer's disease. In 2004, a study involving nearly 1,600 men and women explored the role of omega-3 fats in the middle-aged brain. Eating marine sources of omega-3 fats was found to be associated with less cognitive impairment and better brain processing speed.

How Omega-3s May Prevent Cognitive Decline

Omega-3 fats may help prevent cognitive decline and Alzheimer's disease in many ways. For example, they may turn on genes that keep our brain optimized and keep the brain's cell membranes supple. A recent discovery by Louisiana State University researchers is promising. They found that DHA may protect the brain from the ravages of Alzheimer's disease. DHA creates a compound called *neuroprotectin D1* (NPD1), which promotes brain cell survival and reduces inflammation. Notably, relative to healthy adults, Alzheimer's patients have about ⅒₅ of the protective NPD1 in the brain region critical to memory and cognition. NPD1 also appears to prevent accumulation of a toxin called beta amyloid, which is implicated in Alzheimer's disease.

Omega-3 fats play an amazing role in protecting the brain from the ravages of stress and inflammation, which impacts hostility, learning, and aging. Unbelievably, these fats may offer more benefits from preventing obesity to acquiring better skin, as you will see in the next chapter.

Summary of Chapter 8

• •

Omega-3 fats, especially DHA, lower the chemical stress response in the brain, which:

■ Protects the brain from inflammation ("brain-itis")
■ Minimizes the harmful effects from stress chemicals that affect anxiety, learning, memory, and cognition
■ Puts a lid on hostility and aggression, which are risk factors for heart disease

Fatty-acid deficiency is common in individuals with learning disorders.

■ Omega-3 fatty-acid deficiency causes learning and memory problems in both children and young animals.
■ Omega-3 fats improve reading, spelling, and behavior in children with learning disorders.

Omega-3 fats protect the brain from cognitive decline and Alzheimer's disease by preventing toxins that accumulate in the brain with age and protecting against inflammation.

■ People who eat more omega-3 fats, especially DHA, have a lower incidence of Alzheimer's disease.
■ Eating fish helps the brain to function faster and keeps it biologically younger.

High intakes of omega-6 fats:

■ Increase stress-induced inflammation and may impair learning and behavior
■ Are associated with ADHD, dyslexia, autism, and aggressive and violent behavior
■ May be a contributory factor to Alzheimer's disease

9

On the Horizon
More Benefits of Omega-3s, from Weight Loss to Clear Skin

EMERGING STUDIES of omega-3 fats show promise in a variety of health matters, such as preventing obesity, slowing vision loss, improving insulin resistance, alleviating PMS symptoms, and reducing the risk of cancer. This chapter will explore these promising roles.

Will Omega-3 Fats Prevent Obesity?

A striking body of research indicates that omega-3 fats may help prevent obesity, while omega-6 fats amplify the problem. Keep in mind that obesity is complicated, with many causes and variables. No supplement will offset overeating and inactivity, nor do I want to give the impression that omega-3 fats are a magic bullet for this complex issue.

Omega-6 Fats Trigger Fat Making
The rise in obesity over the last decades is not due to genetics, because it has occurred in too short of a period. A team of French scientists

9

recently reviewed globe-spanning research, leaving no mechanism or relevant study unexplored, including food consumption and obesity trends over the past 40 years. They concluded that omega-6 fats are a "remarkable booster of adipogenesis," meaning the creation of fat. The researchers predict that a disproportionate amount of omega-6 fat in the diet, in conjunction with sedentary lifestyles, will inevitably lead to an increase in the prevalence in obesity worldwide.

So far, animal studies indicate that the omega-6 factor is quite significant. Animals get fatter eating the *same number of calories* when fed diets high in omega-6 fats. Even farm-fed salmon get fatter on diets that are higher in omega-6 fats. Exercising did not offset the effects of a diet high in omega-6; the animals still deposited more fat on their bodies! Why would this occur? Omega-6 fats make the eicosanoid *prostacyclin*, which triggers the cells to make fat, and inflammation perpetuates this cycle. Also, omega-6 fats increase insulin resistance, which makes losing weight more difficult.

Omega-3 Fats Turn Off Fat Making

Studies spanning more than 15 years show ways in which omega-3 fats may help prevent obesity:

- Switching off the genes that make fat
- Lowering insulin (the effects of which are described in the next section)
- Preventing omega-6 fats from creating fat-promoting eicosanoids
- Lowering leptin, a powerful compound produced by fat cells
- Increasing fat burning in the abdominal region of the body

Fish Oil Decreases Body Fat and Increases Metabolism. In a small study from France, healthy adults took six grams of fish oil daily, and they experienced a significant loss of body fat accompanied by an increased metabolic rate without changing their caloric intake! These results are consistent with animal studies in which fish oil lowered body fat while keeping calories constant.

Omega-3 Fats Increase Insulin Effectiveness

Insulin resistance is a growing health problem worldwide. When left unchecked, insulin resistance leads to heart disease, obesity, and diabetes. Many researchers believe that the balance of omega-6 to omega-3 fats is a prime factor in developing insulin resistance. A breakthrough study in the late 1980s averted insulin resistance by replacing high levels of omega-6 fat in the diet with omega-3 fats. In fact, diets high in omega-3 fats and low in omega-6 fats help keep insulin at normal levels.

Omega-3 Fats and Diabetes

The American Pima Indians are well known in research circles for their unusually high rates of obesity and diabetes. Scientists discovered that their muscles are much lower in long-chain omega-3 fats. This is important—the more omega-3s in your muscle cells, the better your insulin works.

The Alaska Siberia Medical Research Program discovered one reason for the alarming rise in diabetes among Alaskan Eskimos: they are eating less of their traditional marine diet, which is high in omega-3s and low in saturated fats. In a promising diabetes prevention study on Alaskan Eskimos with impaired blood sugars, participants resumed their traditional diet for four years. Only one of them developed diabetes, while 60 percent improved their blood sugar levels. They also had better blood pressure and blood cholesterol levels. The researchers attributed the results largely to eating more omega-3s.

Mounting evidence on the benefits of omega-3 fats prompted the American Diabetes Association to recommend eating two to three fish servings per week.

Omega-3s and Clear Skin

Acne affects 79 to 95 percent of adolescents in the United States, with a significant prevalence in children and adults, too. There have been clues that acne is nonexistent in non-industrialized cultures. Notably, when indigenous people make the transition to modern life, acne pops up at incidence rates similar to those of Westerners.

Loren Cordain of Colorado State University discovered holes in the widely accepted belief among dermatologists that there is no connection between diet and acne. Her research team traveled the globe to remote regions to confirm her theory that acne is a phenomenon of Western and Westernized cultures.

In Search of a Pimple

Cordain's group evaluated two such cultures: the native inhabitants of the Kitavan Islands in Papua New Guinea and the Ache population in eastern Paraguay. Both cultures are incredibly healthy; death from heart disease and stroke is extremely rare. All inhabitants were assessed using many health parameters, including a skin evaluation. Upon examination, not a single pimple or blackhead could be found in either population! The researchers concluded that the astonishing difference in acne rates between these cultures and industrialized societies cannot be solely attributed to genetic differences, but likely arises from differing environmental factors, including diet.

Dermatology Dogma Challenged: The Diet-Acne Hypothesis

Cordain believes that diet is a contributing factor to acne, especially because inflammation of the skin occurs in acne development. Recall that omega-3 and omega-6 fats play a key role in modulating inflammation. Notably, a recent study showed that a LOX-blocker medication led to a 70 percent reduction in inflammatory acne lesions. Other research shows that diet-induced insulin resistance may amplify the oil production and development of acne. Interestingly, patients with a medical condition called polycystic ovary syndrome (PCOS) have a prominent feature of insulin resistance and acne. When these patients are treated with medications to improve insulin metabolism, their acne improves.

Also, EPA has been show to improve symptoms in inflammatory skin diseases, with improvement in itching, scaling, and patchy rashes. (Patchy rashes are one of the cardinal signs of inflammation, characterized by an abnormal redness of the skin, which is caused by congestion in the small blood vessels.)

The diet-acne hypothesis is fascinating, but studies are needed to prove cause and effect.

Omega-3s Dampen Pain in Premenstrual Syndrome (PMS)

The prevalence of premenstrual syndrome (PMS) is estimated to range from 20 to 90 percent, and it is the leading cause of recurrent missed school days in teenage girls in the United States. The pain and discomfort of PMS is from an inflammation response. Before menstruation, omega-6 fats are released from the cells and initiate a cascade of inflammatory eicosanoids (prostaglandins and leukotrienes). The omega-6 eicosanoid assault causes constriction of blood vessels and contractions of the cells in the uterus, which leads to the pain of menstrual cramps. The leukotrienes play an important part in generating the symptoms of nausea, vomiting, bloating, and headaches.

According to a 2005 *American Family Physician* review on PMS, the best established initial treatment is the use of nonsteroidal anti-inflammatory drugs (NSAIDs), which include aspirin, naproxen, and ibuprofen. Recall from Chapter 4 that NSAIDs work by blocking the effects of omega-6 fat, by inhibiting COX enzymes, but they have no effect on LOX enzymes. Omega-3 fats found in fish oil block both the inflammatory COX and LOX enzymes.

Fish Oil Eases Menstrual Cramps

In spite of omega-3 fats' known ability to alleviate inflammation, there are surprisingly few studies of their impact on PMS. The studies, though small, consistently show benefits with omega-3 fats.

In one study, researchers gave half of 42 teens fish oil for two months followed by placebo, and the other half of the girls received the same supplementation regime, but in the opposite order. (This is a crossover design, which makes the results more significant.) There was a marked reduction PMS in all groups taking fish oil compared with placebo.

A diet high in omega-6 fats might worsen the PMS cycle because of its role in inflammation. A 1995 Dutch study indicated that a diet high in omega-6 fats was associated with more PMS symptoms. (Keep in mind that the popular over-the-counter PMS pain reliever Midol works by blocking the effects of excess omega-6 fat eicosanoids.)

Omega-3 Fats Dramatically Slow Decline in Eyesight

The long-chain omega-3 fat DHA is required for optimal vision and is highly concentrated in the retina. Eating fish is protective against the risk of developing many eye disorders, while vision problems are associated with low DHA blood levels.

Omega-3 Fats Prolong Vision in Retinitis Pigmentosa

Retinitis pigmentosa is a genetic disorder that leads to progressive vision loss. Many of those afflicted will be legally blind by the age of 40. While there is no cure for this malady, DHA was discovered to play a key role in preventing vision deterioration. Compelling results from a four-year study by a Harvard-led research team, published in 2004, show some encouraging benefits:

- DHA supplementation dramatically slows the decline of vision loss in retinitis pigmentosa.
- Patients eating a diet rich in omega-3 had a 40 to 50 percent slower annual rate of vision loss than patients with a diet lower in omega-3.
- A moderate fish diet (one to two servings a week) could result in 19 additional years of vision!

These results were so extraordinary that the researchers issued an advisory letter to physicians recommending a protocol of 1,200 milligrams of DHA supplementation for the first two years of treatment.[1]

---

1. This advisory letter can be found on the Foundation Fighting Blindness website: blindness
.org/disease/treatment_detail.asp?type=3&id=17.

Omega-3 Fats Decrease the Risk of Age-Related Macular Degeneration

Age-related macular degeneration (AMD) is the leading cause of irreversible visual impairment and blindness in the United States and other developed countries. There are not many studies, but there appears to be a protective relationship between omega-3 fats and risk for AMD, if the diet is low in omega-6 fat. But a diet high in omega-6 fats increases the risk for this disorder.

Omega-3 Fats Are Protective for Dry-Eye Syndrome

Dry-eye syndrome affects 10 million Americans and commonly leads to problems in reading, using a computer, and driving at night. A recent study found that women who ate a diet higher in omega-3 fats had a much lower prevalence of this disorder. In contrast, a high proportion of dietary omega-6 fats was associated with greater prevalence of dry-eye syndrome—more than double the lower rate.

Cataracts

Contrary to popular belief, cataracts are not part of "normal aging." Cataracts are the leading cause of *preventable* blindness in the world. Researchers estimate that if cataract development could be delayed by 10 years, it would reduce surgeries by a whopping 50 percent. Encouraging results from the Nurses' Health Study indicate that eating greater amounts of omega-3 fats and fish lowers the risk of cataract development.

Preventing, Fighting, and Treating Cancer

Cancer is the leading cause of death among Americans under the age of 85, and it affects nearly every organ in the body. A substantial body of research shows that omega-3 fats not only may prevent cancer, but also may improve the survival rate of patients who already have cancer. In fact, promising animal studies show that omega-3 fats can slow the growth of cancer and increase the beneficial affects of chemotherapy while reducing side effects. The cancers most responsive to the benefits of omega-3 fats are hormone-sensitive cancers including breast, prostate, and colon cancer. Yet there are some conflicting results, many of which are attributed to the scientists not controlling for the amount of omega-6 fat in the diet.

How Omega-3 Fats May Prevent or Slow Cancer in Patients

Here are ways that omega-3 fats may impede cancer (notably, they relate to the interplay with omega-6 fat eicosanoids):

- **Slowing growth of tumors.** Cancer cells must multiply to grow, a process known as mitosis. The omega-6 eicosanoid compounds using the COX and LOX enzymes accelerate this process. Omega-3 fats inhibit both of these enzymes and have been shown to inhibit mitosis of breast and colon cancers.

- **Restoring the body's ability to clean house.** We naturally get rid of unneeded or sick cells by a process known as programmed cell death, or apoptosis. But this process is disrupted in cancers, and cells continue to multiply. The omega-6 compounds made by the COX-2 enzyme hamper the body's ability to get rid of unwanted cells, which allows the cancer cells to proliferate. Omega-3 fats, especially DHA, counteract this problem.

- **Suppressing development of new blood vessels.** For cancers to grow, new blood vessels must develop (to feed the cancer). Omega-6 eicosanoids made by the COX and LOX enzymes stimulate growth of new blood vessels, whereas omega-3 fats inhibit this process.

- **Altering estrogen (not just a woman's hormone).** While you may be aware that estrogen can promote breast cancer, the same is true for cancers of the prostate and colon. Omega-6 fats increase estrogen levels, while omega-3 fats are the counterbalance.

Lipidome Theory: Balanced Omega Fats Are the Likely Key to Cancer Prevention

Many researchers believe that the balance of omega-3 and omega-6 fats, not one particular fat, affects the development of cancer. Many studies indicate that to reduce the risk of cancer, you need to reduce the proportion of dietary omega-6 to omega-3 fats, achieving a ratio somewhere in the range of 1-to-1 to 2-to-1.

That's a dramatic departure from the current Western diet—but it can be done. The chapters in Part 3 will show you how to get started.

Summary of Chapter 9

● ●

Omega-3 fats may help prevent obesity by:

- Switching off the genes that make fat
- Lowering hormones associated with obesity (insulin and leptin)
- Preventing omega-6 fats from making their fat-making compounds

Omega-3 fats increase effectiveness of insulin and may prevent diabetes.

- Replacing omega-6 fats with omega-3 fats may prevent insulin resistance.
- Eskimos developed diabetes rapidly when they ate less of their traditional marine diet.

Acne may be a result of Westernized diets, which are low in omega-3 fats and high in omega-6 fats.

- One study found no pimples in two non-Westernized cultures.
- Inflammation and insulin resistance play a role in acne development.

Continued

Omega-3 fats provide relief for PMS.

- Fish eaters have fewer PMS symptoms.
- In studies, groups taking fish oil supplements had fewer PMS symptoms compared to placebo groups.
- PMS symptoms are triggered by omega-6 fat eicosanoids.

Vision disorders are improved with omega-3 fats.

- Omega-3 fats extend years of vision to retinitis pigmentosa sufferers.
- High omega-3 fat diets decrease the risk of cataracts, dry-eye syndrome, and age-related macular degeneration.

The balance between dietary omega-6 and omega-3 fats is critical to cancer prevention.

- Omega-3 fats slow cancer by preventing cells from multiplying, suppressing new blood vessels that feed cancer, and blunting omega-6 fat eicosanoids formation.
- Most studies do not evaluate the dietary omega-6 fats, which explains many of the conflicting results from omega-3 fat studies.

PART 3

How to Omega-Optimize Your Diet

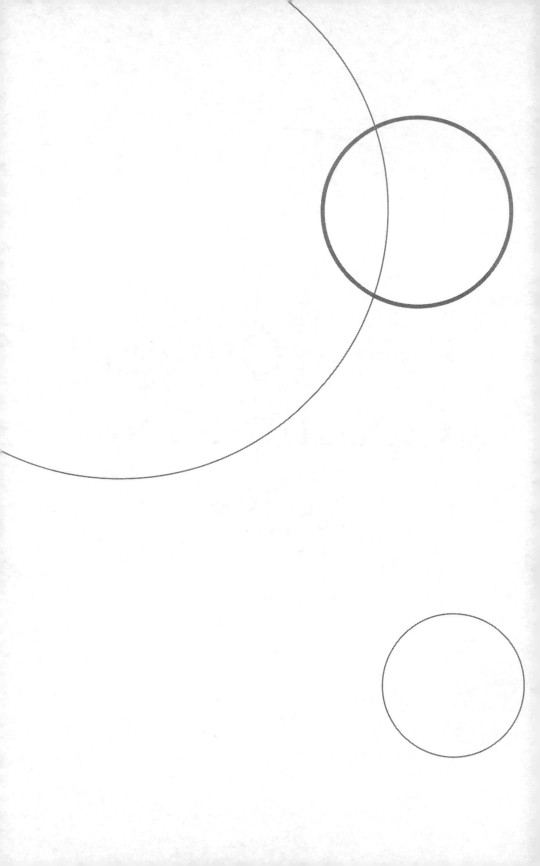

Get Enough Short-Chain Omega-3 Fats in Your Diet

ANY OF MY health-conscious patients have thought they were eating enough omega-3 fats, only to learn, to their dismay, that they were wrong. More often than not, they were eating only *one type* of omega-3 fat, meaning they weren't getting enough omega-3 fats overall, which indeed is a problem. It can be confusing to sort out which omega-3 fats really matter.

Lumping all of the omega-3 fats together as one entity in your diet is the equivalent of assuming that you eat enough of the fat-soluble vitamins if you eat primarily vitamin A–rich foods while ignoring the three other fat-soluble vitamins, D, E, and K, which come from completely different foods. Similarly, the omega-3 fats have significant differences.

Recall that there are three key omega-3 fats: the plant-based ALA and the long-chain EPA and DHA, which are marine-based. The parent omega-3, ALA, is not the same as the fish-based omega-3s. If you focus on eating only ALA (for example, flaxseed oil), you will likely be deficient in EPA and DHA, which are the most important omega-3s. In this chapter you will learn how much of the short-chain omega-3 fat, ALA, you need and where to find it in your diet.

ALA: The Short-Chain Omega-3 Fat

ALA is considered *the* essential omega-3, and it's actually not difficult to get enough of this particular fat. Surprised? That's because ALA is found even in oils that are dominated by omega-6 fats, such as soybean oil. But the ALA in soybean oil is outnumbered by nearly eight times as much of the omega-6 fat linoleic acid. (This is also the reason you will sometimes read that soybean oil is a good source of ALA in the American diet. It's true, but the nutritional price is too high because of the level of omega-6 fat also found in it.) You need to take care in choosing foods containing omega-3 fats, because you don't want to simultaneously flood your body with omega-6 fats.

How Much ALA Do You Need?

You need to get at least 2,200 milligrams (2.2 grams) of ALA a day in your diet. If you don't eat fish, you will need more.

Common Plant-Based Sources of ALA

ALA is found primarily in plant foods, including dark green leafy vegetables, beans, certain oils, and flax and its related products (such as flaxseed oil and flax meal). However, these foods do not contain the other important omega-3 fats, EPA and DHA. The foods described in the following list can be found in most grocery stores and are summarized in Table 10.1:

- **Flax meal and flaxseed oil.** Not only are flax foods an excellent source of ALA, but flax is also very low in omega-6 fats. Unlike any other common vegetable oil, flaxseed oil contains *more* omega-3s than omega-6 fats. That's why flax is an especially stellar omega-3 fat food. Ground flaxseed, or flax meal, is an excellent source of omega-3 fats. A rounded teaspoonful will meet 100 percent of your ALA needs for the day. A notable cold cereal that has been around since long before the omega-3 excitement is Uncle Sam, which is an excellent source of ALA. One cup of this cereal provides more than 100 percent of your ALA needs for the day.

TABLE 10.1 Common Foods High in ALA (and Low in Omega-6 Fat)

You need at least 2,200 milligrams of this short-chain omega-3 fat each day.

Food	Amount	ALA Content (milligrams)
BEANS/LEGUMES		
Black beans, cooked	1 cup	180
Kidney beans, cooked	1 cup	300
Black-eyed peas, cooked	1 cup	200
Navy beans, cooked	1 cup	220
Pinto beans, canned, cooked	1 cup	400
CEREAL		
Flax meal	4 teaspoons	2,470
Kashi Go Lean Crunch	1 cup	230
Uncle Sam cereal	1 cup	3,290
FRUIT		
Blueberries	1 cup	80
Raspberries, fresh	1 cup	150
OILS AND SPREADS		
Canola oil	1 teaspoon	430
Best Foods Canola Real Mayonnaise	1 teaspoon	367
Canola oil margarine	1 teaspoon	333
Flaxseed oil	1 teaspoon	2,420
Mustard oil	1 teaspoon	277
VEGETABLES		
Broccoli florets, fresh	1 cup	90
Grape leaves, canned	2 ounces	480
Romaine lettuce, chopped	3 cups	180
Spinach, cooked	1 cup	160

- **Walnuts and walnut oil.** Walnuts are the only common nuts with a significant source of omega-3 fat. However, for each gram of ALA, you get *five* additional grams of omega-6 fat, LA. If eaten in large quantities, walnuts can be quite an omega-6 overload.

- **Canola oil and spreads.** This oil is a good source of ALA. For every one gram of omega-3 fat, you get two grams of omega-6 fat, which is considered a balanced level. That's why it is important to choose canola oil not only for cooking, but also for margarines, mayonnaise, and salad dressing. Best Foods/Hellman's markets one of the few national brands of canola-based mayonnaise, Best Foods Canola Real Mayonnaise.

- **Legumes.** Beans, especially kidney and pinto beans, are a good source of omega-3 fats, providing 300 and 400 milligrams of ALA, respectively, meeting nearly one-fifth of your daily needs in a one-cup serving.

A Close-Up on Margarines: Which Is Best for You?

Margarine is one of the primary sources of fat in the American diet—and a top source of omega-6 fats. While most margarine brands have been reformulated to get rid of the unhealthful trans fats, many still use soybean oil or some type of vegetable oil blend, which means the oil is high in omega-6 fats. When choosing margarine, keep the following thoughts in mind:

- The first and primary ingredient should be *liquid canola oil.*
- Don't assume that "vegetable oil blend" contains predominantly canola oil.
- Don't assume that a label stating "rich in omega-3" means the margarine is a significant source of omega-3 fat.
- Don't assume that a spread labeled "omega-3" is low in omega-6 fat.

A good example of the margarine quandary is Promise Buttery Spread. It is emblazoned with the description "Rich in Omega 3 ALA." Yet it contains a large amount of omega-6 fat compared with its omega-3 content: 3,400 milligrams, or nearly nine times the amount of ALA.

Table 10.2 provides a look at the omega fat profiles of national brands of margarine. Remember, the lower the omega-6 fat, the better.

TABLE 10.2 Omega Fat Profiles of Margarine Brands

Brand (1 tablespoon)	Omega-6 (milligrams)	Omega-3 (milligrams)	Ratio of Omega-6 to Omega-3*
Canola Harvest			
Margarine	2,000	1,000	2:1
Margarine with calcium	2,000	800	2:1
Margarine with flax	2,000	1,700	1:1
Earth Balance			
Margarine	3,380	410	8:1
Spread stick	2,800	330	8:1
Whipped buttery spread	3,180	370	9:1
Nucoa			
Margarine stick	3,400	520	7:1
Soft margarine	4,090	640	6:1
Promise Buttery Spread	3,400	400	9:1
Smart Balance			
Spread	2,700	470	6:1
Light margarine	1,300	220	6:1
Light with flax	1,200	320	4:1
Margarine (regular)	2,300	400	6:1
Omega Plus	2,200	560	4:1
Superlight margarine	450	140	3:1
Soy Garden margarine	3,400	430	8:1

*Rounded to the nearest whole number.

- **Fruits.** Blueberries and raspberries are among the few fruits that contain omega-3 fats, although the amount per serving is small.

- **Dark green leafy vegetables.** These vegetables include spinach, broccoli, romaine lettuce, and basil. More than half of the fat in these dark green veggies are ALA, but since vegetables are naturally low in fat, you have to consume a large amount to meet your ALA needs—although it gives you another reason to eat your veggies! An entree salad with three cups of romaine will provide nearly 10 percent of your daily ALA needs.

Novel Sources of ALA

Some new foods are wonderful sources of ALA and low in omega-6 fat. Many of the foods listed here can be found at health food stores or can be ordered online or by mail. Others are still in the market research phase, so they aren't yet widely available. Their ALA content is summarized in Table 10.3. Look for any of these new products:

- **Specialty oils.** The seeds from many types of berries are full of omega-3 fat. These include black raspberry oil, blueberry oil, boysenberry oil, cranberry oil, marionberry oil, and red raspberry oil. You may wonder how this can be the case, as these fruits are very low in fat. The source is in the seeds. Fruit seeds are one of the major by-products of manufacturing fruit juice and seedless jams. About five to eight pounds of fruit (raspberries, cranberries, etc.) are needed to provide enough seeds to produce one teaspoon of oil, but the seeds are plentiful. Researchers are exploring the possibility of turning the berry seeds into a coarse meal (like flax meal, which is made from ground flaxseed). Black raspberry meal looks especially promising because it contains over 600 milligrams of ALA per ounce.

- **Hemp.** This may sound like a novel food, but ALA was first isolated from hempseed oil in 1887. Notably, hemp also contains another type of omega-3 fat, called stearadonic acid (see sidebar on page

TABLE 10.3 Less Common Foods High in ALA (and Low in Omega-6)

Food	ALA (milligrams)	Ratio of Omega-6 to Omega-3 Fats
BERRY SEED OILS		
Black raspberry oil (1 teaspoon)	1,702	2:1
Blueberry oil (1 teaspoon)	1,213	2:1
Boysenberry oil (1 teaspoon)	943	3:1
Cranberry oil (1 teaspoon)	1,071	2:1
Marionberry oil (1 teaspoon)	764	4:1
Red raspberry oil (1 teaspoon)	1,566	2:1
SEEDS AND NUTS		
Butternuts (2 tablespoons)	2,470	4:1
Chia seeds (2 tablespoons)	4,980	<1:1
HEMP FOODS		
Hemp seed nut butter (2 tablespoons)	2,000	3:1
Hemp flour (2 tablespoons)	600	3:1
Hemp seed oil (1 teaspoon)	833	3:1
Hemp seed nuts (2 tablespoons)	2,000	3:1
Hemp protein powder (1 ounce)	1,200	2.8
Perilla oil (1 teaspoon)	3,045	<1:1
Purslane (1 cup raw)	172	<1:1

SOURCES: For details, see References under Okuyuma, Parry, Parker, Simopoulos, and USDA.

136). While hemp is related to the marijuana plant, it is not the same thing. Hemp is a distinct variety of the plant species, *Cannabis sativa L*, but due to the similar leaf shape, hemp is frequently confused with marijuana. Although both plants are from the same species, hemp contains virtually no THC, the psychoactive ingredient in marijuana. The fruit of hemp is not a true seed, but a tiny nut covered by a hard shell. Hemp use for foods is becoming mainstream, including hemp nut butter, hemp oil, hemp flour, and hemp cereal. These products can be found at Trader Joe's, Whole Foods Market, and in the health food aisle in grocery stores.

- **Chia seeds.** If you are thinking "Chia Pet," you are right on the mark! These are the same seeds/sprouts that turn a naked pottery animal into one with a full bushy green fur. Two tablespoons of these seeds provide more than 200 percent of your daily needs for ALA.

- **Seaweed.** This abundant plant of the ocean is a good source of omega-3 fats. It is used in many Asian cuisines, from sushi to seaweed salad. You can find seaweeds in the international section of many grocery stores and in specialty ethnic-food shops.

- **Butternuts.** These rich, buttery-tasting nuts, also known as "white walnuts," are grown on butternut trees. Unfortunately, this tree is

---

Another Short-Chain Omega-3 Fat: Stearadonic Acid (SDA)

• •

Researchers are taking a closer look at another member of the omega-3 fat family, stearadonic acid (SDA). It appears to be three to ten times more powerful than its parent, ALA, for its ability to create EPA. One study estimated that 1,000 milligrams of SDA can make 300 milligrams of EPA, whereas the same amount of ALA will make a mere 20 milligrams of EPA. Why so powerful? It's because SDA bypasses a critical bottleneck, where one of the coveted enzymes can limit production of EPA. Researchers are experimenting with ways to incorporate SDA into canola oil to overcome our dietary omega-3 shortfall. Hemp is one of the few available foods that contain SDA.

vulnerable to the disease butternut canker, which has wiped out 80 percent of the butternut trees in some eastern states. Fortunately, more than a dozen different kinds of butternut trees are flourishing in Oregon under the protection the U.S. Department of Agriculture.

- **Purslane.** This wild-growing plant is the richest source of ALA of any green leafy vegetable yet studied (it has nearly five times the ALA content of spinach). Most significantly, it is one of the few plants known to contain EPA. It is used in soups and salads in the Mediterranean and in the Middle East. It is the eighth most commonly distributed plant in the world, and while it is not typically eaten in the United States, purslane is found in all 50 states. You have probably seen it, as it is a common weed!

- **Perilla seed oil.** Perilla oil comes from the perilla plant, which is also known as Chinese basil and purple mint. This plant originated in China and is now cultivated in India, Japan, Korea, and Thailand. It's also a common weed found in pastures and roadsides in the southeastern United States. The fat profile of perilla oil is similar to that of flaxseed oil; it contains a preponderance of ALA (61 percent) while being low in omega-6 fat. In the United States, ethnic-food stores that cater to people from Korea and Japan generally carry some perilla products, including fresh greens in season, seed oil, pickled plums, plum sauce, and other condiments. Perilla foliage and seed oil are used in Asian cooking, and the seeds are eaten in Japan, Korea, and India.

As this chapter has shown, there are several easy ways to get enough ALA in your diet. But regardless of how much ALA you eat, you cannot rely on it to make adequate amounts of the long-chain omega-3 fats, EPA and DHA. You can be deficient in EPA and DHA even while eating large amounts of ALA-rich foods, such as flax. The next chapter explores how much of the long-chain omega-3 fats you need and what to do if you are a vegetarian or if you don't like or choose to eat fish, the main source of these omega-3s.

Summary of Chapter 10

• •

There are three key omega-3 fats that your body needs: ALA, EPA, and DHA.

- ALA is the plant-based omega-3 fat, known as a short-chain omega-3 fat.
- Together, EPA and DHA are collectively known as long-chain omega-3 fats.
- ALA seldom makes the powerful and beneficial long-chain omega-3s, EPA and DHA.

Get enough short-chain omega-3 fat, alpha linoleic acid (ALA).

- Aim for at least 2,200 milligrams each day.
- If you are vegetarian, you need at least 4,400 milligrams each day.

Excellent food sources of ALA are:

- Flax oil, flax meal
- Hemp nut seeds and its oil
- Canola oil and spreads made from it
- Dried beans, especially pinto and kidney beans

Some foods are high in ALA but are also high in omega-6 fat.

- Walnuts and walnut oil can be part of a healthy diet but need to be used carefully.
- Soybean oil has ALA, but it has eight times as much omega-6 and is best avoided.

Get Enough Long-Chain Omega-3 Fats in Your Diet

EPA AND DHA are vitally important nutrients that are critical to health, but sadly, the average American consumes only 9 to 15 percent of the levels recommended for health. It's even worse for vegetarians and others who don't eat fish.

If, like most people, you're not getting enough long-chain omega-3 fats, it's important to seek out ways to get enough in your diet, whether by eating more seafood and omega-enriched foods or by taking a supplement (or any combination of these). In this chapter you will learn how much EPA and DHA you need and how to get them in your diet. You'll discover how to make the best of your fish choices (if you are willing) and what to do if you shun fish or are vegetarian. You will also learn how a loophole in the food-labeling law makes it especially confusing to determine whether a food is a good source of omega-3 fat.

How Much EPA and DHA Do You Need?

You need to get at least a combined total of 650 milligrams (less than 1 gram) of long-chain omega-3 fats (EPA and DHA) a day in your diet. Of this combined total, you need at least 220 milligrams each of

EPA and DHA. If you are pregnant or breastfeeding, the minimum DHA requirement increases to 300 milligrams. If you have heart disease, the total requirement for long-chain omega-3 fats is nearly doubled to 1,000 milligrams. The requirements are summarized in Table 11.1.

Most experts agree that you cannot depend on ALA, the omega-3 fat in plant foods, to create enough EPA or DHA in your body. It just doesn't happen reliably, and when it does, the levels are quite small. For example, one study showed that if you ate 1,000 milligrams of ALA, only a minuscule amount of long-chain omega-3s is created—just 27 milligrams. Since the average American eats 1,300 to 1,700 milligrams of ALA, this means, at best, your body will make 35 to 46 milligrams of long-chain omega-3 fats, *less than 1 percent* of your needs for EPA and DHA. Also, when you factor in that the typical American diet is too high in omega-6 fats, it is even less likely that ALA will be made into the long-chain omega-3s in your body.

That's why if you rely only on eating flax and other plant sources of omega-3 fat, you will still fall short of your EPA and DHA requirements. If you are vegetarian or seldom eat fish, you are at even higher risk for omega-3 fat deficiency.

TABLE 11.1 Recommended Diet Levels of Long-Chain Omega-3 Fats

| | Milligrams of Omega-3s | | |
| | Basic Needs | Special Needs | |
		Pregnancy	Heart Disease
EPA	220 (minimum)	220	Not specified
DHA	220 (minimum)	300	Not specified
Total long-chain (DHA + EPA)	650	650	1,000

SOURCE: Based on the 2000 international recommendations made by the International Society for the Study of Fatty Acids and Lipids (ISSFAL), described in detail in Chapter 3.

Vegetarians and Long-Chain Omega-3 Fats

. . . .

When it comes to the *specific types* of omega-3 fats, there is a big problem for vegetarians. Vegans (those on the strictest, animal-free diet) have negligible amounts of EPA and DHA in their diets, and even the less strict vegetarians don't fare much better, averaging an EPA and DHA intake of only 5 milligrams and 33 milligrams, respectively—far short of the needed 650 milligrams daily.

For vegetarians and others who consume little if any fish, the amount of omega-6 fat in their diet is of greater relevance. Paradoxically, many vegetarians eat far more omega-6 fats than meat eaters do. Vegans have a ratio of omega-6 to omega-3 fat ranging from 14-to-1 to 20-to-1. Vegetarians who include egg and dairy products in their diet (lacto-ovovegetarians) fare a little better, with a ratio between 10-to-1 and 16-to-1. Meanwhile, most omnivores have a ratio of 10-to-1.

Between the low consumption of long-chain omega-3 fats and the competing high proportion of dietary omega-6 fats, vegetarians not surprisingly have EPA and DHA blood levels that are much lower than those of meat eaters. This problem is also true for vegan mothers who breastfeed their babies. Researchers found that these babies have significantly lower levels of long-chain omega-3 fats in their bodies than infants who are breastfed by omnivore mothers. Vegan mothers' milk contains less than half the levels of DHA than are in the milk of their meat-eating counterparts. This is important, because babies need DHA for their developing brains, just as bones need calcium.

Most experts agree that it is *impossible* for vegetarians, especially strict vegans (who eat no animals or their by-products), to get enough EPA and DHA from their diet. Some suggest that vegetarians double the recommended amount of the plant-based omega-3, ALA, which would be about 4,400 milligrams. Vegetarians would benefit from algae-based EPA and DHA supplements.

Food Sources of Long-Chain Omega-3s

The major dietary source of EPA and DHA is seafood, but these long-chain omega-3s can also be found in lean red meat, organ meats such as liver and brain, and eggs. Very small amounts are also found in dairy products, and EPA is found in small amounts in seaweed and purslane (described in the last chapter).

If you don't eat fish, you will need to find other options, or else you will not eat enough long-chain omega-3 fats. There are ways around this issue, however. First, let's look at fish and its surrounding issues, as it's not so straightforward even if you enjoy it. Then we'll look at enriched foods, a promising yet perplexing new way of getting more omega-3s into our diet.

The Seafood Chain

While fish are great *sources* of long-chain omega-3 fats, they, like humans, are not adept at making them. Surprised? EPA and DHA are accumulated up the aquatic food chain (big fish eats little fish), so it's not that fish are inherently high in omega-3 fats.

What a fish eats will determine its flesh content of EPA and DHA. In the ocean, algae or phytoplankton make the omega-3 fat ALA. The small sea critters (zooplankton) eat the algae and elongate its ALA into the long-chain omega-3 fats EPA and DHA. Consequently, fish acquire EPA and DHA directly by eating the plankton (or by eating other fish that have eaten those microbes).

The good news is that several fish are rich sources of long-chain omega-3 fats. See Table 11.2 for a list of these sources.

If you eat four fatty-fish-based meals each week (including salmon, halibut, or sardines), you will meet the current international recommendations for long-chain omega-3 fats (650 milligrams a day).

The Fish Dish: Is It Safe to Eat?

Despite their valuable omega-3 fat and nutritious qualities, fish can pose health risks when contaminated with heavy metals such as mercury and industrial chemicals such as dioxin. This problem is not limited to oceans, rivers, and lakes. It's also an issue of farm-raised

TABLE 11.2 Rich Sources of Long-Chain Omega-3 Fats (EPA and DHA)

You need at least 650 milligrams of the long-chain omega-3 fats (EPA and DHA) each day. Of this, at least 200 milligrams each of EPA and DHA need to be eaten.

Fish (3 ounces), Cooked	Milligrams of Omega-3s		
	EPA	DHA	Total (EPA + DHA)
Anchovies, European, canned with oil, drained	650	1,100	1,750
Bass			
Sea, mixed species	180	470	650
Striped	180	640	820
Bluefish	270	570	840
Carp	260	120	380
Cisco, smoked	650	1,100	1,750
Flounder	210	220	430
Gefilte fish	140	340	480
Halibut			
Atlantic/Pacific	80	320	400
Greenland	570	430	1,000
Herring, Atlantic	770	940	1,710
Mackerel			
Atlantic	430	590	1,020
King	150	190	340
Pacific and Jack	560	1,020	1,580
Spanish	250	810	1,060
Pompano	170	370	540
Sablefish			
Fillet	740	780	1,520
Smoked	760	800	1,560
Salmon			
Atlantic, farmed	590	1,240	1,830
Atlantic, wild	350	1,220	1,570
Chinook	860	620	1,480
Chinook, smoked	160	230	390

Continued

TABLE 11.2 Rich Sources of Long-Chain Omega-3 Fats (EPA and DHA) (continued)

Fish (3 ounces), Cooked	Milligrams of Omega-3s		
	EPA	DHA	Total (EPA + DHA)
Salmon, continued			
Chum	250	430	680
Chum, w/ bone, canned	400	600	1,000
Coho, farmed	350	740	1,090
Coho, wild	340	560	900
Pink, canned	310	590	900
Pink	460	640	1,100
Sockeye	450	600	1,050
Sockeye, with bone, canned	480	750	1,230
Sardines, Atlantic	400	430	830
Sashimi (raw)			
Mackerel, Pacific and Jack	430	790	1,220
Salmon, Chinook	860	800	1,660
Tuna, bluefin	240	760	1,000
Smelt, rainbow	300	460	760
Spot	240	450	690
Suckerfish	210	320	530
Tilefish	150	620	770
Trout			
Mixed species	220	580	800
Rainbow, farmed	280	700	980
Rainbow, wild	400	440	840
Sea	180	230	410
Tuna			
Bluefin	310	970	1,280
Dried	300	950	1,250
Smoked	560	1,020	1,580
White, canned in water, drained	200	530	730
Whitefish, mixed species	350	1,030	1,380
Wolffish, Atlantic	330	340	670

SOURCE: USDA Nutrient Database, nal.usda.gov/fnic/foodcomp/search.

fish. But if you choose carefully, the benefits of eating fish far outweigh the health risks.

Salmon Savvy: Problems on the Farm. Over half of the salmon sold
globally is farm-raised. In fact, during the past 20 years, the output
of farmed salmon has risen from about 24,000 to over 1 million
metric tons! This may seem like good news because more salmon
is available to eat, but that isn't necessarily so. Recently, researchers
have discovered problems with farmed salmon.

One recent study evaluated farmed versus wild salmon from
around the world. Researchers collected salmon totaling two metric
tons, which included Atlantic salmon from 51 farms in six countries,
135 wild Pacific salmon, and farmed salmon purchased from 16 cit-
ies throughout North America and Europe. The research team found
several problems with farmed salmon:

- **Higher levels of contaminants.** The issue here is not mercury,
  but dioxin, which is associated with numerous adverse health
  effects. Just as salmon acquire (or bioaccumulate) omega-3 fats
  from their diet, which then gets deposited into their flesh, the
  same is true for contaminants. Studies show that the likely source
  of dioxin and other pollutants is the feed given to the farmed
  fish. European farmed salmon have significantly higher levels of
  contaminants than those raised on North and South American
  farms.

- **Higher levels of total fat.** As shown in Table 11.3, farmed salmon
  is much higher in fat than wild salmon—nearly three times
  higher (17 percent versus 6 percent fat). This is especially a concern because dioxin accumulates in the fat. The more fat, the
  more contaminants.

- **Higher levels of omega-6 fat.** Farmed salmon has a markedly
  greater amount of omega-6 fat. How can this be? Remember, fish

TABLE 11.3 Fat Profile of Wild and Farmed Salmon

Type of Fat	Fat Content per 3 Ounces	
	Wild Pacific Salmon	Farmed Atlantic Salmon
Total fat (grams)	6	17
Omega-6 fat (milligrams)	128	880
Omega-3 fat (milligrams)	1,222	3,373

SOURCE: Foran, J. A., et al. "Quantitative Analysis of the Benefits and Risks of Consuming Farmed and Wild Salmon." *Journal of Nutrition* 135 (2005): 2639–43.

are really no different from cattle when it comes to diet. What the animals eat will ultimately become an integral part of their flesh. Farmed salmon eat a diet higher in omega-6 fat, so that's what ends up in their flesh.

Benefits Beyond the Risks. While this information may be distressing, the research team analyzed the benefits and risks of eating farmed salmon compared with wild salmon and had encouraging conclusions. Eating wild salmon was considered 900 times more beneficial relative to any adverse health risk. But even the farmed salmon, with its inherent problems, had 300 times greater benefit than health risk.

Not all fish farming is adverse to your health or the environment. Farmed mollusks (clams, oysters, mussels, bay scallops) are one of the least ecologically harmful forms of aquaculture. They require no feed, since they strain their food (plankton) out of the water. Their way of feeding helps filter the water and in some cases improves the water quality.

Tackling the Mercury Dilemma. The health risk from consuming mercury depends on the amount of seafood eaten and its level of mercury. Mercury occurs naturally in the environment, but it also finds its way into streams and the ocean through industrial pollution. The bacteria in the ocean convert mercury into a more toxic

Mercury Matters

• •

The levels of mercury in fish are expressed in terms of parts per million (ppm). The FDA has set a maximum permissible level of one part of mercury in a million parts of seafood (1 ppm), which is equal to one milligram of mercury per 2.2 pounds of fish.

Table 11.4 lists the highest and lowest mercury levels in various types of seafood, based on a 2006 U.S. government report.

TABLE 11.4 Mercury Content of Popular Fish

Fish	Mercury ppm
Shrimp, clams, ocean perch, and canned salmon	0*
Tilapia	0.010
Oysters	0.013
Salmon	0.014
Sardines	0.016
Haddock	0.031
Crawfish	0.033
Pollock	0.041
Anchovies	0.043
Herring	0.044
Mackerel, king	0.730
Swordfish	0.976
Shark	0.988
Tilefish	1.45

*No mercury was detected.

SOURCE: 2006 U.S. Government report (cfsan.fda.gov/~frf/sea-mehg.html, accessed January 14, 2007).

form, methylmercury, which fish accumulate through eating and by the water passing through their gills. Generally, larger predatory fish that live longer have more time to accumulate mercury than small and younger fish. Mercury and all its compounds are toxic to virtually all forms of life, especially to the brain and nervous system of unborn babies and young children.

FDA/EPA Safe-Seafood Recommendations. The Food and Drug Administration (FDA) and the Environmental Protection Agency (EPA) issued guidelines to help consumers reap the benefits of eating seafood while minimizing exposure to mercury. While the guidelines are aimed at pregnant women, breastfeeding mothers, and young children, it makes sense for most people to follow them, with the exception of limiting your fish to 12 ounces per week. After all, if the goal is to eat more fish, it seems prudent to limit your risk of mercury exposure. While your body has ways to get rid of mercury naturally, it may take over a year for the levels to drop significantly.

Here are the recommendations by the FDA and EPA:

- Avoid shark, swordfish, king mackerel, and tilefish, which are high in mercury.
- Eat up to 12 ounces a week of a variety of fish and shellfish that are lower in mercury. Five of the most commonly eaten fish that are low in mercury are shrimp, canned light tuna, salmon, pollock, and catfish. Another commonly eaten fish, albacore ("white") tuna, contains more mercury than canned light tuna. So, when choosing fish and shellfish, you may eat up to 6 ounces (one average meal) of albacore tuna per week. Also, fish sticks are commonly made from fish that are low in mercury: Pacific pollock, which is caught primarily in Alaskan waters. Of course, you want to be sure that the fish sticks are baked, rather than fried.
- Check local advisories about the safety of fish caught by family and friends in your local lakes, rivers, and coastal areas. If no advice is available, eat up to 6 ounces (one average meal) per week of fish you catch from local waters, but don't consume any other fish during that week.

Making the Most of Your Fish Choices. Fish high in omega-3s that are caught or farmed in an ecologically sound manner and are low in contaminants include wild salmon from Alaska (fresh, frozen, and canned), Atlantic mackerel, herring, sardines, sablefish, anchovies, and farmed oysters. Here's what to consider when choosing fish for a meal:

- When it comes to salmon, choose wild rather than farmed. Wild salmon may be labeled as wild, Alaskan, or one of five Pacific salmon species: chinook/king, coho/silver, chum/silverbrite, pink, and sockeye. Alaskan salmon is always wild, since there are no salmon farms in Alaska.
- Choose light tuna rather than albacore, as it has one-third the amount of mercury. Opt for water-packed. Limit tuna steaks to 6 ounces in one week, because they contain higher levels of mercury than canned light tuna.
- Choose low-mercury fish: salmon (including canned), sole, tilapia, haddock, shrimp, clams, ocean perch, crawfish, anchovies, herring, and sardines.
- Eat a wide variety of types of fish, not only to minimize mercury exposure, but also to increase your omega-3 intake.
- Check FDA and EPA Fish Advisories for updated information, which can be found at epa.gov/waterscience/fish/states.htm.
- Prepare your fish in a way that cuts down on contaminants. These techniques do not affect mercury content, because mercury is bound to the protein or flesh part of the fish.
  - *Before cooking:* Remove the skin, fat, internal organs, tomalley of lobster, and mustard of crabs, where toxins are likely to accumulate. This will greatly reduce the risk of exposure to a number of hazardous chemicals.
  - *While cooking:* Let the fat drain away to reduce fish drippings.
  - *Grill or broil, rather than fry:* Frying seals in pollutants that might be in the fish's fat; grilling or broiling allows fat to drain away.
  - *When smoking fish:* Remove the skin before the fish is smoked.
- Look for the Environmental Defense Fund's good "eco-choices," which are recommendations for fish that are healthy choices for both the oceans and you, being safe to eat as well as not

Tuna Terminology Tune-Up

• •

There are many types of tuna, and your choice can make a significant impact on your exposure to mercury.

Canned Tuna

■ *Albacore*, sold as canned white tuna, is higher in mercury.
■ Light tuna is primarily *skipjack* tuna, the smallest of the commercial tuna. These small tunas have short lifespans and rapid reproduction rates, which is why they are also significantly lower in mercury.

Tuna Steaks

■ *Yellowfin* and *bigeye* tuna, also known as ahi, is usually sold as fresh or frozen steaks. These are larger tuna and therefore higher in mercury content.
■ *Bluefin* is highly prized for its flesh and popular for sushi and sashimi. Unlike most tunas, bluefin tunas are slow growing and late to mature, so they are less resilient to fishing pressure, which makes them a type to limit.

endangered. Table 11.5 is adapted from OceansAlive.org, an ocean protection group sponsored by the Environmental Defense Fund. At their website, you can download this information (free) in a pocket-sized format.

Meat, Poultry, and Eggs

Meat *can* be a significant source of long-chain omega-3 fats. Unfortunately, U.S. domestic meats (beef, chicken, pork, and turkey) contain very small or undetectable amounts, since cattle are fed grains that are low in omega-3. In contrast, the fat of wild animals contains EPA

TABLE 11.5 Best and Worst Eco-Choices for Fish

Best Eco-Choices	Worst Eco-Choices
Abalone, U.S. farmed	Caviar, wild sturgeon
Anchovies	Chilean sea bass/toothfish
Arctic char, U.S. and Canadian farmed	Cod, Atlantic
Catfish, U.S. farmed	Grouper
Caviar, U.S. farmed paddlefish and sturgeon eggs	Halibut, Atlantic
Clams, butter, geoducks, hard, littlenecks, Manila	Marlin
Crab, Dungeness, snow from Canada, stone	Monkfish/goosefish
Crawfish, U.S.	Orange roughy
Halibut, Alaskan	Rockfish, Pacific (rock cod/boccacio)
Herring, Atlantic sea herring	Salmon, farmed or Atlantic
Mackerel, Atlantic	Shark
Mahimahi/dolphinfish, U.S., from the Atlantic	Shrimp/prawns, imported
Mussels, farmed blue, New Zealand green	Skate
Oysters, farmed Eastern, European, Pacific	Snapper
Sablefish/black cod from Alaska	Sturgeon, wild
Salmon, wild chinook, chum, coho, pink, sockeye	Swordfish, imported
Sardines	Tilefish
Scallops, farmed bay	Tuna, bluefin
Shrimp, northern from Newfoundland, U.S. farmed	
Spot prawns	
Striped bass, farmed	
Sturgeon, farmed	
Tilapia, U.S.	

SOURCE: OceansAlive.org.

(4 percent of the fat is EPA) because wild animals dine on mosses and ferns that contain long-chain omega-3 fats.

Studies comparing the meat of pasture-fed (also known as free-range) animals with those eating traditional feedlot cuisine consistently demonstrate a higher omega-3 fatty-acid profile in the pasture-fed meat. For example, one study showed that DHA content increased 300 percent and EPA increased by nearly 700 percent when bulls ate in the pasture instead of the feedlot.

The significance of what meat *could* offer in the way of long-chain omega-3 fats is illustrated quite clearly in a recent study. Researchers found that meat, poultry, and game accounted for 43 percent of long-chain omega-3 fat content in the diets of Australians (who on average eat six times more meat, poultry, and game than seafood). So why don't we have similar omega-3 intake (if not double?). In Australia, animals raised for consumption are typically pasture fed, which increases their long-chain omega-3 fat content.

What to do? When possible, choose meats that are free-range or pasture fed. Many stores, including Trader Joe's and Whole Foods Market, carry free-range meats. You can also buy directly from the rancher via the Internet.

Eggs also offer some omega-3 fats. A standard commercial egg provides 18 to 26 milligrams of long-chain omega-3 fats, depending on size (see Table 11.6).

TABLE 11.6 Omega-3 Content of Conventional Eggs

	Milligrams of Omega-3s		
Egg Size	EPA	DHA	Total Long-Chain Omega-3s (EPA + DHA)
Medium	2	16	18
Large	2	18	20
Extra large	3	21	24
Jumbo	2	23	25

Seaweed and Mosses

Wild greens (ferns, mosses, and liverworts)—including those that grow in the sea, such as algae and seaweed—contain long-chain omega-3 fats, primarily EPA. Therefore, both the plant itself and the animals that feed on it (be they with fins or feet) are good sources of long-chain omega-3 fats. Keep in mind that to make a significant difference, you'd need a steady diet of these greens, which is possible with many Asian cuisines that include sushi and seaweed salad.

Omega-3-Enriched Foods for Fish Haters, Vegetarians, and Supplement Refusers

The good news is that foods enriched with the right type of omega-3 fats can make a significant impact on getting your needs met. That's especially important if you seldom eat fish, are vegetarian, or don't like taking supplements. The types of enriched foods to choose are those with the long-chain omega-3 fats, especially DHA. But identifying them can be confusing.

Most of the omega-3-enriched foods you find in supermarkets or health food stores add the short-chain omega-3 fat ALA, most often in the form of flax. On one hand it's wonderful to get more omega-3 fats in your diet to help offset our lopsided omega-6 fat imbalance. But the added flax will do little, if anything, to increase your intake of EPA or DHA. For example, Odwalla's Berries GoMega bar proclaims on its food label that it contains "500 mg of Vegetarian Omega 3's." To the uninformed consumer, that may seem like a great thing. In this case, the omega-3 fat source is flax, which means ALA, not the coveted EPA or DHA.

DHA-Enriched Foods

Surprisingly, the United States has not caught up with the rest of the world in terms of the number of DHA-enriched foods available at the grocery store. Fortunately, that should change soon, thanks to a 2005 FDA ruling that allows the addition of menhaden oil (a type of fish oil) to 29 categories of food. Studies show that eating foods

Food Label Caveat: Conflicting Information on Omega-3 Content

• •

If you buy a food that states it is an "excellent" source of fiber on the label, you could be confident of getting a decent amount of roughage because strict laws govern what information can be placed on a food label. But thanks to a loophole in the law, there are now two conflicting claims for omega-3 fats.

This is a tale of two food companies—one is actually a conglomerate of seafood companies, and the other is Martek Biosciences Corporation, which makes supplements and omega-3s that can be added to food. The problem boils down to this. In 2004 the seafood folks claimed that an "excellent source" of DHA must provide at least 130 milligrams, but one year later, Martek claimed that an "excellent source" of this long-chain fat offers a mere 32 milligrams—just one-fourth as much.

How could the FDA, the protector of consumers and enforcer of the Nutrition Labeling Act, allow this to occur? Under the FDA Modernization Act of 1997, companies can notify the FDA of their intent to use such a claim if it is based on current, published authoritative statements from certain federal scientific bodies. If the FDA does not act within 120 days of receiving a food company's notification, the inaction is deemed to be approval of the proposed nutrient content claim for use on a food label.

Both companies based their claim on the Institute of Medicine's 2002 Dietary Reference Intakes (DRI) report. Ironically, this report did not issue official numbers for DHA. Therefore, both companies had no basis to make their nutrient content claim for DHA.

The FDA should have pulled the plug on the first claim by the seafood company, but it didn't. That's when Martek stepped in, one year later, with a different omega-3 nutrient content claim.

And the FDA let Martek's claim slide, too. Now both claims are in effect! An FDA spokesperson said the agency will initiate rulemaking to clarify the use of these terms, but that has yet to happen.

enriched with long-chain omega-3 fats can be an effective boost. In other countries, there are a variety of foods with enriched DHA, including breads, deli meats, yogurt, sausages, and juice. Currently in the United States, only a few key foods with added long-chain omega-3s are widely available:

- **Omega-3 whole eggs.** Eggs are an easy way to add DHA to your diet. But be careful when selecting a brand of omega-3-enriched eggs; some are enriched with just ALA. Choose eggs that have at least 100 milligrams of DHA per egg. The omega-3 fat is in the yolks, so don't use these eggs in recipes that call for only egg whites, or you'll miss out on the DHA benefit. When the recipes in this book refer to "omega-3 eggs," they mean eggs containing at least 100 milligrams of DHA.

Eggs and Cholesterol

If you are concerned that eating these eggs regularly will raise your cholesterol levels, it shouldn't be a problem for most people, according to a study published in the *Journal of the American Dietetic Association*. The participants, 25 men and women with high blood cholesterol levels, ate 12 DHA-enriched eggs per week over a six-week period. The majority of these people experienced no significant increase in blood cholesterol.

- **Omega-3 egg whites.** Golden Circle Farms has introduced liquid egg whites that contain 50 milligrams of DHA per quarter-cup serving.

- **Smart Beat Omega Plus margarine.** This brand contains 100 milligrams of DHA (from menhaden oil) per serving.

- **Odwalla soymilk.** Odwalla offers soymilk containing 32 milligrams of DHA per serving. Notably, the source of DHA is algae, so it is a good option for strict vegetarians. Three flavors are available: regular, vanilla, and chocolate.

Brave New World of Meats and Poultry

Because of the growing interest of health-conscious consumers, plentiful research has been conducted on ways to increase the omega-3 fat content of various meats and poultry. When animals are fed diets enriched with fish oil or fish meal, the EPA and DHA content of their meat increases considerably (just as with humans). These foods are not commercially available yet but likely will be in the near future.

Harvard University researcher Jing Xuan Kang discovered a novel way to increase the omega-3 fat content of livestock by creating "transgenic animals." These animals are given the gene that allows them to easily make omega-3 fats while keeping the omega-6 fat low, with an optimal ratio of 1-to-1. Kang and his colleagues recently

Best Bests for Choosing Omega-3-Enriched Foods

- Know which type of omega-3 fat is being added and the amount.
- Focus on getting foods enriched with DHA or fish oil.
- Be sure that the food is also low in omega-6 fat.
- Don't assume that all foods enriched with omega-3 fats are a significant source or contain the right kind of omega-3 fat.

achieved success by creating a transgenic pig, and work is under way with chickens and cows. They have great hope that this approach will be a sustainable solution to increasing omega-3 fats in the diet, especially for those who don't care for seafood.

If you are not able or not willing to eat seafood or the selected omega-3-enriched foods, then you will need a supplement. A variety of options are discussed in the next chapter.

Summary of Chapter 11

• •

G et enough of the long-chain omega-3 fats, EPA and DHA.

- Total long-chain omega-3 fat (EPA and DHA) should be 650 milligrams daily.
- Aim for a minimum of 220 milligrams each of EPA + DHA daily.
- If you are pregnant aim for a minimum of 300 milligrams of DHA daily.
- If you have heart disease aim for 1,000 milligrams of EPA + DHA daily.
- Eat at least two fatty fish meals each week, preferably four times each week.
- When possible choose free-range meats and poultry.

Best-bet fish choices are low in contaminants and high in EPA and DHA.

- Choose wild salmon, including Chinook, king, coho, chum, pink, and sockeye. (Alaskan salmon, including fresh frozen and canned, is also wild salmon.)
- Light tuna is a better choice than albacore as it has three times less the mercury level.

Continued

- Lowest-mercury fish are salmon, trout, flounder, tilapia, haddock, and shrimp.
- Limit fried fish as it seals in the contaminants.

The health benefits of eating fish far outweigh risks. To minimize your exposure to contaminants take care in how you prepare your fish.

- Before cooking, remove the skin, fat, and internal organs of fish and shellfish, where toxins are likely to accumulate.
- While cooking, let the fat drain away to reduce fish drippings.
- Avoid or limit frying, as it seals in pollutants that might be in the fish's fat.

If you seldom eat fish or are vegetarian choose omega-3-enriched foods.

- Choose foods enriched with DHA and/or EPA.
- Don't assume all omega-3-enriched foods have the right kind of omega-3 fat.
- You will likely need an EPA/DHA supplement if you seldom eat fish or eat enough long-chain omega-3-enriched foods.

Consider Taking an Omega-3 Supplement

U NLESS YOU CONSUME seafood regularly, you will likely need a supplement to get the required amount of omega-3s in your diet. But when you look at the overflowing supplement shelves, how do you know which omega-3 supplement is best for you? I witnessed this problem repeatedly when I began recommending omega-3 fat supplements to my patients. Without fail, they'd come back with flaxseed oil supplements because the "helpful" clerk told them that flaxseed oil is a good source of omega-3 fat. That's when I started explaining why flaxseed oil is not a substitute for fish oil.

Yet even among the fish oil supplements, there are many different types, with considerable variation in their content of DHA and EPA. Which is best? This chapter will give you the best bets and tell you what to avoid when choosing omega-3 fat supplements. Solutions for vegetarians, kids, and those who don't like swallowing big capsules also will be discussed.

How to Choose an Omega-3 Fat Supplement

There seem to be endless choices of omega-3 supplements. How do you choose between cod-liver oil and shark-liver oil, salmon oil and tuna oil? There's pure EPA or pure DHA, and then there are the 3-6-9 supplements, also known as the essential-fatty-acid supplements. Does "molecularly distilled" make a difference? And how much should you take?

Don't Bother Buying What Your Body Doesn't Need

We don't need any more omega-6 fats in our diet, yet unbelievably, there are omega-3 fat supplements that boast of their added omega-6 fat content, as if that were advantageous. These supplements typically have names like "Omega 3-6-9." The 3 represents the sought-out omega-3 fat; the 6 signifies the omega-6 fat. Omega-9, you may recall, is the family that olive oil belongs to, and our bodies do not require this fat. Omega-9 won't hurt you, but why spend the money on something you don't need and can enjoy eating in olives and olive oil?

Similarly, supplements that say they provide *all* of your essential fatty acids will contain omega-6 fat along with omega-3 fat. These supplements usually have names like "EFAs" or "complete essential fatty acids." Don't waste your money on these types of supplements either.

Forget about the specialty plant oils, too, as they don't contain the coveted EPA and DHA. Flaxseed, hemp, and perilla seed oil are high in the short-chain omega-3 fat ALA. This won't hurt you, but you aren't getting what you need from these oils: EPA and DHA.

Forget about evening primrose oil and borage oil. People often take these oils in hopes of reducing inflammation-related maladies such as PMS or joint pain. But these oils are very high in omega-6 fat. Primrose oil and borage oil contain 86 percent and 67 percent omega-6, respectively. The last thing you need is to dump more omega-6 fat in your diet by way of a supplement. Your best choice is fish oil supplements, which are much more powerful and effective.

What's the Right Dose?

The Food and Drug Administration (FDA) considers a safe level to be 3 grams (3,000 milligrams) of EPA and DHA, combined. International guidelines for general health recommend 650 milligrams of EPA plus DHA, with a minimum of 220 milligrams from each. And as discussed in the previous chapter, the American Heart Association recommends 1,000 milligrams combined EPA and DHA if you have heart disease. Aim for 650 to 3,000 milligrams, combined. Table 12.1 lists dosages typical of oil from different kinds of fish. Of course, it's always a good idea to check with your doctor, especially if you are taking medications. Be sure to inform your doctors and any other health care providers that you are taking fish oil.

Side Effects

If you take more than 3,000 milligrams, some doctors worry that you could bleed a little more easily, and they might want you to temporarily discontinue the supplements if you are having surgery or a dental procedure. Yet there have been many studies using much higher doses with minimal side effects. The U.S. Department of Health and Human Services reviewed 148 studies of more than 20,000 people who reported adverse effects of fish oil supplements.

TABLE 12.1 What You Get in Standard Fish Oil

These measurements are based on 1 teaspoon of oil, which is contained in about 5 capsules.

Type of Oil	EPA	DHA	Total Long-Chain (EPA + DHA)
Salmon oil	590	827	1,417
Menhaden oil	597	387	984
Sardine oil	460	483	943
Cod-liver oil	313	497	810
Herring oil	283	190	473

SOURCE: U.S. Department of Agriculture, National Nutrient Database for Standard Reference, Release 18 (2005) (nal.usda.gov/fnic/foodcomp/search).

They found no significant increased incidence of bleeding. The most common side effect is burping and, sometimes, gastrointestinal upset, but this usually occurs at doses higher than 3,000 milligrams. When the American Heart Association reviewed possible side effects from fish oil supplementation, they found minimal problems, which are summarized in Table 12.2.

How to Choose the Best Fish Oil Supplements

Fish oil is the only type of omega-3 fat supplement that contains both EPA and DHA. There are many good choices from which to select. Often, it really comes down to how many pills you are willing to swallow each day and the price you are willing to pay.

The omega-3 supplement industry recently established uniform standards for purity and quality, through its trade organization, the Council for Responsible Nutrition (CRN). While the standards are voluntary, there's a lot at stake for companies amid the booming but competitive fish oil supplement industry. Environmental Defense, a leading nonprofit organization, uses the CRN criteria to determine the best and worst choices of fish oil supplements and makes its choices public via its website at oceansalive.org/eat.cfm?sub nav=fishoil&sort=Rating.

Consumer Reports evaluated 16 of the top-selling fish oil brands and found no significant differences in the quality or the purity. Ultimately, the magazine recommended buying the brand with the

TABLE 12.2 Risk of Side Effects from Fish Oil Supplements

Dose per Day	GI Upset	Clinical Bleeding	Fishy Aftertaste
<1,000 mg	Very low	Very low	Low
1,000–3,000 mg	Moderate	Very low	Moderate
>3,000 mg	Moderate	Low	Likely

SOURCE: Kris-Etherton, P. M., et al. "Fish Consumption, Fish Oil, Omega-3 Fatty Acids, and Cardiovascular Disease." *Circulation* 106 (2002): 2754.

Minimize the Nuisance Side Effect of Fishy Aftertaste

While a fishy aftertaste, or "fishy burp," is not a health hazard, it can discourage people from consistent fish oil use. To minimize this problem, try any combination of these techniques:

■ Chill the pills, and take them at bedtime. In many instances, the problem disappears altogether with this technique.

■ Take the pills immediately before a meal, with the smallest amount of fluid possible. The fish oil will mix with the solid food and will be emptied from the stomach faster. Otherwise, since oil and water don't mix, the fish oil floats on top of your stomach liquids and takes longer to digest, increasing the chances of the fishy aftertaste.

■ Buy "odorless" fish oil capsules, which work very well.

■ Avoid carbonated beverages.

■ If all else fails, after taking fish supplements, lie down on your left side for 10 minutes. This position helps drain the oil from the stomach into the intestine.

lowest price. When in doubt, follow these guidelines in selecting a fish oil supplement, and you'll do just fine:

• **Forget the hype.** There is no set standard for the definition of pharmaceutical-grade fish oil, although that description does sound official. Molecular distillation does remove contaminants, but it, too, lacks a legal definition.

• **Choose fish oil supplements that contain natural antioxidants.** But note that the benefits of fish oil (long-chain omega-3 fats) are also an Achilles' heel when it comes to stability. These fats are more vulnerable to damage from oxygen. Vitamin E is usually added to protect and keep the omega-3 fats stable. This is a valuable addition, not hype.

- **Look for *USP* on the labels.** The United States Pharmacopeia (USP)–verified mark means the supplement has been independently tested and verified for contaminants and nutrient content. The USP is a nonprofit organization that has been around since 1820.

- **Check the expiration date.** Be sure it's far enough in the future to allow you to use the full product. Also, of course, you want to be sure you are not buying an expired supplement.

When selecting fish oil supplements, you'll also have some other options to consider. Before you buy, weigh the pros and cons of each of these products:

- **Flavored and odorless fish oil.** For many people, "flavor" makes a significant difference. Even though there's not really any taste while swallowing a capsule, that's not the case if you experience a fishy aftertaste or the harmless but annoying side effect of burping. Many manufacturers offer fish oils that have flavors such as citrus and berry or are odorless. If this makes a difference between whether or not you take the pills consistently, it is worth the extra money to buy odorless or flavored fish oils.

- **Fish oil concentrates/marine lipid concentrates.** These fish oils have more EPA and DHA per pill, but you will pay more for that benefit. You do need to be careful, however, because the content of EPA and DHA varies tremendously. (See Table 12.3 for examples.) To be sure you know what you are getting, check the amount of EPA and DHA per dose. Unless directed by your physician, go for the brands that have proportions of EPA and DHA similar to what you'd find in fish or standard fish oil pills.

TABLE 12.3 What You Get in Fish Oil Concentrates

Brand	Dose	Milligrams of Omega-3 EPA	DHA
CVS fish oil concentrate	2 capsules	360	240
Kirkland Signature fish oil concentrate	2 capsules	360	240
Nordic Natural's Ultimate-Omega	2 capsules	650	450
Trader Joe's Trader Darwin's Odorless Omega-3	1 capsule	400	200
Vitamin Shoppe EPA-DHA omega-3 fish oil	1 capsule	300	200
Walgreen's Finest natural fish oil concentrate	2 capsules	520	350

- **Krill oil.** This fish oil is the new kid on the block. Krill are tiny shrimp-like crustaceans (zooplankton) that feed the largest animal in the world, the blue whale. Along with EPA and DHA, krill oil also contains some other types of fats called phospholipids that may be beneficial.

Special Considerations: Vegetarians, Kids, and Pill Haters

Choosing an omega-3 supplement can be a little more challenging for people with certain needs. Vegetarians are looking for choices other than fish oil. Kids and adults who have difficulty swallowing pills want alternatives that are easier to take than the standard fish oil capsule.

Vegetarian Options

If you are a strict vegetarian who consumes no fish or animal products, the only way you're going to get enough omega-3s in your diet is through a supplement. There are vegetarian, algae-based supplements, rather than fish oil, that provide DHA. There is little EPA in this type of supplement, but DHA can "retroconvert" into EPA. Table 12.4 lists examples of vegetarian DHA supplements.

TABLE 12.4 Vegetarian DHA Supplements

| Brand | Dose | Milligrams of Omega-3s | | Comments |
		EPA	DHA	
Deva omega-3	1 gel	—	200	No gelatin. Algae-based.
Nature's Way Neuromins DHA	1 gel	—	100	Contains gelatin. Algae-based.
Neuromins 200 DHA	1 gel	—	200	Contains gelatin. Algae-based.
NuTru O-Mega-Zen3	1 gel	—	300	No gelatin. Algae-based.
Vitamin Shoppe Neuromins DHA	1 gel	—	100	Contains gelatin. Algae-based.

Kids and Adults Who Hate to Swallow Pills

Whether you are a kid or an adult who dislikes swallowing pills, fish oil supplements can be quite a challenge because of their larger-than-average size.

Liquid Assets. Fortunately, kids and adults can try one of the many liquid options, which are now available in a variety of flavors (see Table 12.5). The biggest difference among the liquid options for kids is the potency and the packaging. Regardless of your age, you do need to be cautious with the cod-liver oil. Cod-liver oil naturally contains large amounts of vitamins A and D, which can be dangerous when taken at high levels. This shouldn't be a problem if you take the standard dose, but do be aware of the levels of these vitamins if you are taking other supplements, to prevent a toxic overload.

Omega-3 Supplements for Kids. Beyond liquid fish oils, there are a variety of options for kids: powders that you mix with water (or perhaps could throw into a yogurt), condiment-size pudding packets,

TABLE 12.5 Liquid Options for Fish Oil Supplements

| Brand | Dose | Milligrams of Omega-3s | | Comment |
		EPA	DHA	
Carlson Laboratories Very Finest Fish Oil	1 teaspoon	800	500	Lemon flavor
Jarrow Max DHA Liquid	1 teaspoon	425–600	740–850	Lemon flavor
Nordic Naturals Ultimate Omega Liquid	½ teaspoon	813	563	Lemon flavor
Nordic Naturals Omega3 Liquid	1 teaspoon	825	550	Lemon and orange flavor
Nordic Naturals Artic cod-liver oil	1 teaspoon	410	625	Plain, lemon, orange, and peach flavors. Provides up to 40% of daily value for vitamin A and up to 10% for vitamin D. Also available in individual packets.
Spectrum Essentials cod-liver oil (lemon)	1 teaspoon	340	540	Warning: This dose provides 25% of vitamin A, which means potential for toxicity if taken in excess.

and chewable supplements (see Table 12.6). Lastly, if the child is willing, there are pea-sized gel caps that are easier for the smaller mouth to swallow. These supplements are rather pricey, though, so be sure you can get a refund if your kid absolutely hates them; some of the liquid oils aren't as pleasant-tasting as their name sounds.

While there are a variety of ways to get your long-chain omega-3 fats through supplements (or food), they will do little good if your diet is being assaulted by omega-6 fats, among other omega-3 oppo-

TABLE 12.6 Omega-3 Supplements for Children

| Brand | Dose | Milligrams of Omega-3s | | Comment |
		EPA	DHA	
Coromega	1 packet	350	230	Pleasant orange flavor with pudding texture
Neuromins for Kids	1 gel	—	100	Vegetarian, algae-based; no EPA
Health from the Sea A+ Kids Pure Fish Oil	½ teaspoon	125	187	Fruity flavored; pleasant scent but a fishy aftertaste
Nordic Naturals Berry Keen Children's 100%	½ teaspoon	205	313	Strawberry-flavored cod-liver oil; pleasant scent but a fishy aftertaste
Nordic Naturals Children's DHA Chewable Soft Gels	4 gels	82	125	Source is cod-liver oil; pea-sized gels (very easy to swallow)
Carlson Labs Chewable DHA	1 gel	50	100	Orange flavor

nents. You still need the right background diet to allow the beneficial work of the omega-3 fats to shine through. The next chapter will address how to get rid of the adversarial components in the diet.

Summary of Chapter 12

Don't waste your money on supplements you don't need, such as:

- Supplements with added omega-6 fats
- Supplements with added omega-9 fats

- Short-chain omega-3 fats that you can easily get from your diet (such as flax)
- Evening primrose oil and borage oil because they are very high in omega-6 fats

When choosing a supplement:

- Select a fish-oil based supplement, unless you are a strict vegetarian.
- Aim for a combined dose of EPA + DHA of 650 to 3,000 milligrams.
- Check the expiration date.
- Be sure there's an added antioxidant such as vitamin E, also known as tocopherol.
- Check for third-party testing.
- Choose a supplement with a proportionate amount of EPA and DHA.
- Do not rely on ALA-based supplements such as flax oil capsules to substitute for EPA and DHA.

If you are vegetarian, choose an algae-based supplement.

- Keep in mind that while these are good sources of DHA, most do not contain EPA.
- DHA can be made into EPA by your body.
- If you are vegan, check for gelatin content.

Check for alternative forms if you have difficulty swallowing pills.

- There are many flavored liquid fish oils.
- Take care if you use cod-liver oil because of its vitamin A and vitamin D content.

Kids need fish oil too (if they don't regularly eat fish).

- Choose kid-friendly options, such as powders, pudding-style, liquids, chewable, and small capsules.
- Be sure it contains both EPA and DHA, as some do not.

Nix the Six
Limit Foods High in Omega-6 Fats

Today our food supply contains more omega-6 fats than ever, and it's all too easy to overload on this fat, even if you eat a low-fat diet. Omega-6 fats make powerful hormone-like compounds that, when produced in excess, are associated with heart attacks, stroke, arthritis, asthma, headaches, PMS, inflammation, cancer, insulin resistance, mood disorders, and osteoporosis. Clearly, too much omega-6 fat is not good for your health.

Yet how are you supposed to tell which foods are high in omega-6 fats, especially when this information is not required on food labels? It is especially tricky, as these fats are not even listed as "omega-6" in the ingredient list; labels give only their common names, such as soybean oil. There are no consumer advocates or food police groups waging campaigns to nix the omega-6 in the American diet. In fact, many people don't even know what an omega-6 fat is—including many of the employees of food companies I called requesting this information.

In this chapter, we'll look at how to identify the key sources of omega-6 fats and practical ways to replace them. You'll also learn how little of this nutrient your body needs.

How Much Omega-6 Fat Do You Need?

Linoleic acid (LA), the dominant omega-6 fat in our diet, occurs naturally in nearly every food. It is an essential fat, which means you need it in your diet to stay healthy, but the amount needed is grossly exaggerated by many.

In 2003, Stephen Cunnane from the University of Toronto found a major mistake in the studies used to determine the dietary requirement for LA. The generally accepted dietary requirement for LA is based on diets that were inadvertently deficient in omega-3 fats, and this was not taken into account. (To evaluate nutritional needs, scientists often put animals on a diet deficient in a specific nutrient and then systematically add back the particular nutrient to determine the dose needed to correct the problem.) Cunnane says this error overestimates LA requirements, so they are 5 to 15 times higher than what is needed for healthy people, because the omega-6 oils added back into the deficient diets also contained trace amounts of omega-3 fats. Correcting the deficiency took more omega-6 oil because they were simultaneously correcting the omega-3 fat deficit. The National Academy of Sciences' Institute of Medicine, an American nonprofit organization, not only ignored this big oversight but recommended that Americans continue to eat their current high levels of omega-6 fats, ranging from 11,000 to 16,000 milligrams daily.

Fortunately, international guidelines recommend a more sensible level of LA: 2,200 milligrams is considered adequate for health, with a maximum of 6,600 milligrams per day. Even this level is likely a two- to fourfold overestimate—and the average American eats nearly double that amount (13,000 milligrams).

Keep in mind that no health agency or omega-3 fat expert is recommending that we get rid of omega-6 fats entirely. Rather, the goal is to bring the ratio of omega-6 to omega-3 fats back into balance.

Even if you limit your fat intake by avoiding such foods as margarine or mayonnaise, you can still get an adequate amount of omega-6 fat in your diet. (It's similar to sodium; you can get plenty of this mineral in your diet without lifting a salt shaker, because it's naturally present in many foods, even though you can't taste it.) For example, just two slices of whole-wheat bread provide 500 milligrams of LA, nearly 25 percent of the international recommendation. If you put one teaspoon of margarine on each bread slice, you have met the recommendation with over 3,000 milligrams of LA.

Nix the Six: How to Reduce Omega-6 Fats

Omega-6 fat is abundant in many processed foods, fast foods, nuts, seeds, oils, salad dressings, and margarine. Soybean oil is the greatest contributor of linoleic acid in the American diet. It is all too easy to overload on omega-6 fat, so it's vitally important to become familiar with the foods and oils that are high in omega-6.

Identify High-Omega-6 Fats and Oils

Most of the time, the only hint you'll find regarding a food's omega-6 fat content is on the ingredient list, since omega-6 content need not be listed on the label. To keep your omega fats in balance, for every 1,000 milligrams of omega-6 fat you eat, you'll need another 500 to 1,000 milligrams of omega-3 fat.

Oils, Spreads, and Dressings

When you discover how many foods are high in omega-6 fats, correcting the problem can be overwhelming. The best strategy is to begin by focusing on the changes that will have the biggest benefit, rather than trying to change everything in your diet at once. From there, you can fine-tune your food choices, so that it will be less daunting. Your selection of visible fats has the most significant impact, because they are the biggest sources of omega-6 fats in the diet. So let's start there.

Most dietary omega-6 fat comes from salad dressings, cooking oils, margarines, and spreads. The top three omega-6 fat oils consumed in the United States are cottonseed oil, corn oil, and soybean oil. In 2001–2002, 93 percent of margarines and 72 percent of salad or cooking oils were made with soybean oil. Table 13.1 lists oils, spreads, and salad dressings that are high in omega-6 fat. Keep in mind that experts recommend keeping omega-6 to less than 7,000 milligrams per day.

TABLE 13.1 Oils, Spreads, and Salad Dressings High in Omega-6s

Type of Fat	Omega-6 Fat (% of total fat)	Linoleic Acid (milligrams)	Ratio of Omega-6 to Omega-3 Fats
OILS (PER TABLESPOON)			
Safflower oil	75	10,149	77:1
Grapeseed oil	70	9,470	947:1
Wheat germ oil	55	7,450	8:1
Corn oil	54	7,280	46:1
Walnut oil	53	7,190	5:1
Cottonseed oil	52	7,020	234:1
Soybean oil	51	6,940	8:1
Vegetable oil	58	7,850	8:1
Sunflower oil	66	5,410	180:1
SPREADS (PER TABLESPOON)			
Mayonnaise, regular	48	5,200	8:1
Margarine, tub regular	33	3,760	20:1
Margarine, stick regular	26	2,920	9:1
SALAD DRESSINGS (PER 2 TABLESPOONS)			
Caesar, generic	50	8,500	8:1
Italian, generic	41	3,380	8:1
Thousand Island, generic	45	4,590	7:1

SOURCE: U.S. Department of Agriculture, National Nutrient Database for Standard Reference, Release 18 (2005). The Food Processor SQL versions 9.8 and 10.0.

The key to reducing omega-6 fats in your diet is to use the following alternatives:

- **Canola oil and olive oil.** One of the easiest ways to limit your omega-6 fat intake is to choose foods that use only canola oil or olive oil. Keep in mind that it's not necessary to be this rigid, but it's an easy way to start lowering your omega-6 fats. Of the two oils, olive is the lowest in omega-6 fat, with half the amount found in canola oil.

- **Specialty high-oleic oils.** High-oleic sunflower and high-oleic safflower oils have a fatty-acid profile similar to that of olive oil. (*Oleic* is the name of the dominant fatty acid in olive oil, which is a monounsaturated fat.) You won't find these oils in your grocery store, but they are used in processed foods such as potato chips and frozen meals. In Australia you can find a similar version called Sunola oil, a specialty oil grown from specific Australian sunflower plants.

- **Flaxseed oil.** Flaxseed oil is low in omega-6 fats but is not used often in traditional foods. It can be found in specialty and health food stores. Try the flaxseed oil vinaigrette included with the recipes in Chapter 16.

Olive Oil: The Switzerland of Fat

Olive oil is like the Switzerland of fats, because its impact on omega-3s is neutral. When you use olive oil as the primary fat in your diet, it helps to displace omega-6 fats. Olive oil is a well-established staple in the Mediterranean diet and a favorite among chefs for its culinary properties. It has been promoted for years as a healthful oil because it is low in artery-clogging saturated fat.

> ## What Is the Difference Between a Margarine and a Spread?
>
> Food-labeling laws, particularly standards of identity, require that margarine contain no less than 80 percent fat. Therefore, any margarine-like food that has less than 80 percent fat cannot be called margarine. Instead, *spread* is the catch-all term that legally describes these lower-fat butter alternatives growing in popularity in the dairy case.

- **Margarine.** While they're not as plentiful as their counterparts blended from soybean or vegetable oil, margarines made with canola or olive oil do exist. Some margarines add flaxseed oil, which can be an asset if the primary oil is not high in omega-6 fat. Also, if you use a *light* canola-based spread, your omega-6 fat load will be less, as is the case with fat-free spreads.

- **Salad dressings.** Most salad dressings use soybean oil as their base. If you discover that your favorite salad dressing uses soybean oil or a vegetable oil blend, take the time to find an alternative. Pesto sauces and some vinaigrettes tend to be made with olive oil. But don't assume. Fat-free and light salad dressings can be a good option.

- **Mayonnaise.** The majority of mayo is soybean oil based, but there are national brands made from canola oil. Choices include products from Best Foods/Hellman's, Safeway Select, and Trader Joe's. If you use a *light* canola-based mayonnaise, your omega-6 fat load will be even lower.

For a summary of oils, spreads, and salad dressings that are low in omega-6 fats, see Table 13.2.

TABLE 13.2 Oils, Spreads, and Salad Dressings Low in Omega-6 Fat

Type of Fat	Omega-6 Fat (% of total fat)	Linoleic Acid (milligrams)	Ratio of Omega-6 to Omega-3 Fats
OILS (PER TABLESPOON)			
High-oleic sunflower oil	4	500	17:1
Sunola oil*	5	666	25:1
Olive oil	10	1,320	13:1
Flaxseed oil	13	1,730	0.3:1.0
Avocado oil	13	1,750	14:1
High-oleic safflower oil	14	1,952	N/A
Canola oil	20	2,840	2:1
SPREADS (PER TABLESPOON)			
Mayonnaise, canola	22	2,200	2:1
Mayonnaise, fat-free	44	190	1:1
Margarine, canola oil	18	2,000	2:1
Margarine, fat-free	51	150	6:1
Smart Beat Superlight	22	450	3:1
SALAD DRESSINGS (PER 2 TABLESPOONS)			
Ranch, fat-free	0	0	N/A
Italian, fat-free	21	50	5:1
Blue-cheese fat-free	52	140	7:1
Italian, diet	21	400	4:1
Caesar, low-calorie	47	620	7:1

*Available in Australia.

Use the Food Label to Nix the Six

When the low-carbohydrate craze swept the nation, food companies quickly responded. In no time, you could easily find new low-carbohydrate foods, even ghastly ones like low-carbohydrate milk. The food makers added more carbohydrate information on the food label, even though it was not required.

It's not so easy to find information on the omega-6 fat content of foods. Unlike the carbohydrate craze, there has been no consumer demand for "low-omega-6" foods or for this information, and the information is not required, as it is for trans fat or total fat content.

Regardless of your food choices, you'll need to become familiar with two key parts of the food label—the ingredient list and the nutrition facts panel—to help figure out the omega-6 fat content. Here are some tips:

- **Check the ingredient list.** This is the only place you will get a clue as to the type of fat used. But it will not state "omega-6 oil" or "omega-6 fat." When choosing foods, select those that use only canola oil, flaxseed oil, olive oil, or high-oleic oils. In the beginning, this is the easiest to remember. The oils highest in omega-6 fats include safflower oil, sunflower oil, corn oil, walnut oil, cottonseed oil, and soybean oil.

- **Check the nutrition facts panel for total fat.** This will give you perspective as to the significance of the amount of fat. Does a serving contain 10 grams or 1 gram of fat? For example, the amount of fat in bread is usually insignificant compared with that in margarine.

- **Don't assume foods with the same amount of fat have similar levels of omega-6 fat.** For example, the *light* version of Take Control Spread has nearly twice the omega-6 fat content of its competitor *light* Benecol. You wouldn't know this by looking at the total fat content; both have the same amount of fat per serving (five grams).

- **Choose fat-free foods (that are suitable to your taste buds).** They are usually a better choice than their regular counterparts. Foods that are labeled fat-free must meet a strict definition: less than 500 milligrams of fat per serving. Therefore, these foods will have less omega-6 fat.

- **Don't assume omega-3-enriched foods are low in omega-6 fats.** Omega-3-enriched foods can be loaded with omega-6 fat. For example, Spectrum's Essentials omega-3 spread lists soybean oil as its first ingredient, so it is likely high in omega-6 fat (although the manufacturer did not have omega-6 fat content available upon request). Why eat an enriched food if it adds other ingredients that you don't need—or that can even be hazardous? You are better off taking fish oil or another enriched food with *known* nutrition contents. One serving of LifeStream's Flax Plus or Hemp Plus Waffles has a whopping 3,400 to 3,500 milligrams of omega-6 fat.

- **Don't assume "balanced heart-healthy" margarines are low in omega-6 fats.** For example, Take Control Spread, heavily marketed as good for your heart, delivers an omega-6 fat load of 3,400 milligrams per serving. But it is difficult to evaluate this by looking at its ingredient list: "Water, Liquid Canola Oil, Vegetable Oil Sterol Esters, Liquid Sunflower Oil, Partially Hydrogenated Soybean Oil." The makers of Promise Buttery Spread with Heart Health Essentials state on their website that this product "was developed to provide you with a balanced blend of essential fatty acids." Yet one serving of this margarine packs a hefty 3,400 milligrams of omega-6 fat, and the first ingredient is "Vegetable Oil Blend," which is made up of liquid soybean oil, canola oil, sunflower oil, palm oil, and palm kernel oil.

- **Don't assume natural sources of omega-3 fats are low in omega-6 fats.** I must admit that I was guilty of this assumption. I was so focused on getting omega-3 fats in my diet that I used primarily walnut oil in my foods because it's rich in ALA (and tastes good). I neglected to consider however, that I was loading up my diet with a heavy dose of omega-6 fats at the same time! It wasn't until

I analyzed my diet via a *free* computer program that I realized the error of my ways. I was shocked to see the high level of omega-6 fat in my diet from my walnut oil. If you want to check out the omega fat balance in your diet, see the sidebar about computer analysis.

- **Contact a food company to get omega fat information.** Some companies will provide omega-6 fat content if you ask for it. Other food companies have no idea of the omega-6 fat content of their products. Still, frequent requests might prompt food companies to make this information available, so no phone call or e-mail is a wasted effort.

Free Nutrition Computer Analysis: How Do Your Omegas Rate in Your Diet?

There is a little-known computer program that you can download for *free* from the National Institute of Health's website at http://efaeducation.nih.gov/sig/kim.html.

It's the brainchild of biochemist William Lands, who wanted to educate consumers on how food choices affect the balance of omega-6 and omega-3 fats in their bodies. This program, called KIM2 (for Keep It Managed), might seem a bit complex, but it's quite easy and can be installed on a Mac or PC computer. It organizes and sort foods according to their omega-3 and omega-6 fat content. This program also figures out your ratio of dietary omega-6 to omega-3 fats and the total amounts of each consumed.

Another free option is the U.S. Department of Agriculture's Nutrient Database, which is the source of the information for the KIM2 program. It analyzes only one food at a time, so you can't enter a recipe or a day's worth of eating, but it is very handy, and you don't have to download any software. The website for the database is http://www.nal.usda.gov/fnic/foodcomp/search.

Nuts, Seeds, and Soybeans

As a group of foods, nuts, seeds, and soybeans are generally high in omega-6 fats. (The exceptions are macadamia nuts, chestnuts, chia seeds, and flaxseeds.) However, when these foods are eaten in a less-processed form, they are usually lower in omega-6 fats. For example, soybeans in the form of tofu contain only about one-fifth the level of omega-6 fats found in the concentrated form of soybean oil. Peanuts are another good example. Peanut oil has nearly twice the omega-6 fat content of whole peanuts (see Table 13.3).

When you eat a whole food such as nuts or soybeans, you are obtaining a host of other beneficial nutrients, including fiber, vitamins, minerals, and phytochemicals (natural compounds with health benefits).

Walnuts have the distinction of being high in both omega-6 and omega-3 fats. While walnuts and hemp nut seeds deliver quite an

TABLE 13.3 Omega-6 Content of Soy- and Peanut-Based Foods

Type of Food	Omega-6 Fat (milligrams)
SOYBEAN-BASED FOODS	
¼ cup tofu, regular	1,480
1 cup soy milk, regular	1,800
½ cup green soybeans (edamame)	2,390
1 tablespoon margarine	2,920
2 tablespoons Thousand Island salad dressing	4,590
1 tablespoon mayonnaise	5,200
1 tablespoon soybean oil	6,940
PEANUT-BASED FOODS	
1 tablespoon peanuts	2,225
1 tablespoon peanut butter, chunky	2,350
1 tablespoon peanut oil	4,320

omega-6 load, they are good sources of omega-3 fats. These foods can fit in a healthful diet with careful use, but it's best to opt for the nuts and seeds that are lower in omega-6 fat. Macadamias, cashews, and hazelnuts are primarily made up of monounsaturated fats and are not significant sources of omega-6 fats. The same is true for their pulverized version, nut butters. Cashew butter is lower in omega-6 fat than peanut butter (see Table 13.4, which summarizes the omega-6 fats from nuts and seeds).

Surprising Sources of Omega-6 Fat

You can't assume that a food perceived to be healthful is the lowest in omega-6 fats. Sometimes you might be surprised. For example, it might be hard to believe that a beef hot dog has only one-sixth the

TABLE 13.4 Omega-6 Content of Nuts	
Type of Nut **(1 ounce or 2 tablespoons)**	**Omega-6 Fat** **(milligrams)**
Walnuts	10,800
Sunflower seeds, roasted	9,700
Pine nuts	9,400
Hemp nut seeds	7,700
Pumpkin and squash seeds, dried	5,870
Hickory nuts	5,850
Pecans	5,850
Brazil nuts	5,820
Peanuts	4,450
Pistachio nuts	3,740
Hazelnuts	2,220
Cashews	2,170
Chestnuts	450
Macadamia nuts	370

linoleic acid of a vegetarian frank, but it's true! In fact, vegetarian franks have a higher omega-6 content than hot dogs made from turkey, chicken, or beef (see Table 13.5).

Here are some more examples:

- A granola bar has nearly six times the omega-6 fat content of two medium chocolate chip cookies (2,940 and 520 milligrams, respectively).
- Smart Balance mozzarella cheese shreds, a lower-fat cheese, has nearly ten times the omega-6 fat of regular part-skim mozzarella (1,620 and 130 milligrams, respectively).
- McDonald's grilled chicken sandwich has nearly 15 times the omega-6 fat of a Quarter Pounder (6,110 and 420 milligrams, respectively).

Find out the omega-6 content of the foods you eat. Free information is available online and in this book's tables and Appendix A.

How to Nix the Most Potent Omega-6: Arachidonic Acid

While the majority of arachidonic acid (AA) in our body is made from linoleic acid in the foods we eat, it is also found in meats, poultry, eggs, and dairy, and in small amounts in fish. Generally, the more omega-6 fat fed to the animals, the higher the AA content of the meat. But complete data on AA in foods is lacking. Arachidonic acid is the long-chain omega-6 fat equivalent of EPA and DHA. This

TABLE 13.5 Omega-6 Content of Hot Dogs

Type of Hot Dog	Omega-6 Fat (milligrams per hot dog)
Vegetarian	2,350
Turkey	2,090
Chicken	1,940
Beef	460

SOURCE: USDA Nutrient Database, nal.usda.gov/fnic/foodcomp/search.

is *the* fatty acid that gets directly converted to the compounds that cause inflammation and blood clotting, among other problems.

To illustrate how potent AA is, a fish oil study on arthritis patients found that when this potent omega-6 fat was limited to less than 90 milligrams day in the diet, patients experienced the most improvement in symptom reduction (pain, tender and swollen joints), compared with patients who ate a regular diet supplemented with the same amount of fish oil or no fish oil at all. Notably, to reduce AA to this level, patients had to limit their meat intake to a maximum of eight ounces for the *entire* week. Also, the more AA eaten, the higher the disease activity.

You might think that higher-fat animals have more AA, but that's not necessarily the case, as the examples in Table 13.6 illustrate. Since AA lines the membranes of all cells, it is highly concentrated in the tissue (meat) of the animal. Yes, it's found in its fat, too. Note in the table that farmed and Atlantic salmon have more AA than beef or pork, and at least three times the AA content of wild salmon. Beef sirloin has one of the lowest amounts.

What Can You Do? The Power of One

Does the fact that omega-6 fats are not listed on food labels frustrate you? Until the slow wheels of policy and scientific consensus change, here's what you can do:

- Write to the FDA commissioner, urging clear nutrient content labeling of omega-6 fat content (and omega-3 fat, too).
- Urge free-range meat manufacturers to test and provide information on their meat's omega-6 and omega-3 fat content. It would highlight their nutritional superiority.
- Request the omega-6 fat content of foods from the companies that make them.
- Write to your favorite food companies, requesting that they use oils that are lower in omega-6 fats—for example, canola, olive, or a high-oleic oil.

TABLE 13.6 Arachidonic Acid Content of Common Foods

Food (3 ounces), Cooked	Arachidonic Acid (milligrams)
Beef rib-eye	65
Beef sirloin roast	30
Beefalo*	8
Chicken breast	71
Chicken thigh	103
Egg, one whole large	156
Lamb, domestic	60
Lamb, New Zealand	20
Pork loin, trimmed	63
Salmon, Atlantic	267
Salmon, farmed	1,080
Salmon, wild	30
Tuna, white	28
Turkey breast	61

*A hybrid of American buffalo and beef. Beefalo yields leaner beef than conventional breeds of cattle.

SOURCE: USDA Nutrient Database, nal.usda.gov/fnic/foodcomp/search and see References under Taber.

These action steps might seem fruitless, but keep in mind that every time you make a request to a food company for omega-6 fat content information, the company takes notice; meeting consumer demands and needs is a way to stay competitive in the market. Each single action you take paves the way for critical mass to take place, until the power of one tips the scales for a change. Remember, that's how low-carb foods became popular in grocery stores, and it's the reason why you can get four kinds of milk at Starbuck's, from soymilk to regular cream.

In the meantime, check out Table 13.7 to find quick ways of lowering the omega-6 fat in your diet. You will also find more practical ways to omega-optimize your diet in the following chapters.

TABLE 13.7 Nix-the-Six Substitutions

Here are ways to reduce the omega-6 fat content in your diet, food-by-food. For complete omega-3 fat and omega-6 fat content information, see Appendix A.

Instead of	Use	Comments
CEREALS AND GRAINS		
Granola, regular	Flax-based or canola-oil-based granola	Granola-based cereals are often high in omega-6 fat. The following cereals by Nature's Path have 500 milligrams or less of omega-6 fat, with a good dose of omega-3: Flax Plus with raisins; Optimum Power; Optimum Rebound; Mesa Sunrise.
Wheat germ	Flax meal (ground flaxseed)	Flax meal is widely available at health food stores and many grocery stores. Bob's Red Mill is a brand in many stores nationwide, or you can order it at bobsredmill.com.
SPREADS AND DRESSINGS		
Peanut butter	Almond butter, cashew butter, macadamia nut butter	Available at Trader Joe's and Whole Foods Market. These nut butters are lower in omega-6 fats than peanut butter.
Salad dressings	Fat-free, low-fat dressings	LiteHouse is a brand that uses canola oil.
Shortening	Fat-free shortening	Many brands are available at your local grocery store.
Tahini	Macadamia nut butter	Tahini is made up of ground sesame seeds and used in hummus. Macadamia nut butter can be found where tahini is sold and is an excellent substitute.
DAIRY CASE		
Margarine, standard	Canola oil margarine	Canola Harvest offers a margarine made from canola oil.
Margarine, heart-healthy type	Smart Balance Omega Plus, Benecol light	Even "heart-healthy" types of margarine often use soybean oil or vegetable oil blends that are high in omega-6 fats.

Instead of	Use	Comments
Nondairy creamer	Fat-free nondairy creamer	Nondairy creamers are made from soybean oil.
Eggs	Omega-3 (DHA-enriched) eggs	Gold Circle Farms is one source of enriched whole eggs and egg whites. Available nationwide.

FROZEN FOODS

Instead of	Use	Comments
Frozen meals	Meals using low-omega-6 oil	Amy's Kitchen meals (available at major grocery stores) use primarily high-oleic oils and olive oil.
Waffles	Brands using low-omega-6 oil	Nature's Path Optimum Power Waffles contain 750 milligrams of omega-6 and 500 milligrams of omega-3.

SNACKS

Instead of	Use	Comments
Potato chips, regular	Baked chips; chips made with olive oil and high-oleic oils	Kettle Chips use monounsaturated sunflower oil, which is low in omega-6 fats.
Tortilla chips, regular	Baked or light chips	Tortilla chips are usually made with oils that are very high in omega-6: sunflower oil or corn oil.

MEATS AND POULTRY

Instead of	Use	Comments
Chicken, turkey	Free-range; white meat (breast)	Dark meats of chicken and turkey have a higher arachidonic acid content. You can find free-range meats at Trader Joe's, specialty grocery stores, and online. Free-range turkey is abundant around Thanksgiving. Brands include Shelton's poultry.
Meats	Free-range	Available at Trader Joe's, specialty grocery stores, and online. Brands include Niman Ranch and U.S. Wellness Meats.
Lamb	New Zealand	New Zealand lamb is raised on the pasture, so it's naturally lower in omega-6 fats.
Sausage	Fat-free and low-fat	Sausages are very high in omega-6 fats.
Tuna in oil	Light tuna in water	Many brands are available at your local grocery store.
Sardines in oil	Check the oil	Sardines are a great source of long-chain omega-3s. But take care to check the oil they are packed in.

Summary of Chapter 13

• •

Choose low-omega-6 oils, spreads, and salad dressings, which include:

■ Canola oil–based margarines, salad dressings, and mayonnaise
■ Olive oil–based salad dressings (Use olive oil as your primary cooking oil, as it is lowest in omega-6 fat.)
■ High-oleic oils

Omega-6 fat content is not required to be listed on food labels.

■ In the ingredient list, oils are listed as their common names, not "omega-6."
■ Check the ingredient list for high-omega-6 oils, including soybean, safflower, sunflower, cottonseed, grape seed, corn, walnut, and wheat germ oil.
■ Seek specific omega-6 fat content available (free) on the Web from NIH and USDA.

Don't assume these foods are low in omega-6 fats:

■ Omega-3-enriched foods
■ Balanced, heart-healthy margarine-style spreads
■ Vegetarian foods or naturally high-omega-3 foods, such as walnut or hemp oils

Meats and poultry contain a potent type of omega-6 fat, arachidonic acid (AA).

■ Light-meat poultry is generally lower in AA.
■ Wild salmon is lower in AA than farmed salmon.
■ Free-range or pastured meats are lower in omega-6 fat content.

PART 4

The Ultimate Omega-3 Lifestyle

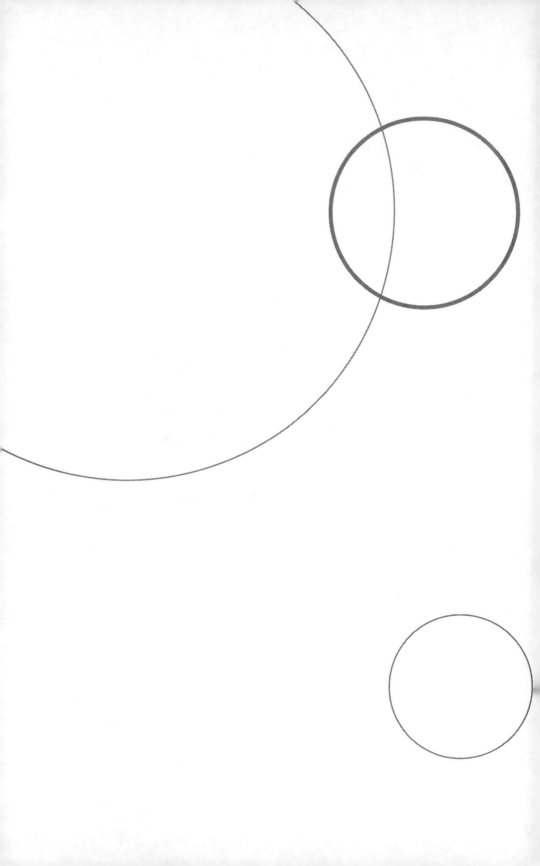

14

The Ultimate Omega-3 Makeover

B Y NOW YOU SHOULD have a pretty good idea of the core aspect of omega-optimizing your diet: increase omega-3 fats (both long- and short-chain) and decrease omega-6 fats to a more healthful level. This chapter will help you put it all together in a practical man- ner, with strategies to fit your lifestyle. The first part of the chapter will show you how omega-optimizing principles fit into an overall healthful diet, including tips for eating out. Then you'll see how dif- ferent eating styles can be converted into a realistic yet better fat balance in your diet.

Omega-Optimize Your Diet for Life

After learning about the benefits of omega-3 fats and the hazards of omega-6 fats, you might be inclined to load up on fish oil pills, switch all your oils to olive, flaxseed, and canola, and believe you hit the omega-optimize mark for balancing your diet. Not quite.

We don't eat in a vacuum. There are factors in food that can opti- mize or detract from the benefits of balanced omega fats in your diet. The nutrients from the foods you eat act as one giant metabolic sym- phony in your body. Some key vitamins and minerals help omega-3 fats do their amazing work in the body. Other substances, including saturated fat, trans fat, and alcohol (in excess) can be problematic. Here are some guidelines to keep in mind, so that you don't inadvertently create a problem while trying to solve the omega fat imbalance. Many of the pillars of healthy eating still remain.

Quantity and Quality of Fats

It's still important to moderate your fat intake, and perhaps you are already skilled at doing so. But if you switch to canola oil and use it indiscriminately, you could still have too much fat in the diet—and too much omega-6 fat as well. Canola oil is among the most healthful oils, but you can still overdo it. Therefore, it's a good idea to seek out lower-fat versions of canola-oil-based mayonnaise, margarine, and salad dressings. The same applies to dairy products and meats. But honor your taste buds; taste counts! And keep in mind that naturally "oily" fish is still lower in fat than most meats.

Total Fat. Overall, most experts agree that a healthful target is for 20 to 35 percent of your calories to come from fat, distributed into the three classes of dietary fat: saturated, monounsaturated, and polyunsaturated (see Figure 14.1). The way the fats are distributed is where the big distinction lies between the omega-optimize and traditional healthful diet paradigms. While the percent of total fat calories remain the same in both the traditional and the omega-optimize diets, their distribution is quite different when you balance omega-6 and omega-3 fats. For instance, most of the fats you eat will come from monounsaturated fats like olive oil, and far less from polyunsaturated fats, which are dominated by omega-6 fats. The distribution in Figure 14.1 is based on guidelines issued by omega-3 fat experts from the International Society for the Study of Fatty Acids and Lipids. The up and down arrows in the figure indicate the change (increase and decrease) from the traditional recommendations.

Saturated Fat. There is universal consensus that saturated fat needs to be kept low in the diet. Besides clogging arteries, saturated fat

FIGURE 14.1 Omega-Optimize: Target Calories from Fat

While the percent of total fat calories remains the same in both the traditional and omega-optimize diets, their distribution is quite different when omega-6 and omega-3 fat is balanced. This distribution is based on guidelines issued from omega-3 fat experts from the International Society for the Study of Fatty Acids and Lipids (ISSFAL). The arrows indicate the change from the traditional recommendations.

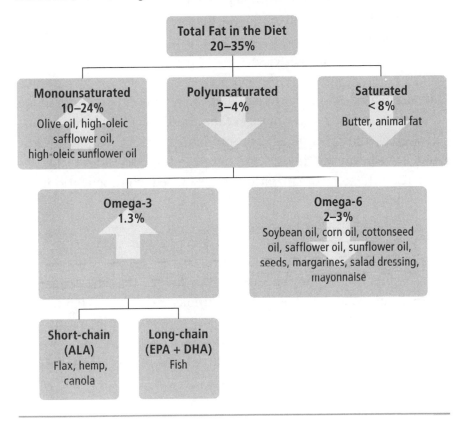

interferes with the metabolism and benefits of omega-3 fats. Saturated fats are found primarily in meats, sausage, poultry skin and fat, full-fat dairy products such as butter and ice cream, and tropical oils such as palm kernel and coconut oil. Saturated fats should be limited to less than 8 percent of your total calories.

Trans fat is a type of fat that also interferes with omega-3 fats, and it's a fat our body does not need. It raises the detrimental cholesterol,

LDL, and lowers the beneficial cholesterol, HDL. Trans fats are on their way out of the food supply, thanks to new food-labeling laws that put this ingredient in the consumer spotlight, but they can still be found in many processed and fried foods.

Monounsaturated Fat. The bulk of our fats should come from mono-unsaturated fats, which have no negative impact on omega-3 fats and also lower cholesterol. Olive oil and the specialty high-oleic oils are monounsaturated fats. Keep in mind, however, that oils, regardless of the source, are calorie-dense.

Polyunsaturated Fat. Polyunsaturated fatty acids (PUFAs) are made up of both omega-3 and omega-6 fats. Traditionally health organizations have indiscriminately recommended increasing polyunsaturated fat, without distinguishing between the two types of PUFA. More recently, some organizations have made recommendations for each type:

- Omega-6 fats should be limited to 2 to 3 percent of fat calories, which is about 4,400 to 6,600 milligrams (or 4.4 to 6.6 grams) of linoleic acid. (Many experts have estimated that an adequate intake of the essential omega-6 fat linoleic acid is from 0.5 to 2 percent of total calories.)
- Calories from omega-3 fats should be distributed as 1 percent ALA (short-chain omega-3, mainly in plants) and 0.3 percent from the long-chain omega-3 fats combined (EPA and DHA, which are mainly marine foods).

The bottom line is that 2 to 3 percent of your fat calories should come from omega-6 PUFAs and 1.3 percent from omega-3 PUFAs. This is quite a substantial change from the standard recommendation to obtain 10 percent of fat calories from polyunsaturated fats. Total PUFA calories are reduced to 3.3 to 4.3 percent of the diet—a consequence of increasing omega-3 fats and lowering omega-6 fats to a balanced level.

Fruits and Vegetables

Yes, you still need to eat your veggies. No amount of fish oil can take the place of what fruits and vegetables do for your health. Plants are truly Mother Nature's medicine chest, and they are an important part of a healthful diet. They offer more than just vitamins and minerals. Researchers are just scratching the surface of identifying their natural beneficial compounds, such as plant sterols and phytochemicals, both of which have health benefits for preventing cancer and heart disease. Fresh, frozen, or canned, they are beneficial. Minimally, aim for two and a half cups to six and a half cups of fruits and vegetables daily.

Whole Grains

Whole grains are found in foods such as whole wheat, rolled oats, and brown rice. Unfortunately, they took a nosedive when low-carbohydrate fad diets were touted as the way to lose weight. Look for flax-based cereals, for their high omega-3 content. Toss flax meal into hot cereal, pancake batters, and muffins. Aim for at least three whole grains a day.

Protein Foods

Many health organizations, from the American Heart Association to the U.S. Department of Health and Human Services, recommend eating at least two fish dishes a week (as discussed earlier, four times a week would be even better). You get more than just long-chain omega-3 fats from eating fish. Every fish dish you eat will usually displace a meal that would have been higher in the saturated and omega-6 fats.

Adequate protein is important for omega-3 fats to work optimally in your body. Dried beans such as pinto and kidney beans are a good source of protein and also have the short-chain omega-3 fat, ALA. Soybeans, when eaten in their less-processed forms such as edamame, low-fat tofu, and low-fat soymilks, are good sources of protein with less omega-6 fat. Many vegetarian foods, such as meatless patties, are high in omega-6 fats.

Calcium-Rich Foods

Aim for at least three servings of calcium-rich foods daily for that all-important bone-contributing nutrient. Yogurt, nonfat and low-fat milk, and low-fat cheeses are good sources of calcium.

Omega-Optimize When Eating Out

Eating out is a wonderful opportunity to explore fish, prepared in a variety of ways, from casual to elegant and even specialty fast food. There are three key questions to ask when eating out:

1. What's the fish dish?
2. What kind of oil is used in salad dressing, cooking, and sauces?
3. What is in the spreads such as mayonnaise and dips?

What's the Fish Dish?

Regardless of the cuisine, it seems that you can get fish—especially salmon, shrimp, and tuna—at almost any restaurant. When ordering fish, be sure to ask how it is prepared. Grilled is preferable, as it tends to use the least amount of added fat.

Here's a brief list of fish-based dishes, by cuisine:

- **Japanese:** This cuisine features sushi, sashimi, seaweed salad, and many other varieties of fish.

- **Mexican:** You can often order shrimp fajitas, fish tacos, or salmon.

- **Chinese:** Many restaurants allow you to select the type of fish or meat you want added to a dish. Choose scallops and shrimp, which are lean shellfish with omega-3 fats.

- **Italian:** Try shrimp scampi and other specialty fish of the day.

- **Steakhouse:** Skip the steak, and go for the lobster, crab, or fresh seafood (grilled, of course).

- **Specialty seafood restaurants:** Dare I state the obvious? Take this as an opportunity to learn about new fish, especially the catch of the day. This is a great place to start if you are uneasy but willing to try seafood. Do choose the wild fish varieties.

What if I Don't Eat Fish? Even if you're not a fish eater, you can still improve your choices. Go for the free-range meat selections that are popping up on many menus. Regional areas such as Denver often have game meats or specialty meats such as buffalo, which are lower in omega-6 fat and higher in omega-3. And unless you are allergic to fish or a strict vegetarian, keep an open mind about trying fish.

Also choose foods with plant-based omega-3s. Choose entree salads made with deep leafy greens such as romaine. Try bean-based dishes, such as hoppin' John, chili, and pinto beans for a good source of omega-3s (short-chain, plant-based ALA).

What Kind of Oil Is Used for Sauces, Cooking, and Salad Dressings?

Take the time to inquire about a restaurant's use of oils. Fortunately, in many places, it's very easy to request and get olive oil. If the salad dressings are not made with canola or olive oil, ask for the simple olive-oil-and-vinegar option. Many restaurants also offer light and fat-free dressings, which can be good choices.

What's in Your Spreads and Dips?

If a sauce or spread is mayonnaise-based, it's likely to be made with soybean oil, which means it is high in omega-6. Pesto sauces are usually made with olive oil. Opt to dip your bread in olive oil rather than spreading it with margarine. Better yet, fresh bread unadorned is fantastic.

Fast Food: Do You Want Omegas with That?

When you find yourself pressed for time, you can still choose well from fast foods or take-out menus.

- **Order the salad instead.** Entree salads with light or fat-free dressing are now standard fare at many fast-food places. It's a better choice than any fried foods, including chicken nuggets or fish sticks.

- **Skip the fried fish.** Fried fish is heavy in omega-6 fat, which negates the health benefit of the omega-3 fats.

- **Ethnic fast-food fish options.** Fish tacos are popular at many Mexican-style fast-food restaurants, including Baja Fresh, Rubio's, and Sharky's. Fresh pinto beans are a great side dish because of their omega-3 fat content. At Pei Wei (a subsidiary of PF Chang's), which serves Asian cuisine, most of the dishes can be made with scallops or shrimp, with the option of brown rice rather than white.

- **Deli tuna sandwiches.** If the tuna is oozing in mayonnaise, it's indicative of a high omega-6 fat load. See if your sandwich can be made with light mayonnaise, dry, or better yet with an olive-oil-based dressing.

Omega-Optimize Makeover

It doesn't take drastic changes to omega-optimize your diet, nor do you suddenly have to become a fish lover (although that would clearly be an asset). If you consider yourself a healthy eater, don't assume that your omega-6 and omega-3 fats are balanced—it's likely not the case. I have to admit that I was stunned at how many *apparently* healthy eaters had diets too high in omega-6. I had this humbling revelation when I first started evaluating my patients' diets for their omega-6 and omega-3 fat content. The following examples describe two different types of healthy eaters. Notice that it took only a couple of changes to make a significant improvement in their fat balance.

The Low-Fat, High-Veggie Eater

A new patient who had just finished therapy for cancer (with an excellent prognosis) sought my help to do everything nutritionally possible to keep the cancer from coming back. She wanted to be sure she was "eating right." Here's the humbling part. If she had consulted me before my foray into balancing the omega-6 and omega-3 fats, I would have concluded that she's doing great, because her diet included lots of veggies and was high in fiber and low in fat. But I took my evaluation one step further, and when I analyzed her diet for her fat balance, I discovered that her ratio was 11-to-1.

With realistic changes in her diet, I was able to get her ratio down to about 1.5-to-1. The most significant changes for her were adding flax meal regularly, incorporating Flax–Olive Oil Vinaigrette (see the recipe in Chapter 16), and changing her margarine.

The Diligent Healthy Eater

A colleague of mine suffers from a chronic inflammation disorder. I had a hunch she was eating too much omega-6 fat, even though she was a careful, healthy eater. At my urging and because she was curious, she let me evaluate a typical day of her eating. She was surprised to learn that her diet was too high in omega-6 fats, with a ratio of 10-to-1 (which even factored in her fish oil supplements).

We made two significant changes to correct her imbalance. First, she replaced her margarine with a spread that is low in omega-6 fat. The biggest change, however, was replacing her daily high dose of walnuts (¼ cup a day) with a combination of hemp nut seeds and dried fruit. While nuts can certainly be part of a healthful diet, she was getting too much of an omega-6 load with that quantity.

The next section shows more examples of simple changes that make a big difference in balancing the fats in your diet, regardless of your eating and cooking style.

Omega-Optimize Makeover of a "Heart-Healthy" Diet

Even a "heart-healthy" diet needs to be omega-optimized. Consider the sample menu in the "Before" column of Table 14.1. At first glance, it might appear to be optimal: low in both overall and saturated fat, and high in fruits in vegetables. This diet is reflective of a health-conscious eater, but it's too high in omega-6 fat and too low in omega-3 fat. The ratio is nearly 11-to-1 (a typical ratio in the American diet). By making several changes, as shown in the table, I got the ratio down to less than 2-to-1.

TABLE 14.1 Omega-Optimize Makeover of a "Heart-Healthy" Diet

Before	After: Omega-Optimized	Omega-Optimize Technique
Breakfast		
Instant oatmeal	Instant oats + *1 tablespoon*	Added flax meal and
Banana	*flax meal* + *2 teaspoons*	walnuts to boost
2 slices whole-wheat toast	*walnuts*	omega-3 fat. Replaced
with light margarine	Banana	margarine with honey
Latte with nonfat milk	2 slices whole-wheat toast	to reduce omega-6 fat.
	with *honey*	
	Latte with nonfat milk	
Lunch		
Turkey-ham sandwich	Turkey-ham sandwich	Switched to light
on wheat	on wheat	canola mayo to
Light mayonnaise	Light *canola* mayonnaise	reduce the omega-6.
1 slice low-fat cheese	1 slice low-fat cheese	Replaced granola bar
Strawberries	Strawberries	with fruit leather to
Granola bar	*Fruit leather* bar	reduce the omega-6.
Dinner		
Salad (iceberg) with fat-free	Salad (*romaine*) with fat-free	Used romaine lettuce
Italian dressing	Italian dressing and	rather than iceberg,
Grilled skinless chicken breast	*kidney beans*	and added kidney
Steamed carrots	Grilled skinless chicken breast	beans for more
Baked potato	Steamed carrots	omega-3.
2 tablespoons light	Baked potato	
sour cream	2 tablespoons light	
1 cup fruit sorbet	sour cream	
	1 cup fruit sorbet	

OMEGA PROFILE

Total fat		
25 grams (17% of calories)	29 grams (20% of calories)	
Ratio of omega-6 to omega-3		
11:1	2:1	

Omega-Optimize Makeover of a "Dash 'n' Go" Diet

Many of my clients eat on the run, grabbing food from take-out places, including fast food. Their intentions to eat healthy are sincere, but they go awry with time-pressured schedules. The "Before" column of Table 14.2 shows a typical diet that results, consisting mostly of fast food and takeout. But even when you eat on the run, you can omega-optimize with a similar style of eating. The two right columns of the table provide easy improvements.

TABLE 14.2 Omega-Optimize Makeover of a "Dash 'n' Go" Diet

Before	After: Omega-Optimized	Omega-Optimize Technique
Breakfast		
Fast Food	*Coffee Shop*	Substituted bagels, which are naturally fat-free; flour tortillas are high in omega-6 fat. Added fruit and nonfat latte to round out the meal nutritionally.
Breakfast burrito	1 bagel with light cream cheese and jam	
Orange juice	1 fresh fruit cup	
	Large nonfat latte	
Lunch		
Fast Food: Traditional	*Fast Food: Fresh-Mex Style*	Fried fish is high in omega-6 fat. Replaced it with grilled fish tacos. Replaced omega-6-laden fries with an omega-3-rich side, pinto beans.
Filet o' Fish sandwich	2 grilled fish tacos on corn tortillas, topped with salsa	
French fries, medium	Side of whole pinto beans	
Diet Coke	Iced tea	
Dinner		
Takeout Pizza	*Takeout Pizza*	Lowered omega-6 fat by replacing pan-style pizza with a thin crust, and added veggies. Used fat-free dressing rather than regular.
2 slices pan cheese pizza, medium	2 slices thin-crust pizza, medium, topped with peppers and mushrooms	
Garden salad with Italian dressing	Garden salad with fat-free dressing	
Diet Coke		

Continued

TABLE 14.2 Omega-Optimize Makeover of a "Dash 'n' Go" Diet (continued)

Before	After: Omega-Optimized	Omega-Optimize Technique
Dessert McDonald's chocolate-chip cookie	McDonald's low-fat vanilla cone	Replaced cookie with low-fat soft-serve cone to lower the omega-6 fat.

OMEGA PROFILE

Total fat 103 grams (43% of calories)	41 grams (21% of calories)	
Ratio of omega-6 to omega-3 9:1	2:1	

What changes do you need to make to your diet to balance your omega-6 and omega-3 fats? Does the task sound too daunting? You can do it, because the next chapter gets you started with seven days' worth of menus for a variety of lifestyles, from hate-to-cook and eating out to kid-friendly and vegetarian.

15

The Ultimate Omega-3 Menus

I T'S EASY TO put together tasty meals and at the same time balance the omega-3 and omega-6 fats in your diet, even if you dislike fish and hate to cook. To show you how easy it is to omega-optimize your diet, I created seven days' worth of menus based on different lifestyle themes, from cooking styles to food preferences. All of these menu days provide a balanced and low ratio of omega-6 to omega-3 fats. *Remember, the lower the ratio, the lower the risk of disease.*

These meals feature all sorts of delicious whole foods, plus particular brands of food products, all currently available in standard supermarkets. Label readers will find more possibilities as food companies meet the growing demand for foods rich in omega-3 and low in omega-6.

Keep in mind that the measurements provided for the foods are not intended to be rigid; they are merely a guide and served as the basis for the nutrient analysis and its data. The omega fat profile that accompanies each recipe is based on these quantities. Dishes printed in *italics* have recipes in the next chapter.

Throw and Go Cook Menu

This day relies on food staples that you are likely to have in the pantry or freezer. These are menus that you can generally throw together at the last minute.

Breakfast
1 cup Kashi Go Lean Crunch cereal
1 cup nonfat milk
1 whole-wheat English muffin with 2 teaspoons honey
1 banana

Lunch
Turkey and avocado sandwich: 2 slices rye bread with 1 teaspoon
   light canola mayonnaise, 1 teaspoon mustard, 2 ounces turkey
   breast, 1 slice low-fat cheddar cheese, and 2 slices avocado
1 ounce pretzels
1 cup watermelon cubes

Afternoon Snack
1 Nature's Path hemp granola bar
1 ounce string cheese

Dinner
2 cups chopped salad greens (sold precut in bags) with 1 serving
   Flax–Olive Oil Vinaigrette
Smoked-Salmon Patties
Spinach Florentine

Omega Fat Profile			
Total Fat grams (% of calories)	Omega-6 milligrams	Omega-3 milligrams	Ratio of Omega-6 to Omega-3
40 (25%)	6,340	5,060	1:1

I-Hate-Fish Menu

Some people just do not like fish—no ifs, ands, or buts. While I'd like you to keep an open mind about trying seafood, this day of meals is fishless, and you still get plenty of the plant type of omega-3 fat, ALA. But since you can't rely on your body to convert a significant amount of ALA to the important long-chain omega-3 fats, EPA and DHA, you will benefit from taking a fish oil supplement regularly (see Chapter 12).

Breakfast
Scrambled eggs, made with 1 omega-3 egg plus 2 egg whites from
   regular eggs
2 slices whole-wheat toast with 1 teaspoon SmartBeat Omega Plus
   buttery spread and honey
½ cantaloupe
1 cup nonfat milk

Lunch
Roast beef sandwich: 2 slices whole-wheat bread, 2 ounces roast
   beef, lettuce, and 1 teaspoon Dijon mustard
½ cup raspberries
1 cup nonfat milk

Afternoon Snack
1 *Blueberry Muffin*

Dinner
Omega Mixed Greens Salad with 1 serving *Flax–Olive Oil*
   Vinaigrette
1½ cups ranch-style barbeque chili beans topped with 2
   tablespoons low-fat cheddar cheese
1 cup sorbet

Omega Fat Profile			
Total Fat grams (% of calories)	**Omega-6 milligrams**	**Omega-3 milligrams**	**Ratio of Omega-6 to Omega-3**
42 (22%)	6,900	5,970	1:1

Eating Out Menu

Remember that eating out is a great opportunity to eat fish and try new varieties. Every meal on this menu can be eaten out.

Breakfast
Bagel with lox and light cream cheese
1 8-ounce nonfat caffe latte
½ cup orange juice

Lunch
Caesar salad with grilled skinless chicken breast and low-calorie, oil-free dressing
French roll, plain
Iced tea

Afternoon Snack
16-ounce berry/banana smoothie

Dinner
Grilled mixed seafood on skewers
Baked potato with 1 tablespoon sour cream
1 cup grilled zucchini
2 chocolate-covered strawberries

Omega Fat Profile			
Total Fat grams (% of calories)	**Omega-6 milligrams**	**Omega-3 milligrams**	**Ratio of Omega-6 to Omega-3**
47 (21%)	4,670	6,190	0.7:1.0

Kid-Friendly Menu

These meals are familiar kiddy fare (such as pancakes) but are omega-optimized. It's best to provide an eating environment that encourages tasting new foods. Ironically, the more a parent pressures a child to eat something, the less likely the child will be to want to eat it! It takes children an average of eight to nine times of actually tasting a new food before they adopt it as their own.

Breakfast
Fluffy Flax Buttermilk Pancakes with 2 tablespoons warm maple
   syrup
½ cup orange juice
1 cup nonfat milk

Lunch
Grilled cheddar cheese sandwich: 2 slices whole-wheat bread and
   1½ tablespoons shredded low-fat cheddar cheese
5 baby carrots with fat-free ranch dressing
½ cup grapes
1 *Chewy Omega Oatmeal Cookie*
1 cup nonfat milk

Afternoon Snack
1 tablespoon almond butter
1 apple, cut into wedges

Dinner
Crispy Fish Sticks with 1 tablespoon catsup
½ cup broccoli
Omega Onion Rings
1 cup nonfat milk
Ice-cream sundae: ½ cup light vanilla ice cream with 1 tablespoon
   chocolate syrup

Omega Fat Profile			
Total Fat grams (% of calories)	Omega-6 milligrams	Omega-3 milligrams	Ratio of Omega-6 to Omega-3
45 (21%)	6,370	7,270	0.9 :1.0

No-Cook Eating at Home Menu

This is a very simple menu; you basically just assemble foods at home. It's designed for a day when you want to relax at home, rather than linger in a restaurant, yet not be fussing about in the kitchen. This menu does not require the use of a microwave.

Breakfast
1 cup nonfat vanilla yogurt
1 cup Uncle Sam cereal
½ cup sliced strawberries

Lunch
Swiss cheese sandwich: 2 slices whole-wheat bread, 1 ounce low-fat
    Swiss cheese, 1 teaspoon mustard, 2 slices tomato, and 2 romaine
    lettuce leaves
½ cup baby carrots
1 medium pear

Afternoon Snack
1 cup baked tortilla chips
¼ cup chunky chili salsa

Dinner
Spinach salad: 3 ounces light tuna (water packed), 2 cups spinach
    leaves (sold prewashed in bags), ¼ cup mandarin oranges, ¼ cup
    sliced mushrooms, 2 tablespoons feta cheese, 1 tablespoon sliced
    olives, 1 tablespoon chopped avocado, and 1 serving *Flax–Olive Oil
    Vinaigrette*
2 plain breadsticks
1 cup nonfat frozen yogurt topped with 1 cup fresh blueberries

Omega Fat Profile			
Total Fat grams (% of calories)	Omega-6 milligrams	Omega-3 milligrams	Ratio of Omega-6 to Omega-3
29 (17%)	4,270	5,750	0.7:1.0

Vegetarian Menu

Ironically, out of all the menu themes, this was one of the most challenging in terms of "nixing the six" (omega-6 fats). Many vegetarian foods are loaded with soybean oil, so take care to check the ingredient labels, and be sure that the primary oils used are canola, flaxseed, and olive oil. Like the no-fish folks, vegetarians are advised to take an omega-3 supplement that contains EPA and DHA. Look for those that provide omega-3s from algae, a vegetable source.

Breakfast
¾ cup Nature's Path FlaxPlus raisin bran cereal
1 cup nonfat soymilk
2 slices whole-wheat toast spread with 2 teaspoons honey
1 cup mixed fresh melon cubes

Lunch
Omega Mixed Greens Salad with 1 tablespoon dried cranberries
    and 1 serving *Flax–Olive Oil Vinaigrette*
Fast Fiesta Burrito (hold the cheese)
1 medium peach

Afternoon Snack
1 kiwi

Dinner
Orzo Pasta Salad (hold the cheese)
1 cup vegetarian chili
Baked potato chips
1 cup strawberries

Omega Fat Profile			
Total Fat grams (% of calories)	Omega-6 milligrams	Omega-3 milligrams	Ratio of Omega-6 to Omega-3
34 (18%)	6,760	5,060	1.3 :1.0

Putter in the Kitchen Menu

This is a menu for a day when you've got the time—and the inclination—to explore new recipes, most likely on the weekend.

Breakfast
1 serving/slice *Double Streusel Coffee Cake*
2 wedges honeydew melon
1 cup nonfat milk

Lunch
1 serving *Omega Kidney Bean Salad*
1 serving *Pesto Bruschetta*
1 fresh pear

Dinner
1 serving *Teriyaki-Glazed Halibut*
½ cup green beans
1 medium sweet potato, baked
1 serving *Omega Frosted Carrot Cake*
1 cup nonfat milk

Omega Fat Profile			
Total Fat grams (% of calories)	Omega-6 milligrams	Omega-3 milligrams	Ratio of Omega-6 to Omega-3
42 (19%)	6,040	5,730	1:1

16

The Ultimate Omega-3 Recipes

IT IS SURPRISINGLY easy to omega-optimize your diet with a few recipes and staples on hand. Each recipe was developed to provide a healthier proportion of fats, less omega-6, and more omega-3 fats. The omega-optimize technique is highlighted in each recipe so that you can incorporate it into your own favorite recipes. The nutrition profile of each recipe is based on eating one serving of the recipe, which includes the amounts of calories, different fats, carbohydrates, protein, fiber, and the ratio of omega-6 to omega-3 fats.

Pantry Staples

Here are some staples to keep on hand. This list is far from comprehensive, but it will give you a good idea of foods to stock in your pantry, refrigerator, and freezer.

- **Olive oil** should be your primary cooking oil (when you use oil). Its biggest advantage in the diet is that it displaces omega-6 fats.
- **Canola oil** is versatile with a neutral flavor and a good balance of omega-6 and omega-3 fats. Remember, too much of it can still add a load of omega-6 fat.

- **Flax oil** needs to be refrigerated once or—because it's so high in the omega-3 fat ALA—it can easily turn rancid. It is best used in recipes that require little, if any, cooking, such as salad dressing. (Be sure to try the Flax–Olive Oil Vinaigrette on page 234, which has only three ingredients to whisk together.)
- **Canola mayonnaise** because most mayonnaise is made with soybean oil. Fat-free mayonnaise is also a good choice.
- **Nonstick spray**, specifically a canola- or olive oil–based spray.
- **Flax meal** is made from ground-up flaxseeds and looks like wheat bran and is very versatile.
- **Canned or dried beans**, such as kidney beans, pinto beans, pink lentils, and black beans, are a good source of omega-3 fats. These legumes can be quickly made into an easy meal or snack.
- **Canned seafood** that has been packed in water, olive oil, or tomato sauce (many are packed with omega-6-rich soybean oil). Choose light tuna, sardines, salmon, smoked salmon, and trout.

The Fridge

Stock your refrigerator with these great omega-3-rich options.

- **Margarine and spreads** that have canola oil as the first ingredient. A brand worth mentioning is SmartBeat Omega spread, which is the only spread to date that has added DHA. This has merits especially if you do not regularly eat fish.
- **Bag-o-salad or greens**, such as romaine, broccoli, spinach, collard greens, and kale. They last longer in the refrigerator and are a good source of omega-3 fat.
- **Fresh basil** is a good source of omega-3 fats. There's nothing like the taste of fresh basil—so I grow it in my kitchen, for convenience; it's ready to use at a moment's notice.
- **Meats and poultry,** especially free-range or "pastured" varieties. I learned the significance of this when I developed the minestrone recipe (page 225). There was originally too much omega-6 fat in the recipe from using traditional skinless, chicken breast! I had to reduce the amount of chicken by half to balance

the fat. Keep in mind that *organic* is not the same thing as *free range*. *Organic* means that no pesticides or chemicals were used to feed the animal.

- **DHA-enriched eggs** are easily found in grocery stores. Remember, the omega-3 fat is in the yolk (unless you buy liquid egg whites with DHA, which are available, but hard to find).
- **Fresh seafood**, the advantage being that fresh fish cooks very quickly; you will need to plan to prepare it that day, as it perishes fast. Remember to choose wild fish.

Frozen Assets—Freezer

Keep these tasty items in your freezer so you'll have healthy options available when you can't get to the store.

- **Raspberries, blueberries, blackberries**, which are indistinguishable from fresh berries when used in cooking, such as in sauces. There's probably not a day when my freezer is devoid of berries.
- **Chopped greens**, such as spinach and collard greens, which are versatile and easy to use.
- **Seafood** is a terrific staple. I have to admit that I was hesitant to use frozen seafood, but I got over my apprehension. Remember to choose wild fish.

Recipe Note

Each recipe that follows has an Omega-Optimize Technique section that highlights the ingredients used to lower the omega-6 fat and increase the omega-3 fat. The Omega-Optimize Nutrition Profile lists the nutrition information for each serving of the recipe.

Breakfast Foods

Many breakfast foods feature eggs. Look for eggs enriched with DHA, usually labeled "omega-3 eggs."

Fluffy Flax Buttermilk Pancakes

Have these pancakes for breakfast, and you'll start the day ahead in omega-3s.

Servings: 4

Omega-Optimize Technique ■ Omega-3 (DHA-enriched) eggs
■ Canola oil ■ Flax meal

---

1 teaspoon baking soda
1 cup low-fat buttermilk
1 omega-3 egg
2 teaspoons canola oil, plus
   extra for coating the griddle

1½ teaspoons vanilla
¾ cup whole-wheat flour
¼ cup flax meal
2 teaspoons sugar
¼ teaspoon cinnamon

In a small bowl dissolve the baking soda into buttermilk. Let stand at least 1 minute. Add the egg, canola oil, and vanilla. In a separate bowl, combine the flour, flax meal, sugar, and cinnamon. Stir in the buttermilk mixture. Coat the griddle with the remaining canola oil.

For each pancake, pour about ¼ cup batter onto the hot griddle. Adjust the heat so that the bottom of the pancakes brown in 2 to 4 minutes. Note that the first batch will require higher heat. Flip the pancakes when they are cooked on the bottom, and continue to cook until the second side is lightly browned.

Omega-Optimize Nutrition Profile			
Calories	283	Fat g	9
Omega-6 mg	1,330	Carbs g	44
Omega-3 mg	2,180	Protein g	9
Ratio of Omega-6 to Omega-3	0.6:1.0	Fiber g	5

Omega Omelet

An omelet is great vehicle for delivering your veggies in the morning. In this case, you get bell pepper.

Servings: 1

Omega-Optimize Technique ■ Omega-3 (DHA-enriched) egg ■ Canola oil, rather than butter ■ Swiss cheese, a better source of omega-3s than the cheddar cheese typically used in omelets

1 omega-3 egg
2 egg whites from
   conventional eggs
⅛ teaspoon salt
Dash black pepper

1 teaspoon canola oil
¼ cup diced green bell pepper
¼ cup diced onion
2 tablespoons shredded
   reduced-fat Swiss cheese

In a small bowl, beat together the egg, egg whites, salt, and pepper.

Heat the canola oil in a small nonstick omelet pan or small skillet. Add the bell pepper and onion. Cook, stirring occasionally, and stir over medium heat until onion is translucent.

Add the egg mixture, and cook *without* stirring until the omelet begins to set around the edges, about 10 seconds. Using a rubber spatula, lift the edges of the cooked portion of the omelet to let the uncooked egg mixture flow under it. Repeat until most of the omelet is set. Cover the pan with a lid, and cook 30 to 45 seconds, or until the eggs are cooked to desired doneness. Top with cheese. Slide the omelet halfway onto a plate, and then flip the omelet over itself so it folds in half.

Florentine Omelet variation: Omit the bell pepper and Swiss cheese. Cook as above, and spoon one serving of Spinach Florentine (see page 233) on egg as it cooks, before folding omelet.

Omega-Optimize Nutrition Profile			
Omega Omelet			
Calories	225	Fat g	12
Omega-6 mg	1,750	Carbs g	7
Omega-3 mg	810	Protein g	22
Ratio of Omega-6 to Omega-3	2:1	Fiber g	1
Variation			
Calories	252	Fat g	15
Omega-6 mg	2,230	Carbs g	12
Omega-3 mg	1,200	Protein g	20
Ratio of Omega-6 to Omega-3	2:1	Fiber g	4

Double Streusel Coffee Cake

This beautiful coffee cake has two cinnamony ribbons of streusel running throughout. Shhh, the streusel is filled with flax meal!

Servings: 12

Omega-Optimize Technique ■ Flax meal in place of walnuts
■ Omega-3 (DHA-enriched) eggs

Streusel
1 cup brown sugar
½ cup flax meal
2 tablespoons ground cinnamon

Coffee Cake
2 cups cake flour
1 cup "white" whole-wheat
  flour (see page 218)

½ teaspoon salt
⅛ teaspoon ground nutmeg
3 omega-3 eggs

1 cup sugar

1½ teaspoons baking powder

1½ teaspoons baking soda

1 16-ounce carton fat-free sour cream

¾ cup applesauce

Glaze

2 tablespoons powdered sugar

¾ teaspoon nonfat milk

Make the streusel in a small bowl by mixing the brown sugar, flax meal, and cinnamon. Set aside.

Preheat the oven to 350°F. Coat a 10-inch Bundt pan with canola oil nonstick spray. In a large bowl, combine the cake and whole-wheat flours, sugar, baking powder, baking soda, salt, and nutmeg.

In another large bowl, using an electric mixer on the high setting, beat the eggs for 2 minutes. Beat in the sour cream and applesauce. Add half of the flour mixture, and beat until moist. Add the remaining flour mixture, and beat until well blended, about 1 minute. (The batter will be quite thick.)

Pour one-third of the batter into the prepared pan. Sprinkle half of the streusel evenly over the batter. Repeat with another one-third of the batter and the remaining streusel. Spoon the remaining batter over the streusel.

Bake cake until a toothpick inserted into the center comes out clean, about 45 minutes. Cool cake in the pan on a wire rack for 10 minutes. Cut around the pan sides to loosen the cake. Turn cake out onto a platter to cool for 1 hour.

Meanwhile, make the glaze. Mix the powdered sugar and milk in a small bowl until smooth. Drizzle over cooled coffee cake.

Omega-Optimize Nutrition Profile			
Calories	333	Fat g	3
Omega-6 mg	540	Carbs g	71
Omega-3 mg	840	Protein g	7
Ratio of Omega-6 to Omega-3	0.6:1.0	Fiber g	3

Baked Goods

Many of these recipes call for "white" whole-wheat flour. This is actually a whole-grain flour but is much finer in texture and less gritty than regular whole-wheat flour. Look for this product at Trader Joe's and in natural-food stores. If it's not available, you can substitute standard whole-wheat flour.

Blueberry Muffins

These muffins are a family favorite.

Yield: 12 muffins

Omega-Optimize Technique ■ Canola oil ■ Flax meal in place of part of the wheat flour ■ Blueberries, one of the few fruits that contain omega-3 fats (80 milligrams per cup) ■ Omega-3 (DHA-enriched) egg

---

¾ cup "white" whole-wheat flour
¼ cup flax meal
¾ cup sugar
1 teaspoon lemon zest
1 tablespoon baking powder

1 omega-3 egg
¾ cup buttermilk
¼ cup canola oil
2 teaspoons vanilla extract
1 cup fresh blueberries

Preheat oven to 400°F. Spray muffin tin (12 2-inch-diameter cups) with canola oil nonstick spray. In a large bowl, combine the flour, flax meal, sugar, lemon zest, and baking powder. Make a well in the center. In a separate bowl, combine the egg, buttermilk, oil, and vanilla. Add the liquid mixture to the dry ingredients. Stir in the blueberries. Divide the batter into muffin cups, filling each three-quarters full. Bake 22 to 25 minutes until a toothpick inserted into center of muffin comes out clean. Cool 5 minutes in pan. Serve immediately, or transfer to a wire rack to continue cooling.

Omega-Optimize Nutrition Profile (for 1 muffin)			
Calories	182	Fat g	7
Omega-6 mg	1,300	Carbs g	27
Omega-3 mg	1,220	Protein g	4
Ratio of Omega-6 to Omega-3	1:1	Fiber g	2

Cranberry Orange Muffins

You can make up a batch of these muffins year-round, since the recipe calls for dried cranberries, not fresh. Dried cranberries are sold in upscale markets and natural-food stores.

Yield: 12 muffins

Omega-Optimize Technique ■ Flax meal ■ Walnuts ■ Omega-3 (DHA-enriched) eggs ■ Canola oil

¾ cup whole-wheat flour or "white" whole-wheat flour
¼ cup flax meal
¾ cup sugar
1 tablespoon baking powder
2 teaspoons grated orange zest (zest of 1 orange)
⅛ teaspoon cinnamon

1 omega-3 egg
⅔ cup buttermilk
⅓ cup canola oil
⅔ cup dried sweetened cranberries
3 tablespoons finely chopped walnuts

Preheat oven to 400°F. Spray muffin tin (12 2-inch-diameter cups) with canola oil nonstick spray. In a large bowl, combine the flour, flax meal, sugar, baking powder, orange zest, and cinnamon. Make a well in the center. In a separate bowl, combine the egg, buttermilk, and oil. Add the liquid mixture to the dry ingredients. Stir in the cranberries. Divide the batter into muffin cups, filling each three-quarters full. Scatter the walnuts on top of the muffin batter. Bake 20 to 22 minutes until a toothpick inserted into center comes out clean. Cool 5 minutes in pan. Serve immediately, or transfer to a wire rack to continue cooling.

Omega-Optimize Nutrition Profile (for 1 muffin)			
Calories	171	Fat g	7
Omega-6 mg	1,590	Carbs g	26
Omega-3 mg	1,170	Protein g	3
Ratio of Omega-6 to Omega-3	1.4:1.0	Fiber g	2

Omega Honey Cornbread

Shhh, don't tell anyone this is so healthful. This cornbread pairs nicely with soup and tastes fabulous as a simple snack.

Servings: 9

Omega-Optimize Technique ▪ Flax meal ▪ Omega-3 (DHA-enriched) eggs ▪ Canola oil

1 cup corn meal
¾ cup all-purpose flour
½ cup sugar
¼ cup flax meal
1 tablespoon baking powder

1¼ cups low-fat buttermilk
⅓ cup honey
¼ cup canola oil
2 omega-3 eggs

Preheat oven 400°F. Lightly coat an 8-inch square pan with canola oil nonstick spray. In a medium bowl, combine the corn meal, flour, sugar, flax meal, and baking powder. Make a well in the center. In a small bowl, mix together the buttermilk, honey, canola oil, and eggs. Mix until smooth, and add to dry ingredients. Pour into the prepared pan. Bake 22 to 25 minutes or until golden. Serve hot or warm.

Omega-Optimize Nutrition Profile			
Calories	283	Fat g	10
Omega-6 mg	1,800	Carbs g	44
Omega-3 mg	1,500	Protein g	6
Ratio of Omega-6 to Omega-3	1.2:1.0	Fiber g	2

Snacks and Small Meals

Fast Fiesta Burritos

Try one of these burritos for a quick and satisfying entree rich in fiber, protein, and omega-3 fats. To save prep time, you can purchase chopped onion in the freezer or produce section of your local supermarket. Vegans can enjoy the burrito, too; just hold the cheese.

Yield: 6 burritos

Omega-Optimize Technique ■ Pinto beans ■ Canola oil

---

2 15-ounce cans whole
  pinto beans, drained
2 teaspoons canola oil
1 medium onion, chopped
1 cup salsa
⅓ cup chopped fresh cilantro

6 whole-wheat tortillas or
  wraps (made with either
  olive oil or canola oil)
¾ cup shredded reduced-fat
cheddar cheese

Drain the pinto beans. In a large skillet, heat the canola oil over medium-high heat. Add the onion. Cook, stirring occasionally, until onions are translucent, about 5 minutes. Add drained beans, salsa, and cilantro. Cook bean mixture until heated through, stirring occasionally. Place one-sixth of the bean mixture on a tortilla. Top with 2 tablespoons of the cheese. Fold the ends of the tortillas over the beans, and roll up. Heat in microwave until cheese is melted, about 30 seconds on high.

Omega-Optimize Nutrition Profile (for 1 burrito)			
Calories	246	Fat g	4
Omega-6 mg	690	Carbs g	45
Omega-3 mg	400	Protein g	14
Ratio of Omega-6 to Omega-3	1.7:1.0	Fiber g	9

Omega Onion Rings

These baked onion rings make an irresistible snack and are so much healthier than the traditional fried rings. Mix up a batch when you feel like nibbling!

Servings: 4

Omega-Optimize Technique ■ Flax meal for part of the crispy coating ■ Omega-3 (DHA-enriched) egg

---

3 large onions, sliced ½ inch
   thick
1 cup buttermilk
½ cup all-purpose flour
½ teaspoon salt

1 omega-3 egg
1 egg white
¾ cup cornflake crumbs
¼ cup flax meal
½ teaspoon salt

Preheat oven to 400°F. Separate the onion slices into rings. Pour the buttermilk into a large bowl, add the onion rings, and mix to coat. Stir occasionally. Set aside.

Spray a baking sheet with canola oil nonstick spray, and set aside. In a shallow dish, combine the flour and salt. In a second shallow dish, lightly beat the whole egg and egg white. In a third shallow dish, mix the cornflake crumbs, flax meal, and salt.

Dip each onion ring first into the flour mixture, next into the eggs, and lastly into the cornflake crumbs to coat. Place on the prepared baking sheet. Spray coated onion rings with nonstick spray. Bake in batches for 15 minutes or until golden. Serve immediately.

Omega-Optimize Nutrition Profile			
Calories	207	Fat g	6
Omega-6 mg	750	Carbs g	32
Omega-3 mg	1,960	Protein g	8
Ratio of Omega-6 to Omega-3	0.4:1.0	Fiber g	4

Easy Omega Onion Dip

In this recipe, instant onion soup turns plain sour cream into a savory dip.

Yield: 1 cup (8 servings of 2 tablespoons each)

Omega-Optimize Technique ▪ Flax meal

---

1 16-ounce carton fat-free sour cream
1 1-ounce packet instant onion soup mix
4 teaspoons flax meal

Combine all ingredients in a medium-size bowl. Cover and chill at least 1 hour before serving.

Omega-Optimize Nutrition Profile			
Calories	30	Fat g	<1
Omega-6 mg	40	Carbs g	6
Omega-3 mg	150	Protein g	1
Ratio of Omega-6 to Omega-3	0.3:1.0	Fiber g	0

Pesto Bruschetta

Bruschetta is one of my favorite snacks. It's also ideal for a small meal, along with a green salad.

Servings: 12

Omega-Optimize Technique ▪ Omega Pesto Sauce, rather than olive oil

---

1 8-ounce baguette, 2 inches in diameter
¼ cup *Omega Pesto Sauce*
2 medium tomatoes, chopped
½ cup finely shredded, part-skim mozzarella cheese

Preheat broiler. Cut baguette crosswise into 24 slices. Spread ½ teaspoon of pesto on each slice. Top with tomatoes and mozzarella, evenly divided among the slices. Broil until cheese is golden, about 3 minutes. Serve immediately.

Omega-Optimize Nutrition Profile			
Calories	108	Fat g	5
Omega-6 mg	750	Carbs g	11
Omega-3 mg	750	Protein g	4
Ratio of Omega-6 to Omega-3	1:1	Fiber g	1

Pesto and Peppers Pizza

Here's a homemade pizza that is yummy and colorful. It's also easy to make using prepared whole-wheat pizza dough. You can find this handy product fresh in the deli section of your supermarket or frozen in the freezer section. Be sure to check the list of ingredients on the package of pizza dough for the type of oil. Preferably it's made with olive or canola oil.

Servings: 8

Omega-Optimize Technique ■ Omega Pesto Sauce

1 pound whole-wheat pizza dough
½ *Omega Pesto Sauce* recipe
1½ cups shredded reduced-fat mozzarella cheese
½ yellow bell pepper, chopped
½ red bell pepper, chopped

Heat oven to 400°F. Spray a pizza pan or baking sheet with canola oil nonstick spray. Place the dough on the baking sheet, and press outward to form a 12-inch circle. Spray the dough with canola oil nonstick spray. Spread the pesto evenly over the dough. Scatter the cheese over the pizza. Top with the chopped peppers. Bake 15 minutes or until bubbly. Slice into 8 wedges. Serve immediately.

Omega-Optimize Nutrition Profile			
Calories	280	Fat g	13
Omega-6 mg	1,420	Carbs g	28
Omega-3 mg	1,700	Protein g	12
Ratio of Omega-6 to Omega-3	0.8:1.0	Fiber g	2

Omega Minestrone

This is my son's favorite soup. It's a great recipe for getting a lot of vegetables into your diet.

Servings: 6

Omega-Optimize Technique ▪ Kidney beans ▪ Canola oil ▪ Kale and basil, which contain omega-3s

2 teaspoons canola oil
1 large onion, chopped
3 garlic cloves, chopped
2 celery stalks, chopped
2 medium carrots, sliced
2 4-ounce boneless, skinless
   chicken breasts (see note)
1 27-ounce can diced tomatoes

3 cups chicken broth
1 cup chopped kale (fresh or
   frozen)
1 cup chopped fresh basil
1 15-ounce can kidney beans,
   drained
2 slices cooked bacon, crumbled
1 teaspoon dried oregano

Heat oil over medium-high heat in a 4-quart soup pan. Add onion, garlic, celery, and carrots. Cook and stir until onions are browned, about 10 minutes. Add chicken breasts, and brown on both sides. Add tomatoes, chicken broth, kale, basil, kidney beans, bacon, and oregano. Bring to a boil, and then reduce the heat. Cover and simmer 1 hour or more.

Note: Use free-range chicken for a better omega-6/omega-3 ratio than with conventionally raised poultry.

Omega-Optimize Nutrition Profile			
Calories	230	Fat g	4
Omega-6 mg	660	Carbs g	32
Omega-3 mg	330	Protein g	19
Ratio of Omega-6 to Omega-3	2:1	Fiber g	8

Salads

Omega Kidney Bean Salad

This colorful salad tastes even better when chilled overnight.

Servings: 6

Omega-Optimize Technique ■ Kidney beans ■ Flax–Olive Oil Vinaigrette

2 15-ounce cans red kidney beans, drained and rinsed
1 yellow bell pepper, trimmed and chopped
1 green bell pepper, trimmed and chopped
¼ cup chopped cilantro leaves
¼ cup minced chives
½ cup (1 recipe) *Flax–Olive Oil Vinaigrette*
2 cloves garlic, minced
½ teaspoon cumin
¼ teaspoon black pepper

Combine kidney beans, yellow and green peppers, cilantro, and chives in a large bowl. In a small bowl, whisk together the vinaigrette, garlic, cumin, and black pepper. Pour the dressing over the bean mixture, and toss until coated. Cover and chill just until cold.

Omega-Optimize Nutrition Profile			
Calories	215	Fat g	10
Omega-6 mg	1,140	Carbs g	25
Omega-3 mg	2,520	Protein g	8
Ratio of Omega-6 to Omega-3	0.4:1.0	Fiber g	7

Omega Mixed Greens Salad

This is a basic garden salad with the dark green lettuces that add omega-3s. Bags of these greens already washed and chopped are sold in the produce section of supermarkets. If you serve this with the Flax–Olive Oil Vinaigrette, you can then omit the walnuts and flax meal in the recipe.

Servings: 6

Omega-Optimize Technique ■ Walnuts ■ Flax meal ■ Dark green leaf lettuce, rather than iceberg

---

8 cups romaine lettuce
4 cups baby spinach
1 cup chopped fresh basil
1 cup chopped fresh parsley

2 medium cucumbers, chopped
½ cup grated carrots
2 tablespoons chopped walnuts
4 teaspoons flax meal

In a large bowl, toss together the romaine, spinach, basil, parsley, cucumbers, and carrots. Scatter walnuts and flax meal over the salad.

Omega-Optimize Nutrition Profile			
Calories	51	Fat g	3
Omega-6 mg	1,130	Carbs g	7
Omega-3 mg	780	Protein g	3
Ratio of Omega-6 to Omega-3	1.5:1.0	Fiber g	4

Tomato-Basil Salad

I usually make a double batch of this salad. On the first day I enjoy it as a salad. Then I marinate the leftovers overnight and spoon it on hot pasta.

Servings: 4

Omega-Optimize Technique ■ Flaxseed oil ■ Olive oil, a neutral fat, low in omega-6s ■ Basil ■ Spinach

---

4 medium tomatoes, chopped
¼ cup fresh basil leaves, stems removed and chopped
2 tablespoons fresh spinach leaves, chopped
2 tablespoons grated Parmesan cheese
1 tablespoon flaxseed oil
1 tablespoon olive oil
2 tablespoons balsamic vinegar

In a medium bowl, combine the tomatoes, basil, spinach, and Parmesan. In a small bowl, whisk together the flaxseed and olive oils with the vinegar until blended. Drizzle dressing over the salad, and serve.

Omega-Optimize Nutrition Profile			
Calories	103	Fat g	8
Omega-6 mg	910	Carbs g	7
Omega-3 mg	1,860	Protein g	2
Ratio of Omega-6 to Omega-3	0.5:1.0	Fiber g	2

Orzo Pasta Salad

Orzo, a tiny rice-shaped pasta, provides plenty of pasta surface for soaking up flavor. It's also easier to eat than less manageable noodles, making orzo a good choice when you're serving buffet-style at a party.

Servings: 8

Omega-Optimize Technique ■ Flax–Olive Oil Vinaigrette ■ Basil

---

1½ cups dry orzo
1 cup shredded carrots
3 medium tomatoes, chopped
1 medium yellow bell pepper, chopped
½ cup sliced black olives

⅓ cup minced chives
¼ cup chopped parsley
2 tablespoons grated Parmesan cheese
½ cup (1 recipe) *Flax–Olive Oil Vinaigrette*

Cook the orzo according to the instructions on the package. When the pasta is cooked to your liking, drain through a sieve, and rinse with cold water to stop the cooking; drain well.

In a large bowl, combine the orzo, carrots, tomatoes, pepper, olives, chives, parsley, and Parmesan. Add the dressing. Using a wooden spoon or spatula, toss to combine.

Omega-Optimize Nutrition Profile			
Calories	126	Fat g	6
Omega-6 mg	590	Carbs g	17
Omega-3 mg	940	Protein g	3
Ratio of Omega-6 to Omega-3	0.5:1.0	Fiber g	2

Vegetable Dishes

Spinach and Feta Sauté

This is one of my favorite vegetable dishes, and it's very easy to assemble at the last minute.

Servings: 4

Omega-Optimize Technique ■ Canola oil ■ Spinach, a plant source of alpha-linolenic fatty acids ■ Feta, a good source of omega-3

2 teaspoons canola oil
1 tablespoon dried minced onion
2 cloves garlic, chopped
1 10-ounce package frozen chopped spinach, partially thawed
4 ounces crumbled light feta cheese

In a large skillet, heat the oil over medium-high heat. Add the onion and garlic. Sauté, stirring gently, until fragrant, about 1 minute. Add spinach and sauté 5 minutes, stirring occasionally. Add the feta cheese and combine. Cook and stir until heated through and cheese is melted, about 1 minute. Serve immediately.

Omega-Optimize Nutrition Profile			
Calories	113	Fat g	6
Omega-6 mg	570	Carbs g	8
Omega-3 mg	490	Protein g	11
Ratio of Omega-6 to Omega-3	1:1	Fiber g	4

Cajun Collard Greens

This recipe gives you a head start on the preparation by using frozen collard greens. If you like your foods on the tame side of spicy, use the smaller amount of red pepper flakes.

Servings: 6

Omega-Optimize Technique ■ Canola oil ■ Collard greens, a good source of omega-3 fats

---

2 slices bacon
2 teaspoons canola oil
1 cup chopped onion (1 medium onion)
¼ to ½ teaspoon crushed red pepper flakes
½ teaspoon salt
1 pound frozen chopped collard greens

In a small skillet, cook bacon over medium heat until crisp. Place on a cutting board and chop into small pieces. Set aside.

Heat the canola oil over medium-high heat in a large skillet. Add the onions, pepper flakes, and salt. Sauté, stirring occasionally, until the onions are translucent, about 5 minutes. Add the bacon and collard greens. Cook, stirring from time to time, until the mixture is heated through, about 5 minutes.

Omega-Optimize Nutrition Profile			
Calories	66	Fat g	3
Omega-6 mg	390	Carbs g	9
Omega-3 mg	220	Protein g	3
Ratio of Omega-6 to Omega-3	2:1	Fiber g	3

Spinach Florentine

This is one of my favorite ways to eat spinach.

Servings: 6

Omega-Optimize Technique ■ Canola oil ■ Spinach, a good source of omega-3 fats

---

2 teaspoons canola oil
2 tablespoons dried minced onion
2 cloves garlic
1 pound frozen chopped spinach, partially thawed
⅓ cup grated Parmesan cheese

In a large skillet, heat oil over medium-high heat. Add the onion and garlic. Sauté, stirring gently, until fragrant, about 1 minute. Add spinach and cook, stirring occasionally, until heated through, about 5 minutes. Add the Parmesan, and stir to combine. Cook until heated through, about 1 minute. Serve immediately.

Omega-Optimize Nutrition Profile			
Calories	60	Fat g	3
Omega-6 mg	360	Carbs g	5
Omega-3 mg	280	Protein g	5
Ratio of Omega-6 to Omega-3	1.3:1.0	Fiber g	2

Dressings and Sauces

Flax–Olive Oil Vinaigrette

This simple dressing is a staple in my home because it is so easy to make and delicious. Just 1 tablespoon meets nearly all your daily requirement for short-chain omega-3 (ALA)!

Yield: 8 1-tablespoon servings

Omega-Optimize Technique ■ Flaxseed oil ■ Olive oil, a neutral fat, predominantly monounsaturated and low in omega 6s

2 tablespoons flaxseed oil
2 tablespoons olive oil
¼ cup balsamic vinegar

Whisk together the flaxseed oil, olive oil, and vinegar until blended. Use on salads and even steamed vegetables.

Omega-Optimize Nutrition Profile			
Calories	65	Fat g	7
Omega-6 mg	760	Carbs g	1
Omega-3 mg	1,840	Protein g	0
Ratio of Omega-6 to Omega-3	0.4:1.0	Fiber g	0

Honey Sesame Vinaigrette

This flavorful Asian dressing with its sweet-sour tang will perk up any salad. While sesame oil is one of the oils higher in omega-6 fats, it doesn't take much of this oil to add its special flavor.

Yield: 12 1-tablespoon servings

Omega-Optimize Technique ■ Flaxseed oil, a rich source of omega-3s ■ Canola oil

¼ cup seasoned rice vinegar

2 tablespoons balsamic vinegar

2 tablespoons unsweetened pineapple juice

2 tablespoons flaxseed oil

1 tablespoon honey

1 tablespoon canola oil

1 tablespoon sesame oil

Dash black pepper

In a small bowl, whisk together all the ingredients until blended. Refrigerate in an airtight container, and use within a week.

Omega-Optimize Nutrition Profile			
Calories	50	Fat g	4
Omega-6 mg	840	Carbs g	3
Omega-3 mg	1,320	Protein g	0
Ratio of Omega-6 to Omega-3	0.6:1.0	Fiber g	0

Omega Pesto Sauce

Enjoy this no-cook sauce that is incredibly delicious and easy to make. It functions as a dip, dressing, or spread.

Yield: 12 1-tablespoon servings

Omega-Optimize Technique ■ Flaxseed oil in place of part of the olive oil ■ Flax meal and walnuts replacing the usual pine nuts ■ Basil, a good source of omega-3 fat

3 cloves garlic

3 tablespoons chopped walnuts

1 tablespoon flax meal

2 cups fresh basil leaves

⅓ cup extra-virgin olive oil

3 tablespoons flaxseed oil

2 tablespoons balsamic vinegar

½ cup grated Parmesan cheese

In a food processor or blender, add ingredients one at a time, blending after each addition until smooth. Pesto can be stored in an airtight container in the refrigerator for use within a couple of days.

Omega-Optimize Nutrition Profile			
Calories	112	Fat g	11
Omega-6 mg	1,750	Carbs g	2
Omega-3 mg	2,210	Protein g	2
Ratio of Omega-6 to Omega-3	0.8:1.0	Fiber g	1

Seafood Entrees

Pesto Sole Florentine

The green of the pesto sauce is a ready-made garnish for this savory fish dish.

Servings: 4

Omega-Optimize Technique ■ Canola oil ■ Spinach, a plant source of omega-3 ■ Sole, a good source of long-chain omega-3 fats

2 teaspoons canola oil
2 tablespoons dried minced onion
2 cloves garlic
1 10-ounce package frozen chopped spinach, partially thawed
¼ cup grated Parmesan cheese
4 4-ounce fillets of sole
4 tablespoons *Omega Pesto Sauce*

Preheat oven to 400°F. Heat oil in a large skillet over medium-high heat. Add the onion and garlic; sauté until fragrant, about 1 minute. Add the spinach and cook until heated through. Add the Parmesan. Cook and stir until heated through. Remove pan from heat, and set aside, stirring occasionally, about 5 minutes.

Place sole fillets on a sheet of waxed paper. Using one-fourth of the spinach mixture for each fillet, spread evenly on fish. Roll up each fillet, and secure with a wooden toothpick. Place in a shallow baking dish that has been sprayed with nonstick canola oil spray. Drizzle pesto sauce over fish. Bake about 10 minutes or until fish is opaque. Serve immediately.

Omega-Optimize Nutrition Profile			
Calories	384	Fat g	21
Omega-6 mg	2,860	Carbs g	11
Omega-3 mg	3.490	Protein g	39
Ratio of Omega-6 to Omega-3	0.8:1.0	Fiber g	5

Salmon with Parmesan-Olive Topping

This is a great meal to make at the last minute when unexpected company arrives. Every time I serve this, I get rave reviews on the savory topping.

Servings: 4

Omega-Optimize Technique ■ Flax meal, rather than bread crumbs
■ Salmon, naturally high in omega-3s

1 clove garlic
1 3-ounce jar stuffed green olives, drained
2 tablespoons chicken broth
3 tablespoons grated Parmesan cheese
1 teaspoon flax meal
4 salmon fillets (about 1 pound)

Preheat the broiler. Coat a broiler pan with canola oil nonstick spray. In a small food processor or blender, pulse the garlic until finely chopped. Add the olives, and pulse until chopped. Add the chicken broth, Parmesan, and flax meal, and pulse until fairly smooth.

Arrange the salmon in the prepared pan in a single layer. Spread a thin layer of the olive paste over each fish fillet.

Broil the fillets 3 to 4 inches from the heat without turning, about 8 to 10 minutes, until the fish flakes easily. Serve immediately.

Omega-Optimize Nutrition Profile			
Calories	306	Fat g	19
Omega-6 mg	650	Carbs g	1
Omega-3 mg	2,270	Protein g	31
Ratio of Omega-6 to Omega-3	0.3:1.0	Fiber g	0

Crispy Fish Sticks

These fish sticks have a great crispy texture without frying. Any firm white fish will work in this recipe.

Servings: 4

Omega-Optimize Technique ■ Flax meal, replacing some of the cornflakes ■ Cod, a rich source of omega-3 fats ■ Omega-3 (DHA-enriched) egg

---

½ cup buttermilk
1 pound cod, cut into 8 pieces
⅓ cup flour
1 omega-3 egg, slightly beaten

½ cup cornflakes, crushed into
   crumbs
¼ cup flax meal
1 teaspoon lemon pepper

Preheat oven to 425°F. Pour buttermilk into a shallow dish or pie pan. Add pieces of fish, and turn each to coat. Arrange three shallow dishes on a workspace. In one, place the flour. In another, place the egg. In the third, combine the cornflake crumbs, flax meal, and lemon pepper. Dredge the fish in the flour, evenly coating both sides; dip in the egg, and then coat the fish with the cornflake crumb mixture.

Lightly coat a baking dish with canola oil nonstick spray. Arrange fish pieces in a single layer so they don't touch; spray the top of the fish with the nonstick spray. Bake 12 to 15 minutes or until the fish is opaque and flaky. Do not turn.

CRUNCHY CHICKEN VARIATION: Use boneless, skinless chicken breasts in place of the fish.

Omega-Optimize Nutrition Profile			
Calories	213	Fat g	6
Omega-6 mg	750	Carbs g	14
Omega-3 mg	2,160	Protein g	25
Ratio of Omega-6 to Omega-3	0.4:1.00	Fiber g	3

Teriyaki-Glazed Halibut

This is a crowd-pleasing recipe and one of my favorites. This sauce is delicious on any fish.

Servings: 4

Omega-Optimize Technique ■ Canola oil ■ Small amount of sesame oil for flavor ■ Halibut, a good source of long-chain omega-3s

1 teaspoon canola oil
⅓ cup brown sugar
2 tablespoons low-sodium soy sauce
½ teaspoon sesame oil
4 4-ounce halibut fillets

Preheat the broiler. In a small bowl, combine the canola oil, brown sugar, soy sauce, and sesame oil. Heat in microwave on high until sugar dissolves, about 30 seconds. Pour half of the sauce into a shallow baking dish. Add halibut. Pour remaining sauce over fish.

Broil the fish about 4 inches from the heat for about 5 minutes; turn once, then baste. Broil an additional 5 minutes until fish is opaque.

Omega-Optimize Nutrition Profile			
Calories	247	Fat g	5
Omega-6 mg	720	Carbs g	18
Omega-3 mg	730	Protein g	31
Ratio of Omega-6 to Omega-3	1:1	Fiber g	0

Smoked-Salmon Patties

This convenient recipe uses canned salmon, which is a good item to keep on hand in your omega-3 pantry.

Servings: 4

Omega-Optimize Technique ■ Canned salmon ■ Omega-3 (DHA-enriched) egg ■ Light canola mayonnaise

---

1 7-ounce can smoked salmon
¼ cup chopped red bell pepper
¼ cup minced chives
2 tablespoons chopped fresh basil
1 tablespoon fat-free canola mayonnaise
1 tablespoon fresh lemon juice

2 egg whites
2 teaspoons Dijon mustard
3 dashes hot pepper sauce
Dash Worcestershire sauce
1 cup cornflakes, crushed into crumbs
2 teaspoons olive oil

In a large bowl, mix together the salmon, red pepper, chives, basil, mayonnaise, lemon juice, egg whites, mustard, hot pepper sauce, and Worcestershire sauce. Shape the mixture into four patties, about ⅓ cup each.

Place the cornflake crumbs in a shallow dish. Coat patties in cornflake crumbs, pressing until the crumbs adhere. Heat the olive oil in a large skillet over medium meat. Add the patties and cook until golden, about 4 minutes per side. Serve immediately.

Omega-Optimize Nutrition Profile			
Calories	126	Fat g	7
Omega-6 mg	890	Carbs g	5
Omega-3 mg	1,200	Protein g	12
Ratio of Omega-6 to Omega-3	0.7:1.0	Fiber g	2

Sweet and Sour Shrimp Stew

These very simple ingredients make for a very flavorful dish, one of my favorites. It's especially easy because it uses frozen shrimp.

Servings: 4

Omega-Optimize Technique ■ Canola oil ■ Flax meal ■ Shrimp, a good source of omega-3 fats

1 teaspoon canola oil
1 large onion, chopped
1 green bell pepper, cut into
    ¾-inch pieces
½ teaspoon salt
¼ teaspoon crushed red pepper
    flakes

½ cup catsup
¼ cup brown sugar
¼ cup balsamic vinegar
1 tablespoon Worcestershire sauce
2 tablespoons flax meal
1 pound frozen large cooked
    shrimp (tail off), thawed

In a 3-quart skillet, heat the canola oil over medium-high heat. Add the onion, green pepper, salt, and red pepper flakes. Cook, stirring occasionally, until the onion is translucent, about 5 minutes. In a small bowl, combine the catsup, brown sugar, vinegar, Worcestershire sauce, and flax meal. Add shrimp to mixture. Bring to a boil. Reduce heat. Cover and simmer 5 minutes.

Omega-Optimize Nutrition Profile			
Calories	259	Fat g	4
Omega-6 mg	670	Carbs g	30
Omega-3 mg	1,410	Protein g	26
Ratio of Omega-6 to Omega-3	0.5:1.0	Fiber g	2

Desserts and Sweet Treats

Incredible Omega Brownies

These are hands-down the best brownies I've ever made. Don't skimp on the chocolate. The brand you choose makes a big difference in taste and texture. I find that Scharffenberger, Ghirardelli, and Valrohna work very well.

Yield: 12 brownies

Omega-Optimize Technique ■ Canola oil and applesauce in place of butter ■ Omega-3 (DHA-enriched) eggs ■ Flax meal Incorporated into the flour ■ Reduced amount of walnuts (scattered on top)

¼ cup canola oil
4 ounces fine-quality bittersweet chocolate (not unsweetened), coarsely chopped
1 cup white sugar
½ cup all-purpose flour
3 tablespoons flax meal

½ teaspoon baking powder
½ teaspoon salt
2 omega-3 eggs
1 egg white
¼ cup applesauce
2 teaspoons vanilla
2 tablespoons chopped walnuts

Preheat oven to 350°F. Coat an 8-inch square pan with canola oil nonstick spray. In a medium-size bowl that can be used in the microwave, combine the oil and chocolate. Microwave on High 30 seconds, and stir to thoroughly combine mix. If chocolate is not smooth and melted, microwave again for 30 seconds and stir. Set aside to cool.

In a large bowl, combine the sugar, flour, flax meal, baking powder, and salt. In a medium bowl, combine the eggs, egg white, applesauce, and vanilla. Whisk until smooth. Add a small dollop of chocolate mixture, and whisk until smooth. Repeat this process until all of the chocolate is mixed together with the egg mixture. Add this mixture to the flour mixture. Whisk until smooth.

Transfer the batter to the prepared pan. Scatter the walnuts on top. Bake 25 minutes. Cool the brownies completely in the pan, and then cut into 12 bars.

Omega-Optimize Nutrition Profile (for 1 brownie)			
Calories	211	Fat g	10
Omega-6 mg	1,680	Carbs g	28
Omega-3 mg	980	Protein g	3
Ratio of Omega-6 to Omega-3	1.7:1.0	Fiber g	1.5

Chewy Omega Oatmeal Cookies

These chewy and satisfying cookies are one of my favorites.

Yield: 30 cookies

Omega-Optimize Technique ■ Flax meal ■ Omega-3 (DHA-enriched) egg ■ Canola oil

¾ cup all-purpose flour
½ cup brown sugar
¼ cup flax meal
¼ cup granulated sugar
1 teaspoon cinnamon
½ teaspoon baking soda

½ cup canola oil
1 omega-3 egg
1 egg white
2 teaspoons vanilla
1¼ cups rolled oats
⅓ cup currants (or chopped raisins)

Preheat oven to 350°F. Spray a cookie sheet with canola oil nonstick spray. In a large bowl, combine the flour, brown sugar, flax meal, granulated sugar, cinnamon, and baking soda. In a medium bowl, beat together the canola oil, whole egg, egg white, and vanilla. Pour the egg mixture into the flour mixture and mix. Add the oats and currants. Mix all ingredients until blended.

Drop the dough by rounded teaspoonfuls onto the prepared cookie sheet, allowing room for the dough to expand. Bake 10 to 12 minutes or until golden. Cool 1 minute, and then remove to wire rack.

Omega-Optimize Nutrition Profile (for 1 cookie)			
Calories	92	Fat g	5
Omega-6 mg	930	Carbs g	12
Omega-3 mg	610	Protein g	1
Ratio of Omega-6 to Omega-3	1.5:1.0	Fiber g	1

Gingerbread Bars

Not only are these easy-to-make bars a good source of omega-3 fats, but they contain as much fiber as a slice of whole-wheat bread.

Yield: 16 bars

Omega-Optimize Technique ■ Flax meal ■ Omega-3 (DHA-enriched) eggs ■ Canola oil

1 cup all-purpose flour
¾ cup whole-wheat flour
½ cup brown sugar
¼ cup flax meal
1 tablespoon baking powder
1 teaspoon chopped
  crystallized ginger

1 teaspoon cinnamon
1 teaspoon powdered ginger
1¼ cups low-fat buttermilk
½ cup molasses
⅓ cup canola oil
2 omega-3 eggs
1 tablespoon powdered sugar

Preheat oven to 350°F. Lightly coat a 9″ × 13″ cake pan with canola oil nonstick spray. In a medium bowl, combine the flours, sugar, flax meal, baking powder, ginger, and cinnamon. In a small bowl, mix together the buttermilk, molasses, canola oil, and eggs. Mix until smooth, and add to the dry ingredients. Pour the batter into the prepared pan. Bake 22 to 25 minutes or until golden. Cool to room temperature, and cut into 16 bars.

Omega-Optimize Nutrition Profile (for 1 bar)			
Calories	167	Fat g	6
Omega-6 mg	1,010	Carbs g	27
Omega-3 mg	840	Protein g	4
Ratio of Omega-6 to Omega-3	1.2:1.0	Fiber g	2

Lemon Bars

If you enjoy the taste of lemon, you will love these bars.

Yield: 12 bars

Omega-Optimize Technique ■ Flax meal in graham cracker crust
■ Omega-3 (DHA-enriched) eggs

---

1 *Graham Cracker Flax Crust*
3 omega-3 eggs
¾ cup sugar
4 teaspoons cornstarch

1 tablespoon lemon zest
¼ cup fresh lemon juice
¼ teaspoon baking powder
1 tablespoon powdered sugar

Preheat oven to 350°F. Lightly coat an 8-inch square baking pan with canola oil nonstick spray. Lightly press the graham cracker crust into the pan, and bake 10 minutes.

In a medium bowl, combine the eggs, sugar, and cornstarch. Beat for 2 minutes with an electric mixer. Add the lemon zest, juice, and baking powder. Beat until thoroughly combined. Pour the mixture over the warm crust. Bake 20 minutes or until lightly brown. Cool on a wire rack. Sprinkle the powdered sugar on top. Cut into 12 bars.

Omega-Optimize Nutrition Profile (for 1 bar)			
Calories	164	Fat g	8
Omega-6 mg	1,610	Carbs g	22
Omega-3 mg	1,700	Protein g	3
Ratio of Omega-6 to Omega-3	1.1:1.0	Fiber g	2

Raspberry Bars

These bars are absolutely delicious. The raspberry filling is easy to make, but if you want to skip that step or are short on time, you can substitute raspberry preserves.

Yield: 12 bars

Omega-Optimize Technique ■ Flax meal in place of part of the oats ■ Margarine made with canola oil ■ Raspberries, one of the fruits highest in omega-3 fats (150 milligrams per cup) ■ Walnuts

---

½ cup brown sugar
1 cup "white" whole-wheat flour
⅔ cup rolled oats
⅓ cup flax meal
⅓ cup canola margarine

1 recipe *Raspberry Topping and Filling*, made with 3 teaspoons cornstarch, or ¾ cup raspberry preserves
3 tablespoons chopped walnuts

Preheat oven to 350°F. Lightly coat an 8-inch square pan with canola oil nonstick spray. In a medium bowl, combine the brown sugar, flour, oats, and flax meal. Add the margarine, and using a pastry blender or fork, cut the margarine into the flour until the mixture is crumbly. Press 2 cups of the mixture into the bottom of the prepared pan. Spread the raspberry filling or preserves to within ¼ inch of the edge. Scatter the remaining crumb mixture evenly over the top. Sprinkle with the walnuts. Lightly press the topping into the filling. Bake 35 to 40 minutes until a toothpick inserted into center comes out clean. Cool on a wire rack, and then cut into 12 bars.

Omega-Optimize Nutrition Profile (for 1 bar)			
Calories	207	Fat g	8
Omega-6 mg	830	Carbs g	33
Omega-3 mg	330	Protein g	3
Ratio of Omega-6 to Omega-3	2.5:1.0	Fiber g	4

Raspberry Topping and Filling

Raspberries are a staple in my freezer, which makes it easier to throw together a sauce or filling. This recipe is especially simple because you throw three ingredients in the pan at the same time. This topping tastes great over pancakes, ice cream, and vanilla yogurt.

6 ¼-cup servings

Omega-Optimize Technique ■ Raspberries, one of the few fruits that contain omega-3 fats

---

1 12-ounce package frozen raspberries
⅔ cup sugar
1 to 3 teaspoons cornstarch (see note)

Combine the raspberries, sugar, and cornstarch in a medium saucepan. Cook and stir over medium-high heat until bubbly.

Note: The basic sauce uses 1 teaspoon of cornstarch. For a thicker filling, use 3 teaspoons (1 tablespoon).

Omega-Optimize Nutrition Profile			
Calories	110	Fat g	<0.5
Omega-6 mg	140	Carbs g	28
Omega-3 mg	70	Protein g	1
Ratio of Omega-6 to Omega-3	2:1	Fiber g	4

Graham Cracker Flax Crust

Flax meal blends beautifully with graham cracker crumbs for a perennial favorite: graham cracker crust.

Yield: 1 crust

Omega-Optimize Technique ■ Flax meal in place of part of the graham cracker crumbs ■ Canola margarine (soft tub) in place of butter

½ cup graham cracker crumbs
½ cup flax meal
3 tablespoons sugar
2 tablespoons finely chopped walnuts
3 tablespoons canola margarine, melted

Preheat oven to 350°F. In a medium bowl, combine the graham cracker crumbs, flax meal, sugar, and walnuts. Stir in the melted margarine, and mix until even in texture. Press into 9-inch pie pan. Bake 10 minutes, and remove from oven.

Omega-Optimize Nutrition Profile			
Calories	134	Fat g	9
Omega-6 mg	2,103	Carbs g	11
Omega-3 mg	2,410	Protein g	2
Ratio of Omega-6 to Omega-3	1:1	Fiber g	3

Omega Strawberry Cheesecake Squares

This cheesecake recipe is especially easy because it's made in a 9″ × 13″ pan rather than the traditional springform pan. Just remember to drain the yogurt the night before you plan to make this fabulous dessert.

Servings: 16

Omega-Optimize Technique ■ Flax meal in graham cracker crust ■ Omega-3 (DHA-enriched) eggs ■ Equal parts light cream cheese and vanilla yogurt in place of full-fat cream cheese

1 16-ounce carton low-fat (not fat-free) vanilla yogurt
1 recipe *Graham Cracker Flax Crust* (unbaked)
2 8-ounce packages light cream cheese, softened
1 cup sugar
4 teaspoons all-purpose flour
4 omega-3 eggs
2 pints fresh strawberries, hulled
¼ cup raspberry or strawberry jam

Line a strainer with a large coffee filter or cheesecloth. Place the lined strainer over a bowl, and put the yogurt in the strainer so that any excess liquid drains into the bowl. Cover, chill, and let drain at least 8 hours or overnight. Discard liquid.

Preheat oven to 325°F. Line a 9″ × 13″ pan with foil, and lightly coat with canola oil nonstick spray. Press the graham cracker crust mixture firmly onto the bottom of the pan. Bake 10 minutes, and remove from oven.

In a large bowl, beat together the drained vanilla yogurt, light cream cheese, sugar, and flour. Beat in the eggs, one at a time. Pour the mixture into the prepared crust. Bake 55 minutes or until almost set. Let cool 1 hour on a wire rack. Cover and chill overnight or at least 4 hours.

Arrange the strawberries, points up, on top of the cheesecake. In a small microwavable bowl, melt the jam about 30 seconds on high in the microwave. Brush the melted jam over the strawberries.

Omega-Optimize Nutrition Profile			
Calories	256	Fat g	13
Omega-6 mg	1,060	Carbs g	30
Omega-3 mg	1,290	Protein g	7
Ratio of Omega-6 to Omega-3	0.8:1.0	Fiber g	2

Omega Frosted Carrot Cake

Traditional carrot cake is usually made with at least 1 cup of oil. I've used applesauce in place of the oil for years, and the taste and texture are wonderful.

Yield: 16 servings

Omega-Optimize Technique ■ Flax meal ■ Omega-3 (DHA-enriched) eggs ■ Applesauce, replacing oil, which is high in omega-6 fats

---

1 cup all-purpose flour
¾ cup whole-wheat flour
¼ cup flax meal
2 teaspoons baking soda
2½ teaspoons cinnamon
½ teaspoon nutmeg
¼ teaspoon cloves
2 omega-3 eggs

2 egg whites
1½ cups sugar
½ cup buttermilk
1 cup unsweetened applesauce
2 teaspoons vanilla
3 cups shredded carrots
⅓ cup currants or raisins

Preheat oven to 350°F. Lightly coat a 9″ × 13″ baking pan with canola oil nonstick spray. In a large bowl, combine the flours, flax meal, baking soda, cinnamon, nutmeg, and cloves; set aside. In a large bowl, beat the whole eggs and egg whites 2 minutes. Gradually beat in the sugar. Add the buttermilk, applesauce, and vanilla to the egg mixture. Combine the egg mixture with flour mixture. Stir in the carrots and then the currants or raisins. Transfer the batter to the prepared baking pan. Bake 40 minutes or until a wooden toothpick inserted into the center comes out clean. Cool on a wire rack. Frost if desired with *Light Cream Cheese Frosting.*

Omega-Optimize Nutrition Profile

Unfrosted cake

Calories	161	Fat g	2
Omega-6 mg	320	Carbs g	34
Omega-3 mg	510	Protein g	3
Ratio of Omega-6 to Omega-3	0.6:1.0	Fiber g	3

With frosting

Calories	239	Fat g	6
Omega-6 mg	570	Carbs g	42
Omega-3 mg	640	Protein g	5
Ratio of Omega-6 to Omega-3	1:1	Fiber g	3

Light Cream Cheese Frosting

This is a versatile frosting that tastes great not only on carrot cake, but also with other sweet breads such as gingerbread. This frosting also pairs nicely with strawberries.

Yield: Approximately 16 tablespoons

Omega-Optimize Technique ■ Canola soft tub margarine (and less of it) ■ Light cream cheese ■ Vanilla low-fat yogurt

1 (8-ounce) package light cream cheese, softened
3 tablespoons low-fat vanilla yogurt
1½ tablespoons canola margarine
1 cup powdered sugar

In a small bowl, beat together the cream cheese, yogurt, and margarine until smooth. Gradually mix in the powdered sugar, and beat all ingredients until smooth.

Omega-Optimize Nutrition Profile			
Calories	78	Fat g	4
Omega-6 mg	260	Carbs g	8
Omega-3 mg	120	Protein g	2
Ratio of Omega-6 to Omega-3	2:1	Fiber g	0

Blackberry-Raspberry Crisp

It's hard to believe that this delicious dessert delivers 8 grams of fiber per serving (from the berries, flax, and oats).

Servings: 8

Omega-Optimize Technique ■ Canola soft tub margarine ■ Flax meal ■ Berries, a good source of omega-3 fats

Filling
1 16-ounce package frozen blackberries, unthawed
1 12-ounce package frozen raspberries, unthawed
⅓ cup sugar
3 tablespoons all-purpose flour
2 tablespoons flax meal
½ teaspoon lemon zest

Topping
½ cup old-fashioned oats
½ cup brown sugar
⅓ cup all-purpose flour
2 tablespoons flax meal
1 teaspoon cinnamon
4 tablespoons canola margarine, melted

Preheat oven to 375°F. To make the filling, combine the berries, sugar, 3 tablespoons flour, 2 tablespoons flax meal, and lemon zest in a large bowl; toss to coat berries. Transfer the berry mixture to an 8-inch square pan.

To make the topping, combine the oats, brown sugar, ⅓ cup flour, 2 tablespoons flax meal, and cinnamon in a medium bowl. Add the melted margarine to the oat mixture; using a pastry blender or fork, combine until crumbly. Sprinkle the topping over the berry mixture.

Bake until the berry mixture bubbles thickly and the topping is golden brown, about 35 minutes. Let stand 15 minutes. Serve warm or at room temperature.

Omega-Optimize Nutrition Profile			
Calories	245	Fat g	8
Omega-6 mg	1,610	Carbs g	42
Omega-3 mg	1,550	Protein g	4
Ratio of Omega-6 to Omega-3	1:1	Fiber g	8

Appendix A
Omega-3 and -6 Fat Content and Ratio of Foods

DAIRY

Food	Amount	Total Fat (g)	Total (mg) Omega-6	Total (mg) Omega-3	Ratio 6:3	Omega-6 LA	AA	Omega-3 ALA	EPA	DHA
Butter	1 Tbsp	11.3	380	40	10	380	0	40	0	0
Buttermilk, cultured, reduced fat	1 cup	4.9	100	70	1	100	0	70	0	0
Buttermilk, prepared from powder with water	1 cup	1.4	30	20	2	30	0	20	0	0
Cheese substitute, mozzarella, 1" cube	1 ounce	3.5	470	20	24	470	0	20	0	0
Cheese, American, pasteurized, processed, fat-free, 1" cube	l ounce	0.2	0	0	na	0	0	0	0	0
Cheese, American, pasteurized, processed, low-fat, 1" cube	1 ounce	2.0	40	20	2	40	0	20	0	0
Cheese, blue, crumbled	1 ounce	8.2	150	70	2	150	0	70	0	0
Cheese, brie, sliced	1 ounce	7.9	150	90	2	150	0	90	0	0
Cheese, camembert	1 ounce	6.9	130	80	2	130	0	80	0	0
Cheese, cheddar, 1" cube	1 ounce	9.4	160	100	2	160	0	100	0	0
Cheese, cheddar, low-fat, 1" cube	1 ounce	2.0	40	20	2	40	0	20	0	0
Cheese, cheshire	1 ounce	8.7	150	100	2	150	0	100	0	0

Food	Serving								
Cheese, colby, 1" cube	1 ounce	9.1	190	80	2	190	0	80	0
Cheese, colby, low-fat, 1" cube	1 ounce	2.0	40	20	2	40	0	20	0
Cheese, emmentaler, 1" cube	1 ounce	7.9	180	100	2	180	0	100	0
Cheese, feta, crumbled	1 ounce	6.0	90	80	1	90	0	80	0
Cheese, fontina, 1" cube	1 ounce	8.8	240	220	1	240	0	220	0
Cheese, gjetost	1 ounce	8.4	140	120	1	140	0	120	0
Cheese, goat, hard	1 ounce	10.1	240	0	na	240	0	0	0
Cheese, goat, semi-soft	1 ounce	8.5	200	0	na	200	0	0	0
Cheese, goat, soft	1 ounce	6.0	140	0	na	140	0	0	0
Cheese, gruyere, 1" cube	1 ounce	9.2	370	120	3	370	0	120	0
Cheese, monterey jack, 1" cube	1 ounce	8.6	180	70	3	180	0	70	0
Cheese, mozzarella, low moisture, part-skim, 1" cube	1 ounce	5.7	130	50	3	130	0	50	0
Cheese, parmesan, fat-free, topping	1 ounce	1.4	30	20	2	30	0	20	0
Cheese, parmesan, grated	1 ounce	8.1	270	50	5	270	0	50	0
Cheese, parmesan, hard, 1" cube	1 ounce	7.3	80	80	1	80	0	80	0
Cheese, provolone	1 ounce	7.6	140	80	2	140	0	80	0

DAIRY, continued

Food	Amount	Total Fat (g)	Total (mg) Omega-6	Total (mg) Omega-3	Ratio 6:3	Omega-6 LA	AA	Omega-3 ALA	EPA	DHA
Cheese, ricotta, part-skim	1 ounce	2.2	50	20	3	50	0	20	0	0
Cheese, ricotta, whole milk	1 ounce	3.7	80	30	3	80	0	30	0	0
Cheese, Swiss	1 ounce	7.9	180	100	2	180	0	100	0	0
Cheese, Swiss, low-fat	1 ounce	1.5	30	20	2	30	0	20	0	0
Cottage cheese, 1% fat	1 ounce	0.3	10	0	na	10	0	0	0	0
Cottage cheese, 2% fat	1 ounce	0.6	10	0	na	10	0	0	0	0
Cottage cheese, small curd	1 ounce	1.3	30	10	3	30	0	10	0	0
Cream cheese	1 ounce	9.9	220	140	2	220	0	140	0	0
Cream cheese, fat-free	1 ounce	0.4	10	0	na	10	0	0	0	0
Cream cheese, low-fat	1 ounce	5.0	110	70	2	110	0	70	0	0
Egg, hard-boiled, large	1	5.3	670	40	17	590	70	20	0	20
Egg, Healthy Horizons DHA	1	4.5	na	350	na	na	na	na	0	100
Egg, Omega-3-enriched 350, large	1	6.0	750	350	2	na	na	250	0	100
Egg, whole, raw, large	1	5.0	640	40	16	570	70	20	0	20

Food	Amount									
Ice cream, vanilla	½ cup	7.3	180	120	2	180	0	110	0	0
Milk, nonfat/skim	1 cup	0.4	10	0	na	10	0	0	0	0
Milk, 1%	1 cup	2.4	70	10	7	70	0	10	0	0
Milk, 2%	1 cup	4.8	150	20	8	150	0	20	0	0
Milk, whole, 3.25%	1 cup	7.9	290	180	2	290	0	180	0	0
Milk, condensed , sweetened	1 cup	26.6	660	370	2	660	0	370	0	0
Milk, evaporated, 2%	1 cup	4.9	110	70	2	110	0	70	0	0
Milk, evaporated, fat-free/skim, canned	1 cup	0.5	10	10	1	10	0	10	0	0
Milk, goat	1 cup	10.1	270	100	3	270	0	100	0	0
Milk, Indian buffalo	1 cup	16.8	170	190	1	170	0	190	0	0
Yogurt, frozen, all flavors except chocolate	½ cup	3.1	60	30	2	60	0	30	0	0
Yogurt, frozen, chocolate, nonfat	½ cup	0.8	20	0	na	20	0	20	0	0
Yogurt, fruit, low-fat	1 cup	2.7	50	20	3	50	0	20	0	0
Yogurt, plain, skim	1 cup	0.4	10	0	na	10	0	0	0	0
Yogurt, plain, whole milk	1 cup	8.0	160	70	2	160	0	70	0	0

Food	Amount	Total Fat (g)	Total (mg) Omega-6	Total (mg) Omega-3	Ratio 6:3	Omega-6 LA	AA	Omega-3 ALA	EPA	DHA
DAIRY SUBSTITUTES										
Milk substitute, non-soy	1 cup	4.9	2,830	30	94	2,830	0	30	0	0
Rice milk	1 cup	2.1	1,100	20	55	1,100	0	20	0	0
Soy milk, regular	1 cup	4.7	1,660	210	8	1,660	0	210	0	0
Soy milk, chocolate	1 cup	4.7	1,800	240	8	1,800	0	240	0	0
FAST FOODS										
BURGER KING										
Cheeseburger, Whopper	1 order	48.4	10,480	1,480	7	10,480	0	1,480	0	0
Cheeseburger, Whopper, double	1 order	68.1	10,350	1,560	7	10,350	0	1,560	0	0
Chicken, tenders, 5-piece serving	1 order	12.8	1,560	30	52	1,520	40	30	0	0
French fries, medium, serving	1 order	20.4	1,310	30	44	1,310	0	30	0	0
Hamburger	1 order	14.7	1,360	140	10	1,360	0	140	0	0
Hamburger, Whopper	1 order	37.4	8,023	800	10	210	10	800	0	0
Sandwich, chicken, original	1 order	31.4	9,878	1,280	8	240	30	1,280	0	0

Food	Serving									
Sandwich, chicken, Whopper	1 order	28.6	11,520	1,420	8	11,520	0	1,420	0	0
DOMINO'S										
Pizza, cheese, crunchy thin crust, 14"	2 slices	13.1	2,480	360	7	2,470	10	360	0	0
Pizza, cheese, hand tossed, 14"	2 slices	17.8	2,670	320	8	2,650	20	320	0	0
Pizza, cheese, ultimate deep dish, 14"	2 slices	25.0	4,220	430	10	4,200	20	430	0	0
Pizza, ExtravaganZZa Feast, 14"	2 slices	33.5	3,870	380	10	3,810	60	380	0	0
Pizza, pepperoni, hand tossed, 14"	2 slices	25.3	3,460	380	9	3,410	50	370	0	0
Pizza, pepperoni, ultimate deep dish, 14"	2 slices	31.2	4,660	460	10	4,610	50	460	0	0
McDONALD'S										
Hamburger, Quarter Pounder	1 order	19.8	420	40	11	410	10	40	0	0
Sandwich, Filet-O-Fish	1 order	20.5	6,250	730	9	6,250	0	730	0	0
Big Mac	1 order	25.4	6,780	910	7	6,740	40	910	0	0
Biscuit	1 order	10.6	750	30	25	750	0	30	0	0
Breakfast, big, w/eggs, sausage, hash browns, and biscuit	1 order	50.4	6,120	220	28	6,010	110	220	0	0
Burrito, sausage, breakfast	1 order	17.1	2,240	110	20	2,140	90	110	0	0
Cheeseburger	1 order	14.0	360	40	9	350	10	40	0	0

FAST FOODS, continued

Food	Amount	Total Fat (g)	Total Omega-6 (mg)	Total Omega-3 (mg)	Ratio 6:3	Omega-6		Omega-3		
						LA	AA	ALA	EPA	DHA
Cheeseburger, Big Mac	1 order	32.8	580	80	7	580	0	80	0	0
Cheeseburger, Quarter Pounder	1 order	28.3	720	90	8	700	20	90	0	0
Chicken, breast strips, premium, Selects	1 order	7.2	2,310	80	29	2,300	10	80	0	0
Chicken, nuggets, McNuggets, 6-piece serving	1 order	16.4	5,170	230	22	5,120	50	230	0	0
Cookie, chocolate chip, package	1 order	12.8	670	60	11	650	20	60	0	0
Cookie, McDonaldland, package	1 order	8.8	1,190	30	40	1,190	0	30	0	0
Dessert, apple dipper, w/low-fat caramel sauce	1 order	0.7	30	30	na	30	0	30	0	0
Eggs, scrambled, serving	1 order	13.6	1,340	20	67	1,260	80	20	0	0
French fries, medium	1 order	18.0	1,020	190	5	1,020	0	190	0	0
Frozen dessert, McFlurry, M&M's, regular	1 order	22.5	900	80	11	880	20	80	0	0
Frozen dessert, McFlurry, Oreo, regular	1 order	19.1	1,160	70	17	1,140	20	70	0	0
Frozen dessert, sundae, hot caramel	1 order	8.9	390	30	13	380	10	30	0	0

Food	Serving									
Frozen dessert, sundae, hot fudge	1 order	10.6	360	30	12	350	10	30	0	0
Frozen dessert, sundae, strawberry, low-fat	1 order	7.0	310	20	16	300	10	20	0	0
Hamburger	1 order	9.8	200	20	10	200	0	20	0	0
Honey mustard, tangy, dipping	1 packet	2.5	990	160	6	990	0	160	0	0
Ice cream cone, vanilla, low-fat	1 order	4.4	250	20	13	240	0	20	0	0
Milk shake, chocolate, triple thick, med	1 order	21.3	920	80	12	900	20	80	0	0
Milk shake, strawberry, triple thick, med	1 order	20.8	920	80	12	900	20	80	0	0
Milk shake, vanilla, triple thick, med	1 order	20.8	930	80	12	900	20	80	0	0
Nuts, sundae style, serving	1 order	3.7	980	0	na	980	0	0	0	0
Pancakes, Hotcake	1 order	2.9	1,320	160	8	1,320	0	160	0	0
Pie, apple	1 order	12.1	800	0	na	800	0	0	0	0
Potatoes, hash browns, serving	1 order	9.2	2,120	90	24	2,120	0	90	0	0
Sandwich, chicken, crisp deluxe	1 order	25.0	9,510	1,040	9	9,470	40	1,040	0	0
Sandwich, chicken, grilled, McGrill	1 order	16.8	6,110	770	8	6,060	50	770	0	0
Sandwich, sausage and egg, w/biscuit	1 order	35.5	3,720	160	23	3,640	80	160	0	0
Sandwich, sausage, w/biscuit	1 order	28.5	2,960	130	23	2,920	40	130	0	0

Food	Amount	Total Fat (g)	Total (mg) Omega-6	Total (mg) Omega-3	Ratio 6:3	Omega-6 LA	Omega-6 AA	Omega-3 ALA	Omega-3 EPA	Omega-3 DHA
FAST FOODS, continued										
Sauce, barbeque	1 packet	0.3	120	20	6	120	0	20	0	0
Sauce, creamy ranch	1 ounce	14.8	7,070	920	8	7,070	0	920	0	0
Sauce, spicy buffalo	1 ounce	4.4	2,120	270	8	2,120	0	270	0	0
Sausage, pork patty	3 ounces	33.7	3,780	170	22	3,710	70	170	0	0
Sweet roll, cinnamon	1 order	19.1	2,860	90	32	2,830	30	90	0	0
Sweet roll, cinnamon, deluxe	1 order	26.3	3,090	130	24	3,090	0	130	0	0
PIZZA HUT										
Pizza, cheese, pan, large, 14"	2 slices	23.6	4,670	600	8	4,650	20	600	0	0
Pizza, cheese, pan, medium, 12"	2 slices	25.1	4,900	610	8	4,870	30	610	0	0
Pizza, pepperoni, pan, medium, 12"	2 slices	27.3	5,920	690	9	5,870	50	690	0	0
TACO BELL										
Burrito, bean	1 order	13.6	1,490	260	6	1,490	0	260	0	0
Burrito, beef, supreme	1 order	20.0	1,770	250	7	1,770	0	250	0	0

Burrito, steak, supreme	1 order	18.0	1,690	220	8	1,670	20	220	0	0
Nachos, supreme, serving	1 order	26.6	2,530	260	10	2,530	0	260	0	0
Nachos, serving	1 order	22.0	2,480	60	41	2,480	0	60	0	0
Salad, taco, w/salsa and shell	1 order	48.9	3,490	520	7	3,490	0	520	0	0
Taco, beef	1 order	10.5	1,540	100	15	1,520	10	100	0	0
Taco, soft, beef	1 order	10.3	930	70	13	920	10	70	0	0
Taco, soft, chicken	1 order	7.3	990	60	17	960	30	60	0	0
Taco, soft, steak	1 order	15.4	3,960	470	8	3,930	30	470	0	0
WENDY'S									
Cheeseburger, classic double	1 order	44.0	3,320	470	7	3,220	90	470	0	0
Cheeseburger, classic single	1 order	27.4	2,870	380	8	2,820	50	380	0	0
Chicken nuggets, 5-piece serving	1 order	17.4	4,220	100	42	4,180	40	100	0	0
French fries, medium	1 order	23.1	5,190	110	47	5,190	0	110	0	0
Frozen dessert, Frosty, dairy, medium	1 order	7.8	300	50	6	300	0	50	0	0
Hamburger, classic single	1 order	23.1	2,900	370	8	2,850	50	370	0	0
Sandwich, chicken fillet, homestyle	1 order	18.6	6,540	540	12	6,500	40	540	0	0
Sandwich, chicken, Ultimate Grill	1 order	11.3	3,640	430	8	3,600	40	430	0	0

FISH

Food	Amount	Total Fat (g)	Total (mg) Omega-6	Total (mg) Omega-3	Ratio 6:3	Omega-6 LA	Omega-6 AA	Omega-3 ALA	Omega-3 EPA	Omega-3 DHA
Anchovies, European, canned w/oil, drained	3 ounces	8.3	320	1,760	<1	310	10	10	650	1,100
Bass, sea, mixed species, fillet, baked/broiled	3 ounces	2.2	30	650	<1	30	na	na	180	470
Bass, striped, fillet, baked/broiled	3 ounces	2.5	20	840	<1	20	0	20	180	640
Bluefish, fillet, baked/broiled	3 ounces	4.6	70	840	<1	70	0	0	270	570
Carp, fillet, baked/broiled	3 ounces	6.1	730	680	1	560	170	290	260	120
Cisco, smoked	3 ounces	10.1	400	1,760	<1	310	90	10	650	1,100
Cod, Atlantic, fillet, baked/broiled	3 ounces	0.7	30	140	<1	10	20	0	0	130
Flounder, fillet, baked/broiled	3 ounces	1.3	50	440	<1	10	40	10	210	220
Gefilte fish	3 ounces	3.3	330	580	1	220	100	100	140	340
Haddock, fillet, baked/broiled	3 ounces	0.8	30	200	<1	10	20	0	60	140
Halibut, Atlantic/Pacific, fillet, baked/broiled	3 ounces	2.5	180	470	<1	30	150	70	80	320
Halibut, Greenland, fillet, baked/broiled	3 ounces	15.1	200	1,050	<1	130	70	50	570	430

Food	Serving									
Herring, Atlantic, fillet, baked/broiled	3 ounces	9.9	210	1,830	<1	140	70	110	770	940
Mackerel, Atlantic, fillet, baked/broiled	3 ounces	15.2	170	1,120	<1	130	40	100	430	590
Mackerel, King, fillet, baked/broiled	3 ounces	2.2	40	340	<1	40	0	0	150	190
Mackerel, Pacific and Jack, fillet, baked, mixed	3 ounces	8.6	220	1,630	<1	130	90	50	560	1,020
Mackerel, Spanish, fillet, baked/broiled	3 ounces	5.4	230	1,160	<1	90	140	100	250	810
Orange roughy, fillet, baked/broiled	3 ounces	0.8	70	30	2	50	20	0	10	20
Pompano, Florida, fillet, baked/broiled	3 ounces	10.3	350	660	1	110	230	120	170	370
Sablefish, smoked	3 ounces	17.1	300	1,670	<1	180	120	110	760	800
Sablefish, fillet, baked/broiled	3 ounces	16.7	290	1,620	<1	180	110	100	740	780
Salmon, Atlantic, fillet, baked/broiled, farmed	3 ounces	10.5	1,650	1,930	1	570	1,080	100	590	1,240
Salmon, Atlantic, fillet, baked/broiled, wild	3 ounces	6.9	480	1,890	<1	190	290	320	350	1,220
Salmon, chinook, fillet, baked/broiled	3 ounces	11.4	290	1,570	<1	120	170	90	860	620
Salmon, chinook, smoked	3 ounces	3.7	400	390	1	400	0	0	160	230
Salmon, chum, fillet, baked/broiled	3 ounces	4.1	100	720	<1	70	30	40	250	430
Salmon, chum, w/bone, canned, drained	3 ounces	4.7	110	1,040	<1	50	60	40	400	600

FISH, continued

Food	Amount	Total Fat (g)	Total (mg) Omega-6	Total (mg) Omega-3	Ratio 6:3	Omega-6		Omega-3		
						LA	AA	ALA	EPA	DHA
Salmon, coho, fillet, baked/broiled, farmed	3 ounces	7.0	400	1,150	< 1	320	80	60	350	740
Salmon, coho, fillet, baked/broiled, wild	3 ounces	3.7	70	950	< 1	50	20	50	340	560
Salmon, pink, canned, drained	3 ounces	4.1	90	950	< 1	60	30	50	310	590
Salmon, pink, fillet, baked/broiled	3 ounces	3.8	140	1,140	< 1	50	80	40	460	640
Salmon, sockeye, fillet, baked/broiled	3 ounces	9.3	130	1,100	< 1	100	30	50	450	600
Salmon, sockeye, w/bone, canned, drained	3 ounces	6.2	130	1,300	< 1	100	30	70	480	750
Sardines, Atlantic, w/bones, w/oil, drained	3 ounces	9.7	3,010	1,260	2	3,010	0	420	400	430
Sashimi, eel, fillet, mixed species	3 ounces	9.9	250	490	1	170	80	370	70	50
Sashimi, mackerel, Pacific and Jack, fillet	3 ounces	6.7	170	1,270	< 1	100	70	40	430	790
Sashimi, salmon, chinook, fillet	3 ounces	8.9	230	1,740	< 1	100	130	80	860	800
Sashimi, snapper, fillet, mixed species	3 ounces	1.1	60	270	< 1	20	40	0	40	220
Sashimi, tuna, bluefin, fillet	3 ounces	4.2	90	1,000	< 1	50	40	0	240	760

Food	Serving									
Sashimi, tuna, skipjack, fillet	3 ounces	0.9	40	220	<1	10	20	0	60	160
Sashimi, tuna, yellowfin, fillet, w/o bone, 1" cube	3 ounces	0.8	30	200	<1	10	20	10	30	150
Smelt, rainbow, baked/broiled	3 ounces	2.6	110	810	<1	50	60	50	300	460
Snapper, fillet, baked/broiled, mixed species	3 ounces	1.5	60	270	<1	20	40	0	40	230
Spot, fillet, baked/broiled	3 ounces	5.3	170	710	<1	40	130	20	240	450
Sucker fish, white, baked/broiled	3 ounces	2.5	190	590	<1	70	110	60	210	320
Tilefish, fillet, baked/broiled	3 ounces	4.0	170	770	<1	40	130	0	150	620
Trout, fillet, baked/broiled, mixed species	3 ounces	7.2	400	970	<1	190	210	170	220	580
Trout, rainbow, fillet, baked/broiled, farmed	3 ounces	6.1	840	1,050	1	810	30	70	280	700
Trout, rainbow, fillet, baked/broiled, wild	3 ounces	5.0	350	1,000	<1	240	100	160	400	440
Trout, sea, fillet, baked/broiled, mixed species	3 ounces	3.9	280	410	1	70	210	0	180	230
Tuna, bluefin, fillet, baked/broiled	3 ounces	5.3	110	1,280	<1	60	50	0	310	970
Tuna, dried	3 ounces	5.2	110	1,250	<1	60	50	0	300	950

Food	Amount	Total Fat (g)	Total (mg) Omega-6	Total (mg) Omega-3	Ratio 6:3	Omega-6		Omega-3		
						LA	AA	ALA	EPA	DHA
FISH, continued										
Tuna, light, w/oil, drained, can	3 ounces	7.0	2,280	170	13	2,280	0	60	20	90
Tuna, light, w/water, drained, unsalted, canned	3 ounces	0.7	40	230	<1	10	30	0	40	190
Tuna, skipjack, fillet, baked/broiled	3 ounces	1.1	50	280	<1	20	30	0	80	200
Tuna, smoked	3 ounces	8.6	220	1,630	<1	130	90	50	560	1,020
Tuna, white, w/water, drained, canned	3 ounces	2.5	90	790	<1	50	40	60	200	530
Whitefish, fillet, baked/broiled, mixed species	3 ounces	6.4	540	1,580	<1	300	240	200	350	1,030
Wolffish, Atlantic, fillet, baked/broiled	3 ounces	2.6	120	690	<1	20	100	10	330	340
FISH OIL										
Salmon oil	1 Tbsp	13.6	300	4,390	<1	210	90	140	1,770	2,480
Menhaden oil	1 Tbsp	13.6	450	3,160	<1	290	160	200	1,790	1,160
Sardine oil	1 Tbsp	13.6	510	3,010	<1	270	240	180	1,380	1,450
Cod-liver oil	1 Tbsp	13.6	260	2,560	<1	130	130	130	940	1,490

Herring oil	1 Tbsp	13.6	200	1,530	<1	160	40	100	850	570

FRUIT

Bilberries	1 cup	0.48	130	80	2	130	0	80	0	0
Blackberries	1 cup	0.7	270	140	2	270	0	140	0	0
Blueberries	1 cup	0.5	130	80	2	130	0	80	0	0
Boysenberries	1 cup	0.7	270	140	2	270	0	140	0	0
Cherries, red, sour, fresh	1 cup	0.5	70	70	1	70	0	70	0	0
Cherries, sweet, fresh	1 cup	0.3	40	40	1	40	0	40	0	0
Cranberries	1 cup	0.1	30	20	2	30	0	20	0	0
Elderberries	1 cup	0.7	230	120	2	230	0	120	0	0
Gooseberries	1 cup	0.9	410	70	6	410	0	70	0	0
Gooseberries, Chinese	1 cup	0.9	430	70	6	430	0	70	0	0
Guava	1 cup	1.6	480	180	3	480	na	180	na	na
Huckleberries	1 cup	0.5	130	80	2	130	0	80	0	0
Mango, slices	1 cup	0.5	20	60	<1	20	0	60	0	0
Melon, honeydew, diced	1 cup	0.2	40	60	1	40	0	60	0	0

Food	Amount	Total Fat (g)	Total (mg) Omega-6	Total (mg) Omega-3	Ratio 6:3	Omega-6		Omega-3		
						LA	AA	ALA	EPA	DHA
FRUIT, continued										
Raspberries, red	1 cup	0.8	310	150	2	310	0	150	0	0
Strawberries	1 cup	0.4	130	90	1	130	0	90	0	0
Watermelon, diced	1 cup	0.2	80	0	na	80	0	0	0	0
Whortleberries	1 cup	0.5	130	80	2	130	0	80	0	0
GRAINS										
Amaranth	½ cup	6.4	2,760	60	46	2,760	0	60	0	0
Barley, pearled, cooked	½ cup	0.4	150	20	8	150	0	20	0	0
Bran, rice, crude	2 Tbsp	3.1	1,050	50	21	1,050	0	50	na	na
Bran, wheat, crude	2 Tbsp	0.3	150	10	15	150	0	10	0	0
Buckwheat	½ cup	2.9	820	70	12	820	0	70	0	0
Buckwheat, groats, roasted, cooked	½ cup	0.5	150	10	15	150	0	10	0	0
Millet, cooked	½ cup	0.9	420	20	21	420	0	20	0	0
Millet, puffed	½ cup	0.4	200	10	20	200	0	10	0	0

Oats, unprocessed whole grain	½ cup	5.4	1,890	90	21	1,890	0	90	0
Quinoa, dry	½ cup	4.9	1,880	110	17	1,880	0	110	0
Rice, brown, long grain, cooked	½ cup	0.9	300	10	30	300	0	10	0
Rice, white, long grain, unenriched, cooked	½ cup	0.2	50	10	5	50	na	10	na
Triticale, grain, dry	½ cup	2.0	820	60	14	820	0	60	0
Wheat, bulgur, dry	½ cup	0.9	360	20	18	360	0	20	0
Wheat, durum, grain	½ cup	2.4	890	50	18	890	0	50	0
Wheat, germ, crude	2 Tbsp	1.4	760	100	8	760	0	100	0
Wheat, hard red winter, whole grain, dry	½ cup	1.5	580	30	19	580	0	30	0
LEGUMES									
Beans, black, cooked	½ cup	0.5	110	90	1	110	0	90	0
Beans, black-eyed, cooked	½ cup	0.5	120	70	2	120	0	70	0
Beans, black-eyed, plain, canned	½ cup	0.7	180	100	2	180	0	100	0
Beans, catjang cowpeas, cooked	½ cup	0.6	160	90	2	160	0	90	0
Beans, cowpeas, cooked	½ cup	0.5	120	70	2	120	0	70	0

LEGUMES, continued

Food	Amount	Total Fat (g)	Total (mg) Omega-6	Total (mg) Omega-3	Ratio 6:3	Omega-6 LA	AA	Omega-3 ALA	EPA	DHA
Beans, cowpeas, plain, canned	½ cup	0.7	180	100	2	180	0	100	0	0
Beans, cranberry, cooked	½ cup	0.4	100	80	1	100	0	80	0	0
Beans, cranberry/roman, canned	½ cup	0.4	90	70	1	90	0	70	0	0
Beans, fava, cooked	½ cup	0.3	130	10	13	130	0	10	0	0
Beans, fava/broad, canned, not drained	½ cup	0.3	110	10	11	110	0	10	0	0
Beans, garbanzo, cooked	½ cup	2.1	910	40	23	910	0	40	0	0
Beans, garbanzo, canned	½ cup	1.4	590	20	30	590	0	20	0	0
Beans, Great Northern, cooked	½ cup	0.4	90	70	1	90	0	70	0	0
Beans, Great Northern, canned	½ cup	0.5	120	90	1	120	0	90	0	0
Beans, kidney, all types, cooked	½ cup	0.4	90	150	1	90	0	150	0	0
Beans, kidney, all types, canned	½ cup	0.8	80	60	1	80	na	60	na	na
Beans, lentils, cooked f/dry w/o salt	½ cup	0.4	140	40	4	140	na	40	na	na
Beans, lima, baby, cooked	½ cup	0.4	110	50	2	110	0	50	0	0
Beans, lima, large, canned	½ cup	0.2	60	30	2	60	0	30	0	0

Food	Serving									
Beans, mung, cooked	½ cup	0.4	120	10	12	120	0	10	0	0
Beans, navy, cooked	½ cup	0.6	80	110	1	80	na	110	na	na
Beans, navy, canned	½ cup	0.6	130	110	1	130	0	110	0	0
Beans, pink, cooked	½ cup	0.4	100	80	1	100	0	80	0	0
Beans, pinto, cooked	½ cup	0.6	70	90	1	70	0	90	0	0
Beans, pinto, canned	½ cup	1.0	150	200	1	150	0	200	0	0
Beans, pinto, red, small, cooked	½ cup	0.4	60	80	1	60	0	80	0	0
Beans, roman, cooked	½ cup	0.4	100	80	1	100	0	80	0	0
Beans, white, cooked	½ cup	0.3	70	60	1	70	0	60	0	0
Beans, white, canned	½ cup	0.4	90	70	1	90	0	70	0	0
Soybeans, cooked	½ cup	7.7	3,840	510	8	3,840	na	510	na	na
Soybeans, green, cooked, drained	½ cup	5.8	2,390	320	7	2,390	0	320	0	0
Soybeans, roasted, unsalted	½ cup	21.8	10,870	1,460	7	10,870	na	1,460	na	na
Tofu, fermented and salted, block	3 ounces	6.8	3,390	450	8	3,390	0	450	0	0
Tofu, okara	3 ounces	1.5	570	80	7	570	0	80	0	0
Tofu, regular, w/calc. sulfate, ¼ block	3 ounces	4.1	2,020	270	7	2,020	0	270	0	0

Food	Amount	Total Fat (g)	Total (mg) Omega-6	Total (mg) Omega-3	Ratio 6:3	Omega-6 LA	Omega-6 AA	Omega-3 ALA	Omega-3 EPA	Omega-3 DHA
MARGARINES AND SPREADS										
Buttery spread, Earth Balance, natural	1 Tbsp	11.0	na	440	na					
Buttery spread, Earth Balance, whipped	1 Tbsp	9.0	3,180	370	9					
Buttery spread, Promise, 60% vegetable oil	1 Tbsp	8.0	3,400	400	9					
Buttery spread, Promise, light	1 Tbsp	5.0	200	250	1					
Buttery spread, Smart Balance Omega-Plus	1 Tbsp	9.0	2,200	550	4					
Buttery spread, Smart Balance Organic, whipped	1 Tbsp	9.0	2,720	340	8					
Buttery spread, Smart Balance, light, 37% vegetable oil	1 Tbsp	5.0	1,200	300	4					
Margarine, 80% fat, tub	1 Tbsp	11.4	3,760	190	20	3,760	na	190	na	na
Margarine, 80% fat, stick	1 Tbsp	11.4	2,920	310	9	2,920	na	310	na	na
Margarine, Canola Harvest	1 Tbsp	11.0	2,000	1,000	2					
Margarine, Canola Harvest Natural Selections	1 Tbsp	12.0	2,250	1,050	2					

Margarine, Canola Harvest w/calcium	1 Tbsp		2,000	800	3				
Margarine, Canola Harvest w/flax	1 Tbsp	12.0	2,250	1,500	2				
Margarine, Earth Balance, 1-lb	1 Tbsp		3,380	410	8				
Margarine, fat-free, Smart Squeeze	1 Tbsp	0.3	150	24	6				
Margarine, Nucoa, quarters	1 Tbsp	11.0	3,400	520	7				
Margarine, Nucoa, soft	1 Tbsp	10.0	4,090	640	6				
Margarine, Smart Balance	1 Tbsp	9.0	2,300	400	6				
Margarine, Smart Balance Light	1 Tbsp	5.0	1,300	220	6				
Margarine, Smart Beat Superlight	1 Tbsp	2.0	450	140	3				
Margarine, Soy Garden	1 Tbsp	11.0	3,400	430	8				
Mayonnaise, Best Foods/Hellman's, canola	1 Tbsp	10.0	2,200	1,100	2				
Mayonnaise, fat-free, Smart Beat	1 Tbsp	0.2	190	30	6				
Mayonnaise, imitation, soybean	1 Tbsp	2.9	1,350	240	6	1,350	240	0	0
Mayonnaise, imitation, tofu	1 Tbsp	4.7	2,190	300	7	2,190	300	na	na
Mayonnaise, Smart Balance Light	1 Tbsp	5.0	1,190	420	3				
Mayonnaise, soybean oil	1 Tbsp	10.8	5,200	690	8	5,200	690	0	0

Food	Amount	Total Fat (g)	Total Omega-6 (mg)	Total Omega-3 (mg)	Ratio 6:3	Omega-6		Omega-3		
						LA	AA	ALA	EPA	DHA
MARGARINES AND SPREADS, continued										
Spread, Benecol, light	1 Tbsp	5	1,100	600	2					
Spread, Benecol, regular	1 Tbsp	8	1,800	300	6					
Spread, Earth Balance, quarters	1 Tbsp	11	2,800	330	8					
Spread, Smart Balance 5-lb	1 Tbsp	9	2,700	470	6					
Spread, Take Control, light	1 Tbsp	5	2,000	200	10					
Spread, Take Control, regular	1 Tbsp	8	3,400	350	10					
MEAT										
Beef, bottom round roast, braised, select, 0" trim	3 ounces	6.6	210	30	7	180	30	30	0	0
Beef, brains, cooked	3 ounces	9.0	340	730	<1	30	300	0	0	730
Beef, brisket, flat half, lean, braised, 0" trim	3 ounces	5.0	160	10	16	140	20	10	0	0
Beef, chuck arm pot roast, lean, braised, select, 0" trim	3 ounces	4.9	160	10	16	140	20	10	0	0

Food	Serving									
Beef, flank steak, broiled, select, 0" trim	3 ounces	6.1	170	70	2	150	20	70	0	0
Beef, hamburger patty, broiled, 5% fat	3 ounces	5.6	240	40	6	200	40	40	na	na
Beef, hamburger patty, broiled, 10% fat	3 ounces	10.0	310	50	6	270	40	50	0	0
Beef, hamburger patty, broiled, 15% fat	3 ounces	13.2	350	50	7	310	40	50	na	na
Beef, hamburger patty, broiled, 20% fat	3 ounces	15.2	380	50	8	340	40	50	na	na
Beef, hamburger patty, broiled, 25% fat	3 ounces	15.9	390	40	10	350	40	40	na	na
Beef, porterhouse steak, broiled, select, 0" trim	3 ounces	15.3	450	160	3	420	30	160	0	0
Beef, rib-eye steak, lean, broiled, selec-, 0" trim	3 ounces	5.2	170	10	17	150	20	10	na	na
Beef, short ribs, lean, braised, choice, 1/4" trim	3 ounces	15.4	410	40	10	370	40	40	na	na
Beef, T-bone steak, broiled, select, 0" trim	3 ounces	11.9	390	140	3	330	60	140	0	0
Beef, tenderloin, filet mignon, broiled, select, 0" trim	3 ounces	8.4	260	50	5	230	30	50	0	0
Beef, top loin, strip steak, broiled, select, 0" trim	3 ounces	5.2	160	30	5	140	20	30	0	0

MEAT, continued

Food	Amount	Total Fat (g)	Total (mg) Omega-6	Total (mg) Omega-3	Ratio 6:3	Omega-6 LA	Omega-6 AA	Omega-3 ALA	Omega-3 EPA	Omega-3 DHA
Beef, top round steak, broiled, select, 0" trim	3 ounces	3.9	130	20	7	110	20	20	0	0
Beef, tri-tip roast, sirloin, roasted, select, 0" trim	3 ounces	8.3	230	40	6	200	30	40	0	0
Hot dog, pork	3 ounces	20.1	1,700	130	13	1,660	40	130	na	na
Hot dog, pork and turkey	3 ounces	25.4	3,420	200	17	3,350	70	190	0	0
Hot dog, pork, turkey, and beef, light	3 ounces	12.7	1,630	110	15	1,630	0	110	0	0
Kidney, beef, cooked	3 ounces	4.0	670	10	67	390	280	10	na	na
Kidney, lamb, braised	3 ounces	3.1	370	160	2	220	140	80	50	30
Kidney, pork, braised	3 ounces	4.0	310	10	31	210	100	10	0	0
Kidney, veal, braised	3 ounces	4.8	740	170	5	470	270	60	80	30
Lamb, Australian, average of all cuts, lean, cooked, 1/8" trim	3 ounces	8.2	240	100	2	210	30	100	na	na
Lamb, Australian, center slice, lean, broiled, 1/8" trim	3 ounces	6.5	240	90	3	200	40	90	na	na

Food										
Lamb, Australian, leg, shank half, lean, roasted, 1/8" trim	3 ounces	6.2	210	80	3	180	30	80	na	na
Lamb, Australian, leg, whole, lean, roasted, 1/8" trim	3 ounces	6.9	220	90	2	190	30	90	na	na
Lamb, Australian, rib, lean, roasted, 1/8" trim	3 ounces	9.9	260	110	2	230	30	110	na	na
Lamb, Australian, sirloin half, lean, roasted, 1/8" trim	3 ounces	9.1	280	110	3	250	na	110	na	na
Lamb, average of all cuts, cooked, choice, 1/4" trim	3 ounces	17.8	1,030	260	4	970	60	260	na	na
Lamb, brains, braised	3 ounces	8.7	260	500	1	30	230	0	0	500
Lamb, NZ, average of all cuts, cooked f/fzn	3 ounces	18.9	540	340	2	520	20	340	na	na
Lamb, NZ, foreshank, braised f/fzn, 1/8" trim	3 ounces	13.5	390	240	2	370	20	240	0	0
Lamb, NZ, leg, whole, roasted f/fzn, 1/8" trim	3 ounces	11.9	370	210	2	350	20	210	0	0
Lamb, NZ, loin chop, broiled f/fzn, 1/8" trim	3 ounces	18.1	510	320	2	490	20	320	na	na
Lamb, NZ, rib, roasted f/fzn, 1/8" trim	3 ounces	21.9	620	400	2	590	30	400	0	0

Food	Amount	Total Fat (g)	Total (mg) Omega-6	Total (mg) Omega-3	Ratio 6:3	Omega-6 LA	Omega-6 AA	Omega-3 ALA	Omega-3 EPA	Omega-3 DHA
MEAT, continued										
Lamb, NZ, shoulder, whole, braised f/fzn, 1/8" trim	3 ounces	20.4	700	370	2	660	30	370	0	0
Lamb, sweetbread, braised	3 ounces	12.9	380	250	2	240	140	250	0	0
Liver, beef, braised	3 ounces	4.5	520	20	26	320	190	20	na	na
Liver, lamb, braised	3 ounces	7.5	1,010	100	10	480	530	100	0	0
Liver, pork, braised, 1" cubic piece	3 ounces	3.7	800	60	13	350	450	30	0	30
Liver, veal, braised	3 ounces	5.3	830	30	28	550	280	30	na	na
Pork, backribs, roasted	3 ounces	25.2	1,810	80	23	1,740	70	80	na	na
Pork, chop, blade loin, lean, broiled	3 ounces	11.8	870	30	29	830	30	30	na	na
Pork, chop, center loin, broiled	3 ounces	11.1	760	30	25	710	40	30	na	na
Pork, chop, sirloin, lean, w/bone, broiled	3 ounces	8.6	700	20	35	650	40	20	na	na
Pork, chop, top loin, broiled	3 ounces	5.3	460	20	23	390	60	20	na	na
Pork, cured ham, center slice	3 ounces	11.0	730	120	6	660	70	120	na	na

Food	Serving									
Pork, ham, shank half, lean, roasted, diced	3 ounces	8.9	760	20	38	700	60	20	0	0
Pork, shoulder, arm, lean, roasted	3 ounces	10.7	950	30	32	880	70	30	na	na
Pork, shoulder, blade, Boston roast, roasted	3 ounces	16.0	1,370	50	27	1,320	50	50	na	na
Pork, shoulder, ham hocks, cooked	3 ounces	19.8	1,800	60	30	1,720	80	60	na	na
Pork, tenderloin, lean, roasted	3 ounces	4.1	330	10	32	300	30	10	na	na
Sausage, beef and pork, smoked, link, small 2" × ¾"	3 ounces	24.4	3,050	180	17	2,960	70	180	na	na
Sausage, beef, precooked	3 ounces	32.0	690	60	12	660	30	60	na	na
Sausage, bratwurst, beef and pork, smoked	3 ounces	22.4	1,190	150	8	1,190	0	150	0	0
Sausage, bratwurst, pork, cooked	3 ounces	24.8	2,140	100	21	2,040	100	100	na	na
Sausage, Polish, pork and beef, smoked	3 ounces	22.6	2,120	280	8	2,120	0	280	0	0
Veal, average of all cuts, lean, cooked	3 ounces	5.6	480	30	2	380	90	30	0	0
Veal, brains, braised	3 ounces	8.2	80	0	na	80	na	na	na	na
Veal, breast, whole, lean, braised	3 ounces	8.3	610	30	20	530	80	30	na	na
Veal, ground, broiled, 8% fat	3 ounces	6.4	430	40	11	350	80	40	0	0
Veal, leg, top round steak, lean, roasted	3 ounces	2.9	230	20	12	180	50	20	0	0

Food	Amount	Total Fat (g)	Total (mg) Omega-6	Total (mg) Omega-3	Ratio 6:3	Omega-6		Omega-3		
						LA	AA	ALA	EPA	DHA
MEAT, continued										
Veal, loin chop, lean, roasted	3 ounces	5.9	450	30	15	360	90	30	0	0
Veal, short ribs, lean, roasted	3 ounces	6.3	540	30	18	430	100	30	na	na
Veal, sirloin steak, lean, roasted	3 ounces	5.3	370	30	12	300	70	30	na	na
MEAT SUBSTITUTES										
Bacon substitute, vegetarian, strips	3 ounces	25.1	11,700	1,430	8	11,700	0	1,430	0	0
Beef substitute, vegetarian, fillet	3 ounces	15.3	7,050	880	8	7,050	0	880	0	0
Beef substitute, vegetarian, meatballs	3 ounces	7.7	3,530	440	8	3,530	0	440	0	0
Beef substitute, vegetarian, meatloaf, slice	3 ounces	7.7	3,530	440	8	3,530	0	440	0	0
Beef substitute, Morningstar Farms, recipe crumbles	3 ounces	10.0	3,400	410	8	3,400	0	410	0	0
Burger substitute, Morningstar Farms, black bean, spicy	1	0.8	310	40	8	310	0	40	0	0
Burger substitute, Morningstar Better 'n Burger, frozen	1	0.5	140	20	7	140	0	20	0	0

Burger substitute, Morningstar Farms, Garden Veggie Patties	1	3.8	2,120	40	53	2,120	0	40	0	0
Burger substitute, Gardetto's, Harvest Burger, original	1	4.1	240	20	12	240	0	20	0	0
Burger substitute, vegetarian, soy	3 ounces	5.1	1,780	220	8	1,780	0	220	0	0
Chicken substitute, vegetarian	3 ounces	10.8	3,790	480	8	3,790	na	480	na	na
Chili, vegetarian, w/beans, canned	1 cup	0.7	200	170	1	200	na	170	na	na
Fish sticks substitute, vegetarian	3 ounces	15.3	7,050	880	8	7,050	0	880	0	0
Hot dog substitute, Worthington, vegetarian	1	6.2	3,230	80	40	3,230	0	80	0	0
Mayonnaise, imitation, tofu	1 Tbsp	4.7	2,190	300	7	2,190	na	300	na	na
Sausage substitute, Morningstar Farms, breakfast patty	1	2.8	1,250	60	21	1,250	0	60	0	0

NUTS

Almond butter	1 Tbsp	9.2	1,860	70	27	1,860	na	70	na	na
Almond butter, unsalted	1 Tbsp	9.5	1,900	70	27	1,900	na	70	na	na

NUTS, continued

Food	Amount	Total Fat (g)	Total (mg) Omega-6	Total (mg) Omega-3	Ratio 6:3	Omega-6 LA	AA	Omega-3 ALA	EPA	DHA
Almonds, dry roasted, whole	1 ounce	15.0	3,590	0	na	3,590	0	0	0	0
Beechnuts	1 ounce	14.2	5,210	480	11	5,210	0	480	0	0
Brazil nuts	1 ounce	18.8	5,820	10	582	5,820	0	10	0	0
Butternuts	1 ounce	16.2	9,560	2,470	4	9,560	na	2,470	na	na
Cashew butter	1 Tbsp	7.9	1,310	30	44	1,310	na	30	na	na
Cashews	1 ounce	13.1	2,170	50	43	2,170	na	50	na	na
Chestnuts, European, dried	1 ounce	1.3	450	50	9	450	0	50	0	0
Chia seeds	1 ounce	8.7	1,640	4,980	< 1	1,640	0	4,980	0	0
Hazelnuts	1 ounce	17.2	2,220	20	111	2,220	0	20	0	0
Hemp nuts	1 ounce	13.2	7,700	2,430	3	7,700	na	2,430	na	na
Hickory nuts	1 ounce	18.3	5,850	300	20	5,850	na	300	na	na
Macadamia nuts	1 ounce	21.5	370	60	6	370	0	60	0	0
Mixed nuts, with peanuts	1 ounce	14.6	2,990	50	60	2,990	na	50	na	na
Nuts formed f/wheat, unflavored	1 ounce	16.4	5,950	480	12	5,950	0	480	0	0

Peanut butter, chunky	1 Tbsp	8.0	2,350	10	235	2,350	0	10	0	0
Peanut butter, chunky, vitamin and mineral fortified	1 Tbsp	8.2	2,330	10	233	2,330	0	10	0	0
Peanut butter, creamy	1 Tbsp	8.1	2,210	10	221	2,210	0	10	na	na
Peanut butter, creamy, reduced fat	1 ounce	9.6	2,590	10	259	2,590	na	10	na	na
Peanut butter, reduced sodium	1 Tbsp	8.0	2,280	10	228	2,250	30	10	na	na
Peanuts	1 ounce	14.1	4,450	0	na	4,450	na	0	na	na
Peanuts, oil roasted	1 ounce	14.0	4,420	0	na	4,420	na	0	na	na
Peanuts, Spanish, oil roasted	1 ounce	13.9	4,820	0	na	4,820	na	0	na	na
Peanuts, Spanish, raw	1 ounce	14.1	4,870	0	na	4,870	na	0	na	na
Peanuts, Valencia	1 ounce	13.5	4,670	0	na	4,670	na	0	na	na
Peanuts, Virginia	1 ounce	13.8	4,160	10	416	4,150	10	10	0	0
Pecans	1 ounce	20.4	5,850	280	21	5,850	0	280	0	0
Pine nuts, pignolia	1 ounce	19.4	9,400	50	188	9,400	0	50	na	na
Pine nuts, pinon/pinyon	1 ounce	17.3	7,050	220	32	7,050	na	220	0	0
Pistachio nuts	1 ounce	12.6	3,750	70	53	3,750	10	70	0	0
Pumpkin and squash seeds, kernels, dried	1 ounce	13.0	5,870	50	117	5,870	na	50	na	na

Food	Amount	Total Fat (g)	Total (mg) Omega-6	Total (mg) Omega-3	Ratio 6:3	Omega-6 LA	Omega-6 AA	Omega-3 ALA	Omega-3 EPA	Omega-3 DHA
NUTS, continued										
Pumpkin and squash seeds, kernels, roasted	1 ounce	11.9	5,390	50	108	5,390	na	50	na	na
Pumpkin and squash seeds, whole, roasted	1 ounce	5.5	2,480	20	124	2,480	na	20	na	na
Sunflower seed butter	1 Tbsp	7.6	5,030	10	503	5,030	na	10	na	na
Sunflower seeds, dried	1 ounce	14.1	9,250	20	463	9,250	na	20	na	na
Sunflower seeds, oil roasted	1 ounce	14.5	9,700	20	485	9,700	na	20	na	na
Walnuts, black	1 ounce	16.7	9,380	570	16	9,380	0	570	0	0
Walnuts, English	1 ounce	18.5	10,800	2,570	4	10,800	na	2,570	na	na
OILS										
Avocado oil	1 Tbsp	14	1,750	130	13	1,750	0	130	0	0
Black raspberry seed oil	1 Tbsp	14.5	8,098	5,107	2	8,098	na	5,107	na	na
Blueberry oil	1 Tbsp	14.5	6,308	3,640	2	6,308	na	3,640	na	na
Boysenberry oil	1 Tbsp	14.5	7,801	2,828	3	7,801	na	2,828	na	na

Canola oil	1 Tbsp	13.6	2,840	1,300	2	2,840	na	1,300	na
Caraway oil	1 Tbsp	14.5	8,494	35	243	8,094	na	35	na
Carrot oil	1 Tbsp	14.5	1,913	41	47	1,913	na	41	na
Cocoa butter oil	1 Tbsp	13.6	380	10	38	380	na	10	na
Coconut oil	1 Tbsp	13.6	240	0	na	240	0	0	na
Corn oil	1 Tbsp	13.6	7,280	160	46	7,280	na	160	na
Cottonseed oil	1 Tbsp	13.6	7,020	30	234	7,000	na	30	na
Cranberry oil	1 Tbsp	14.5	6,567	3,231	2	6,425	na	3,231	na
Flaxseed oil	1 Tbsp	13.6	1,730	7,250	<1	1,730	0	7,250	0
Grapeseed oil	1 Tbsp	13.6	9,470	10	947	9,470	na	10	na
Hemp oil	1 Tbsp	14.5	8,694	2,803	3	8,694	na	2,803	na
Hemp nut oil	1 Tbsp	11.7	8,265	2,755	3	8,265	na	2,755	na
Marionberry oil	1 Tbsp	14.5	9,106	2,291	4	9,106	na	2,291	na
Mustard oil	1 Tbsp	14	2,150	830	3	2,150	0	830	0
Oat oil	1 Tbsp	13.6	5,310	240	22	5,310	0	240	0
Olive oil	1 Tbsp	13.5	1,320	100	13	1,320	0	100	0
Palm kernel oil	1 Tbsp	13.6	220	0	na	220	0	0	0

OILS, continued

Food	Amount	Total Fat (g)	Total (mg) Omega-6	Total (mg) Omega-3	Ratio 6:3	Omega-6		Omega-3		
						LA	AA	ALA	EPA	DHA
Palm oil	1 Tbsp	13.6	1,240	30	41	1,240	0	30	na	na
Peanut oil	1 Tbsp	13.5	4,320	0	na	4,320	0	0	0	0
Red raspberry oil	1 Tbsp	14.5	7,685	4,698	2	7,685	na	4,698	na	na
Rice bran oil	1 Tbsp	13.6	4,540	220	21	4,540	0	220	0	0
Safflower oil	1 Tbsp	13.6	10,149	trace	77	10,150	0	0	0	0
Sesame oil	1 Tbsp	13.6	5,620	40	141	5,620	na	40	na	na
Sheanut oil	1 Tbsp	13.6	670	40	17	670	0	40	0	0
Soybean oil	1 Tbsp	13.6	6,940	920	8	6,940	na	920	na	na
Soybean oil, hydrogenated	1 Tbsp	13.6	4,750	350	14	4,750	na	350	na	na
Soybean oil, part hydrogenated, industrial, all-purpose	1 Tbsp	13.6	1,170	30	39	1,170	na	30	na	na
Sunflower oil, greater than 70% oleic	1 Tbsp	14	500	30	17	500	0	30	0	0
Sunflower oil, hydrogenated, linoleic	1 Tbsp	13.6	4,800	120	40	4,800	na	120	na	na
Sunflower oil, less than 60% linoleic	1 Tbsp	13.6	5,410	30	180	5,410	na	30	na	na

Food	Serving	g								
Tea seed oil	1 Tbsp	13.6	3,020	100	30	3,020	100	na	na	na
Tomato seed oil	1 Tbsp	13.6	6,910	310	22	6,910	310	0	0	0
Walnut oil	1 Tbsp	13.6	7,190	1,410	5	7,190	1,410	0	0	0
Wheat-germ oil	1 Tbsp	13.6	7,450	940	8	7,450	940	0	0	0

POULTRY

Food	Serving	g								
Chicken, broiler/fryer, breast, w/o skin, roasted	3 ounces	3.0	550	50	71	500	50	30	10	20
Chicken, broiler/fryer, breast, w/skin, roasted	3 ounces	6.6	1,260	90	14	1,200	60	50	10	30
Chicken, broiler/fryer, dark meat, w/o skin, roasted	3 ounces	8.3	1,710	130	13	1,590	120	80	10	40
Chicken, broiler/fryer, dark meat, w/skin, roasted	3 ounces	13.4	2,710	180	15	2,590	120	120	20	40
Chicken, broiler/fryer, drumstick, w/o skin, roasted	3 ounces	4.8	1,020	90	11	920	100	40	10	40
Chicken, broiler/fryer, drumstick, w/skin, roasted	3 ounces	9.5	1,920	120	16	1,820	100	80	10	30
Chicken, broiler/fryer, light meat, w/o skin, roasted	3 ounces	3.8	700	70	10	630	70	30	10	30

POULTRY, continued

Food	Amount	Total Fat (g)	Total (mg) Omega-6	Total (mg) Omega-3	Ratio 6:3	Omega-6		Omega-3		
						LA	AA	ALA	EPA	DHA
Chicken, broiler/fryer, light meat, w/skin, roasted	3 ounces	9.2	1,760	120	16	1,680	80	80	10	30
Chicken, broiler/fryer, thigh, w/o skin, roasted	3 ounces	9.3	1,900	140	14	1,790	121	90	10	40
Chicken, broiler/fryer, thigh, w/skin, roasted	3 ounces	13.2	2,650	170	16	2,540	110	120	10	40
Chicken, broiler/fryer, wing, w/o skin, roasted	3 ounces	6.9	1,240	130	10	1,100	140	50	20	60
Chicken, broiler/fryer, wing, w/skin, roasted	3 ounces	16.6	3,170	200	16	3,040	130	130	20	50
Chicken, capon, whole, w/skin, roasted	3 ounces	9.9	1,960	130	16	1,890	70	90	10	30
Chicken, stewing, light meat, w/o skin, stewed	3 ounces	6.8	1,320	120	11	1,070	250	50	na	70
Chicken, stewing, whole, w/skin, stewed	3 ounces	16.1	3,210	230	15	3,000	210	140	20	70
Cornish game hen, w/o skin, roasted	3 ounces	3.3	730	60	15	590	140	30	10	20

Food	Serving									
Cornish game hen, w/skin, roasted	3 ounces	15.5	2,880	180	17	2,720	160	140	20	20
Duck, whole, w/o skin, roasted, domesticated	3 ounces	9.5	1,100	120	9	1,100	0	120	0	0
Duck, whole, w/skin, roasted, domesticated	3 ounces	24.1	2,860	250	11	2,860	0	250	0	0
Sausage, turkey, cooked	3 ounces	8.9	2,140	150	14	2,030	110	150	na	na
Turkey, avg, breast, w/skin, roasted	3 ounces	6.3	1,370	100	15	1,230	140	70	na	30
Turkey, avg, dark meat, w/o skin, roasted	3 ounces	6.1	1,690	110	15	1,470	220	60	0	50
Turkey, avg, dark meat, w/skin, roasted	3 ounces	9.8	2,420	160	15	2,220	200	120	na	40
Turkey, avg, light meat, w/skin, roasted	3 ounces	7.1	1,530	120	14	1,390	140	90	na	30
Turkey, avg, wing, w/skin, roasted	3 ounces	10.6	2,260	170	14	2,120	140	140	na	30
Turkey, fryer/roaster, breast, w/o skin, roasted	3 ounces	0.6	140	10	14	110	61	na	na	10
Turkey, fryer/roaster, leg, w/o skin, roasted	3 ounces	3.2	890	60	18	780	110	30	0	30
Turkey, fryer/roaster, leg, w/skin, roasted	3 ounces	4.6	1,170	80	15	1,050	110	50	0	30
Turkey, fryer/roaster, light meat, w/o skin, roasted	3 ounces	1.0	230	20	12	180	50	10	na	10

Food	Amount	Total Fat (g)	Total (mg) Omega-6	Total (mg) Omega-3	Ratio 6:3	Omega-6		Omega-3		
						LA	AA	ALA	EPA	DHA
POULTRY, continued										
Turkey, fryer/roaster, wing, w/o skin, roasted	3 ounces	2.9	670	50	13	520	150	20	na	30
Turkey, leg, w/o skin, cooked	3 ounces	6.1	1,690	110	15	1,470	220	60	0	50
Turkey, patty	3 ounces	12.9	3,070	260	12	3,030	40	240	0	20
Turkey, thigh, prebasted, w/skin, roasted	3 ounces	7.3	1,860	120	15	1,680	180	90	0	30
WILD MEATS										
Antelope, roasted	3 ounces	2.3	410	80	5	280	130	80	0	0
Bear, cooked	3 ounces	11.4	1,610	70	23	1,340	270	40	na	30
Beaver, roasted	3 ounces	5.9	910	240	4	910	0	240	0	0
Beefalo, roasted	3 ounces	5.4	120	50	2	120	8	50	0	0
Bison, ground, pan-broiled	3 ounces	12.9	540	70	8	470	70	70	0	0
Bison, rib-eye steak, lean, 1" thick, broiled	3 ounces	4.8	200	30	7	170	20	30	0	0

Food										
Bison, roasted	3 ounces	2.1	170	30	6	110	60	30	0	0
Bison, shoulder clod roast, lean, braised	3 ounces	4.6	190	20	10	170	20	20	0	0
Bison, top sirloin steak, lean 1" thick, broiled	3 ounces	4.8	200	30	7	170	20	30	0	0
Boar, wild, roasted	3 ounces	3.7	520	30	17	430	90	30	0	0
Caribou, roasted	3 ounces	3.8	420	80	5	260	150	30	na	50
Deer, chop, cooked	3 ounces	8.0	1,970	200	10	1,860	110	200	na	na
Deer, ground, pan broiled	3 ounces	7.0	290	80	4	220	70	80	na	na
Deer, loin, lean, 1" thick steak, broiled	3 ounces	2.0	60	20	3	50	10	20	0	0
Deer, roasted	3 ounces	2.7	450	80	6	340	110	80	0	0
Deer, tenderloin, lean, broiled	3 ounces	2.0	80	20	4	60	20	20	na	na
Deer, top round steak, lean, 1" thick, broiled	3 ounces	1.6	80	30	3	60	20	30	0	0
Elk, ground, pan broiled	3 ounces	7.4	280	60	5	210	70	60	na	na
Elk, loin, lean, broiled	3 ounces	3.3	120	30	4	90	30	30	na	na
Elk, round, lean, broiled	3 ounces	2.3	80	20	4	60	20	20	na	na
Elk, roasted	3 ounces	1.6	290	50	6	200	90	50	0	0
Elk, tenderloin, lean, broiled	3 ounces	2.9	110	20	6	80	30	20	na	na

WILD MEATS, continued

Food	Amount	Total Fat (g)	Total (mg) Omega-6	Total (mg) Omega-3	Ratio 6:3	Omega-6		Omega-3		
						LA	AA	ALA	EPA	DHA
Goat, broiled	3 ounces	2.6	180	20	9	110	70	20	0	0
Moose, roasted	3 ounces	0.8	240	30	8	160	80	30	0	0
Opossum, roasted	3 ounces	8.7	2,480	60	41	2,480	0	60	0	0
Pheasant, whole, cooked	3 ounces	10.3	900	110	8	900	na	110	na	na
Rabbit, roasted, domestic	3 ounces	6.9	1,050	270	4	1,050	0	270	0	0
Squirrel, roasted	3 ounces	4.0	1,130	100	11	990	140	20	0	80
Venison, chop, cooked	3 ounces	8.0	1,970	200	10	1,860	110	200	na	na
Venison, roasted	3 ounces	2.7	450	80	6	340	110	80	0	0
Water buffalo, roasted	3 ounces	1.5	270	40	7	180	90	40	0	0

PROCESSED AND CONVENIENCE FOODS

Food	Amount	Total Fat (g)	Total (mg) Omega-6	Total (mg) Omega-3	Ratio 6:3	LA	AA	ALA	EPA	DHA
Bar, granola, chocolate chip, uncoated, soft, 1/5 oz	1	7.1	800	40	20	800	0	40	0	0
Bar, granola, nut and raisin, uncoated, soft, 1 oz	1	5.8	1,520	50	30	1,520	0	50	0	0

Food	Serving									
Bar, granola, plain, hard	1	4.9	2,940	10	294	2,940	0	10	0	0
Bar, granola, raisin, uncoated, soft	1	7.6	1,290	70	18	1,290	0	70	0	0
Biscuit, buttermilk, art flvr, refrig dough	1	1.4	290	20	15	290	0	20	0	0
Biscuit, buttermilk, refrig dough	1	8.7	190	20	10	190	0	20	0	0
Bread, 7 grain, slice, toasted	1 piece	1.0	230	20	12	230	0	20	0	0
Bread, Armenian	1 piece	0.7	260	20	13	260	0	20	0	0
Bread, banana, homemade w/margarine, loaf, indiv size	1 piece	6.0	1,700	80	21	1,690	10	80	na	20
Bread, buckwheat	1 piece	1.1	290	20	15	290	0	20	0	0
Bread, cracked wheat, slice, large/thick	1 piece	1.2	190	10	19	190	0	10	0	0
Bread, Cuban/Spanish/Portuguese	1 piece	0.6	130	10	13	130	na	10	na	na
Bread, egg, slice	1 piece	2.4	420	20	21	400	20	20	0	0
Bread, French, slice, medium	1 piece	1.9	420	20	21	420	0	20	0	0
Bread, low-fat	15 grams	0.5	190	20	10	190	0	20	0	0
Bread, mixed grain, slice, toasted	1 piece	1.0	230	20	12	230	0	20	0	0
Bread, pita, wheat, small, 4"	1 piece	0.7	280	10	28	280	0	10	0	0
Bread, potato	1 piece	0.9	180	10	18	180	0	10	0	0

PROCESSED AND CONVENIENCE FOODS, continued

Food	Amount	Total Fat (g)	Total (mg) Omega-6	Total (mg) Omega-3	Ratio 6:3	Omega-6 LA	Omega-6 AA	Omega-3 ALA	Omega-3 EPA	Omega-3 DHA
Bread, pumpernickel, slice, regular	1 piece	0.8	300	20	15	300	0	20	0	0
Bread, rye, slice	1 piece	1.1	240	20	12	240	0	20	0	0
Bread, sourdough, slice, medium	1 piece	1.9	420	20	21	420	0	20	0	0
Bread, white, soft, enriched, slice	1 piece	0.8	300	30	10	300	0	30	0	0
Bread, whole wheat, slice	1 piece	1.2	270	10	27	270	0	10	0	0
Cereal, General Mills, Basic 4	1 cup	2.8	1,000	60	17	1,000	0	60	na	na
Cereal, General Mills, Cheerios	1 cup	1.8	630	30	21	630	0	20	10	0
Cereal, General Mills, Cheerios, multigrain	1 cup	1.2	140	10	14	140	0	10	0	0
Cereal, General Mills, Chex, corn	1 cup	0.3	100	10	10	100	0	10	0	0
Cereal, General Mills, Chex, honey nut	1 cup	1	220	10	22	220	0	10	0	0
Cereal, General Mills, Chex, multibran	1 cup	1	470	20	24	470	na	20	na	na
Cereal, General Mills, Chex, rice	1 cup	0	50	10	5	50	0	10	0	0
Cereal, General Mills, Chex, wheat	1 cup	1	230	20	12	230	0	20	0	0
Cereal, General Mills, Fiber One	1 cup	2	760	60	13	760	0	60	0	0

Food	Serving								
Cereal, General Mills, Total, Raisin Bran	1 cup	1	480	40	12	480	0	40	0	0
Cereal, hot Cream of Rice, cooked, w/water, w/o salt	1 svg	0	50	10	5	50	0	10	0	0
Cereal, Kashi, Go Lean	1 cup	1	550	40	14	550	0	40	0	0
Cereal, Kashi, Go Lean Crunch	1 cup	3	750	230	3	750	0	230	0	0
Cereal, Kashi, Good Friends	1 cup	1	570	70	8	570	0	70	0	0
Cereal, Kashi, Heart to Heart	¾ cup	2	360	30	12	360	0	30	0	0
Cereal, Kashi, Honey Puffs, 7 whole grain	1 cup	1	240	20	12	240	0	20	0	0
Cereal, Kashi, Medley	¾ cup	1	460	30	15	460	0	30	na	na
Cereal, Kashi, Nuggets, 7 whole grain	½ cup	2	650	40	16	650	0	40	na	na
Cereal, Kashi, Puffs, 7 whole grain	1 cup	1	310	20	16	310	0	20	0	0
Cereal, Nature Valley, granola, w/fruit, low-fat	1 cup	4	900	40	23	900	0	40	0	0
Cereal, Nature's Path, Flax Plus	¾ cup	2	1,000	500	2					
Cereal, Nature's Path, Flax Plus with raisins	¾ cup	3	500	600	1					
Cereal, Nature's Path, Hemp Plus Granola	½ cup	5	1,800	600	3					

PROCESSED AND CONVENIENCE FOODS, continued

Food	Amount	Total Fat (g)	Total (mg) Omega-6	Total (mg) Omega-3	Ratio 6:3	Omega-6 LA	Omega-6 AA	Omega-3 ALA	Omega-3 EPA	Omega-3 DHA
Cereal, Nature's Path, Mesa Sunrise	¾ cup	2	300	450	1					
Cereal, Nature's Path, Optimum Power	1 cup	3	130	500	<1					
Cereal, Nature's Path, Optimum Rebound	¾ cup	6	250	400	1					
Cereal, Nature's Path, Pumpkin Flax Plus Granola	½ cup	5	1,500	450	3					
Cereal, Post, Grape Nuts	1 cup	2	1,290	60	22	1,290	0	60	0	0
Cereal, Quaker Oats, granola, Sun Country, almond	1 cup	21	3,440	180	19	3,440	na	180	na	na
Cereal, Quaker Oats, Honey Graham O's!	1 cup	3	250	10	25	250	0	10	0	0
Cereal, Quaker Oats, hot, oat bran, w/water, w/o salt	½ cup	1	370	20	19	370	na	20	na	na
Cereal, Quaker Oats, hot, oatmeal, apple cinnamon, instant	1 svg	2	420	20	21	420	0	20	0	0

Food										
Cereal, Quaker Oats, hot, oatmeal, banana bread, instant	1 svg	2	540	40	14	540	0	40	0	0
Cereal, Quaker Oats, hot, oatmeal, cinnamon spice, instant	1 svg	2	610	30	20	610	0	30	0	0
Cereal, Quaker Oats, hot, oatmeal, plain, low-sodium, instant	1 svg	2	760	30	25	760	0	30	0	0
Cereal, Quaker Oats, hot, oatmeal, plain, quick, dry	1 svg	6	1,760	80	22	1,760	0	80	0	0
Cereal, Quaker Oats, Life, plain	1 cup	2	580	30	19	580	0	30	0	0
Cereal, Quaker Oats, Oatmeal Squares	1 cup	2	940	40	24	940	0	40	na	na
Cookie, almond	1	3	740	50	15	730	0	50	na	0
Cookie, butter, enriched, cmrcl prep	1	1	40	10	4	30	0	10	0	0
Cookie, chocolate chip, baked f/refrig dough, medium, 2¼"	1	3	260	10	26	260	0	10	0	0
Cookie, chocolate chip, box	1	12	930	90	10	930	0	90	0	0
Cookie, chocolate chip, lower fat, cmrcl prep	1	2	430	30	14	430	0	30	0	0
Cookie, chocolate sandwich, creme filled	1	2	220	10	22	220	na	10	0	0
Cookie, fig bar	1	1	410	30	14	410	na	30	na	na

PROCESSED AND CONVENIENCE FOODS, continued

Food	Amount	Total Fat (g)	Total (mg) Omega-6	Total (mg) Omega-3	Ratio 6:3	Omega-6 LA	Omega-6 AA	Omega-3 ALA	Omega-3 EPA	Omega-3 DHA
Flax, Nature's Path, Flax Plus Flax Seeds	2 Tbsp	7	850	3,500	<1					
Flax, Nature's Path, Flax Plus Flaxseed Meal	2 Tbsp	5	650	2,500	<1					
Frankfurter, beef and pork, 5" × 3/4"	1	12.4	1,050	180	6	1,050	0	180	0	0
Frankfurter, beef and pork, low-fat	1	6	460	80	6	460	0	80	0	0
Frankfurter, beef, cooked	1	15	460	90	5	460	0	90	0	0
Frankfurter, beef, low-fat	1	11	340	0	na	0	0	0	0	0
Frankfurter, chicken	1	9	1,680	70	24	1,680	na	70	na	na
Frankfurter, meat, cooked	1	13	1,990	70	28	1,940	50	70	0	0
Frankfurter, turkey	1	8	2,090	160	13	2,090	0	160	0	0
Granola bar, Nature's Path, Hemp Plus	1	5	880	650	1					
Granola bar, Nature's Path, Hemp Raisin	1	3	900	400	2					
Granola bar, Nature's Path, Pumpkin Flax Plus	1	5	1,200	400	3					

Hot dog substitute, vegetarian	1	5	2,350	290	8	2,350	0	290	0	0
Hot dog, pork	1	18	1,520	110	14	1,490	30	110	na	na
Oatmeal, Nature's Path, Optimum Power	1 packet	3	140	300	<1					
Pasta, LifeStream (5 varieties)	2 ounces	4	200	700	<1					
Popcorn, air popped	3 cups	1	540	10	54	540	0	10	0	0
Popcorn, low-fat, low-sodium, microvave	3 cups	3	940	70	13	940	na	70	na	na
Popcorn, Smart Balance Light	4 cups	5	1,340	30	45					
Popcorn, Smart Balance Low-fat	5 cups	2	140	0	na					
Waffles, LifeStream, Flax Plus	2 waffles	9	3,400	1,000	3					
Waffles, LifeStream, Hemp Plus	2 waffles	9	3,500	1,500	2					
Waffles, Mesa Sunrise	2 waffles	8	3,500	1,000	4					
Waffles, Nature's Path, Optimum Power	2 waffles	6	1,500	1,000	2					

SALAD DRESSINGS

Blue cheese, fat-free	2 Tbsp	0.3	140	20	7	140	0	20	0	0
Blue cheese, low-cal	2 Tbsp	2.2	640	90	7	640	0	90	na	0

SALAD DRESSINGS, continued

Food	Amount	Total Fat (g)	Total (mg) Omega-6	Total (mg) Omega-3	Ratio 6:3	Omega-6		Omega-3		
						LA	AA	ALA	EPA	DHA
Blue cheese, regular	2 Tbsp	16.0	7,190	1,130	6	7,190	na	1,130	na	na
Caesar	2 Tbsp	17.0	8,500	1,140	7	8,500	0	1,140	0	0
Caesar, low-cal	2 Tbsp	1.3	620	90	7	620	na	90	0	0
French	2 Tbsp	14.0	5,710	850	7	5,710	0	850	0	0
French, diet, 5 cal/tsp	2 Tbsp	4.4	1,260	380	3	1,260	0	380	0	0
Green Goddess	2 Tbsp	13.0	6,130	820	7	6,130	0	820	0	0
Honey mustard	2 Tbsp	5.6	2,490	330	8	2,490	na	330	na	na
Italian	2 Tbsp	8.3	3,390	420	8	3,390	na	420	na	na
Italian, diet, 2 cal/tsp	2 Tbsp	1.9	400	110	4	400	0	110	0	0
Italian, fat-free	2 Tbsp	0.2	50	10	5	50	0	10	0	0
Ranch	2 Tbsp	14.6	110	870	<1	110	0	870	0	0
Ranch, fat-free	2 Tbsp	0.5	0	20	na	0	0	20	0	0
Thousand Island	2 Tbsp	10.9	4,950	730	7	4,950	0	730	0	0

VEGETABLES

Food	Serving									
Artichokes, globe/french, cooked, drained, medium	1	0.2	60	20	3	60	na	20	na	na
Arugula, chopped, fresh	1 cup	0.1	30	30	1	30	0	30	na	na
Asparagus, cooked, drained	½ cup	0.2	70	30	2	70	na	30	na	na
Beans, French, cooked	½ cup	0.7	150	250	1	150	0	250	0	0
Beans, green, snap, cooked, drained	½ cup	0.2	30	60	1	30	0	60	0	0
Bitter melon, pods, cooked, drained, ½" pieces	½ cup	0.1	50	0	na	50	0	0	0	0
Broccoli, Chinese, cooked	½ cup	0.3	30	110	<1	30	0	110	0	0
Broccoli, chopped, cooked, drained	½ cup	0.3	40	90	<1	40	0	90	0	0
Brussels sprouts, cooked, drained	½ cup	0.4	60	130	<1	60	0	130	na	na
Cabbage, bok choy, cooked, drained	½ cup	0.1	30	30	1	30	na	30	0	na
Cabbage, cooked, drained, shredded	½ cup	0.3	60	80	1	60	0	80	0	0
Cabbage, fresh, chopped	1 cup	0.1	20	30	1	20	0	30	0	0
Celery root, cooked, drained, pieces	½ cup	0.2	70	10	7	70	na	10	na	na
Chayote, cooked, drained, 1" pieces	½ cup	0.4	60	100	1	60	0	100	0	0
Collards, chopped, cooked, drained	½ cup	0.3	60	70	1	60	0	70	na	na

VEGETABLES, continued

Food	Amount	Total Fat (g)	Total (mg) Omega-6	Total (mg) Omega-3	Ratio 6:3	Omega-6		Omega-3		
						LA	AA	ALA	EPA	DHA
Collards, chopped, fresh	1 cup	0.2	30	40	1	30	0	40	na	na
Grape leaves, canned	2 ounces	1.1	80	480	<1	80	0	480	0	0
Leeks, cooked, drained, chopped	½ cup	0.1	20	30	1	20	0	30	0	0
Lettuce, Bibb, fresh	1 cup	0.1	20	50	<1	20	na	50	na	na
Lettuce, Boston, fresh	1 cup	0.1	20	50	<1	20	na	50	na	na
Lettuce, butterhead, fresh	1 cup	0.1	20	50	<1	20	na	50	na	na
Lettuce, iceberg, fresh, chopped	1 cup	0.1	10	30	<1	10	na	30	na	na
Lettuce, romaine, fresh, chopped	1 cup	0.2	30	60	<1	30	0	60	0	0
Mustard spinach, tender green, fresh	1 cup	0.5	40	40	1	40	0	40	0	0
Peas, green, cooked, drained	½ cup	0.2	70	20	4	70	na	20	na	na
Peas, snow, pods, steamed	½ cup	0.2	60	10	6	60	na	10	na	na
Soybeans, green, cooked, steamed	½ cup	5.8	2,390	320	7	2,390	0	320	0	0
Spinach, cooked, drained	½ cup	0.2	10	80	<1	10	na	80	na	na
Spinach, fresh, chopped	1 cup	0.1	10	40	<1	10	na	40	na	na

Swiss chard, cooked, drained, chopped	½ cup	0.1	20	0	na	20	0	0	0
Turnip greens, chopped, cooked, drained	½ cup	0.2	20	50	<1	20	50	0	0
Zucchini, slices, steamed	½ cup	0.1	20	30	1	20	30	na	na

Abbreviation	Full Name
Omega-6 Fat	
LA	Linoleic acid
AA	Arachidonic acid
Omega-3 Fat	
ALA	Alpha-linolenic acid
EPA	Eicosapentaenoic acid
DHA	Docosahexaenoic acid

Any data boxes left blank mean that there is no established value.

If the amount of the omega-3 fats is zero, a ratio cannot be mathematically determined and is designated "na" for not applicable.

All ratios are rounded to the nearest whole number and reflect a ratio of that number to 1. For example, a listing of 2 is an omega-6 to omega-3 ratio of 2:1.

Source: SDA Nutrient Database (http://www.nal.usda.gov/fnic/foodcomp); ESHA Food Processor SLQ software; food manufacturer.

Appendix B
Converting to Metrics

Volume Measurement Conversions

U.S.	METRIC
¼ teaspoon	1.25 ml
½ teaspoon	2.5 ml
¾ teaspoon	3.75 ml
1 teaspoon	5 ml
1 tablespoon	15 ml
¼ cup	62.5 ml
½ cup	125 ml
¾ cup	187.5 ml
1 cup	250 ml

Weight Conversion Measurements

U.S.	METRIC
1 ounce	28.4 g
8 ounces	227.5 g
16 ounces (1 pound)	455 g

Cooking Temperature Conversions

Celsius/Centigrade	0°C and 100°C are arbitrarily placed at the melting and boiling points of water.
Fahrenheit	Fahrenheit established 0°F as the stabilized temperature when equal amounts of ice, water, and salt are mixed.

To convert temperatures in Fahrenheit to Celsius, use this formula:

$$C = (F - 32) \times 0.5555$$

So, for example, if you are baking at 350°F and want to know that temperature in Celsius, use this calculation:

$$C = (350 - 32) \times 0.5555 = 176.65°C$$

References

Chapter 1, Omega-3 and Omega-6 Fats

Evans, H. and G. Burr. "A New Dietary Deficiency with Highly Purified Diets: The Beneficial Effect of Fat in the Diet." *Proceedings of the Society for Experimental Biology and Medicine* 25 (1928): 390–97.

Holman, R. T. "How I Got My Start in Lipids, and Where It Led Me." *Federation of American Societies for Experimental Biology Journal* 10 (1996): 931–34.

Holman, R. T. "The Slow Discovery of the Importance of ω3 Essential Fatty Acids in Human Health." *Journal of Nutrition* 128 (1998): 427S–433S.

Lands, W. E. M. *Fish, Omega-3 and Human Health*, 2nd ed. Champaign, IL: AOCS Press, 2005.

Simopoulos, A. P. "N-3 Fatty Acids and Human Health: Defining Strategies for Public Policy." *Lipids* 36 (2001): S83–S89.

Simopoulos, A. P. "The Importance of the Ratio of Omega-6/Omega-3 Essential Fatty Acids." *Biomedicine and Pharmacotherapy* 56 (2002): 365–79.

Chapter 2, Omega Fats Are Not Created Equal

Muskiet, F. A. J., et al. "Is Docosahexaenoic Acid (DHA) Essential?" *Journal of Nutrition* 134 (2004): 183–86.

Pawlowsky, R. J., et al. "Physiological Compartmental Analysis of α-Linolenic Acid Metabolism in Adult Humans." *Journal of Lipid Research* 42 (2001): 1257–65.

Pawlowsky, R. J., et al. "Effects of Beef- and Fish-Based Diets on the Kinetics of n-3 Fatty Acid Metabolism in Human Subjects." *American Journal of Clinical Nutrition* 77 (2003): 565–72.

Salem, N. "Introduction to Polyunsaturated Fatty Acids." *PUFA Info Backgrounder* 3 (1999): 1–8.

Chapter 3, Omega-6 Fat Syndrome

Ambring, A., et al. "Mediterranean-Inspired Diet Lowers the Ratio of Serum Phospholipids n-6 to n-3 Fatty Acids, the Number of Leukocytes and Platelets, and Vascular Endothelial Growth Factor in Healthy Subjects." *American Journal of Clinical Nutrition* 83 (2006): 575–81.

American Institute for Cancer Research (AICR). "Experts Concerned Over Unhealthy 'Fat Ratio' in American Diets." News release, AICR, 2004.

Berry, E. M. "Are Diets High in Omega-6 Polyunsaturated Fatty Acids Unhealthy?" *European Heart Journal* 3 (supp. D) (2001): D37–D41.

Bougnoux, P., et al. "Omega-6/Omega-3 Polyunsaturated Fatty Acids Ratio and Breast Cancer." *World Review of Nutrition and Dietetics* 94 (2005): 158–65.

Chajes, V., et al. "Omega-6/Omega-3 Polyunsaturated Fatty Acid Ratio and Cancer." *World Review of Nutrition and Dietetics* 92 (2003): 133–51.

Cleland, L. G., et al. "Linoleate Inhibits EPA Incorporation from Dietary Fish Oil Supplements in Human Subjects." *American Journal of Clinical Nutrition* 55 (1992): 395–99.

Cleland, L. G., et al. "Omega-6/Omega-3 Fatty Acids and Arthritis." *World Review of Nutrition and Dietetics* 92 (2003): 152–68.

Cordain, L., et al. "Origins and Evolution of the Western Diet: Health Implications for the 21st Century." *American Journal of Clinical Nutrition* 81 (2005): 341–54.

Davis, B. C., and P. M. Kris-Etherton. "Achieving Optimal Essential Fatty Acid Status in Vegetarians: Current Knowledge and Practical Implications." *American Journal of Clinical Nutrition* 78 (2003): 640–46.

De Lorgeril, M., et al. "Dietary Prevention of Coronary Heart Disease: Focus on Omega-6/Omega-3 Essential Fatty Acid Balance." *World Review of Nutrition and Dietetics* 92 (2003): 57–73.

Dubnov, G., et al. "Omega-6/Omega-3 Fatty Acid Ratio: The Israeli Paradox." *World Review of Nutrition and Dietetics* 92 (2003): 81–91.

Gebauer, S., et al. "Dietary n-6:n-3 Fatty Acid Ratio and Health." *Healthful Lipids* (2005): 221–48.

Ghafoorunissa, et al. "Substituting Dietary Linoleic Acid with α-Linolenic Acid Improves Insulin Sensitivity in Sucrose Fed Rats." *Biochimica et Biophysical Acta* 1,733 (2005): 67–75.

Groom, N. "Kellogg Touts Soy Oil Alternative to Trans Fats." *Reuters* (December 2005).

Hamazaki, T., et al. "The Japan Society for Lipid Nutrition Recommends to Reduce the Intake of Linoleic Acid." *World Review of Nutrition and Dietetics* 92 (2003): 109–32.

Hauswirth, C. B., et al. "High ω-3 Fatty Acid Content in Alpine Cheese: The Basis for an Alpine Paradox." *Circulation* 109 (2004): 103–7.

Hibbeln, J., et al. "Healthy Intakes of n-3 and n-6 Fatty Acids: Estimations Considering Worldwide Diversity." *American Journal of Clinical Nutrition* 83 (2006): 1483S–1493S.

IOM. *Dietary Reference Intakes for Energy, Carbohydrate, Fiber, Fat, Fatty Acids, Cholesterol, Protein, and Amino Acids.* Washington, DC: National Academies Press, 2002/2005.

Kang, J. X. "Achieving Balance in the Omega-6/Omega-3 Ratio Through Nutrigenomics: *Fat-1* Transgenic Mice Convert Omega-6 to Omega-3 Fatty Acids." *World Review of Nutrition and Dietetics* 92 (2004): 92–98.

Kelavkar, U. P., et al. "Prostate Tumor Growth and Recurrence Can Be Modulated by the ω-6:ω-3 Ratio in Diet: Athymic Mouse Xenograft Model Simulating Radical Prostatectomy." *Neoplasia* 8 (2006): 112–24.

Kolzumi, I., et al. "Studies of Composition of Intramuscular Lipids of Pigs, Cattle, and Birds." *Journal of Nutritional Science and Vitaminology* 37 (1991): 545–54.

Kris-Etherton, P. M., et al. "Polyunsaturated Fatty Acids in the Food Chain in the United States." *American Journal of Clinical Nutrition* 71 (supp.) (2000): 179S–188S.

Lands, W. E. M. "Dose-Response Relationships for ω3/ω6 Effects." *World Review of Nutrition and Dietetics* 66 (1991): 177–94.

Lands, W. E. M. "Please Don't Tell Me to Die Faster." *Inform* 13 (2002): 896–97.

Lands, W. E. M. "Dietary Fat and Health: The Evidence and the Politics of Prevention; Careful Use of Dietary Fats Can Improve Life and Prevent Disease." *Annals of the New York Academy of Sciences* 1,055 (2005): 179–92.

Larson, S. C., et al. "Dietary Long-Chain n-3 Fatty Acids for the Prevention of Cancer: A Review of Potential Mechanisms." *American Journal of Clinical Nutrition* 79 (2004): 935–45.

Leaf, A. "Dietary Prevention of Coronary Heart Disease: The Lyon Diet Heart Study." *Circulation* 99 (1999): 733–35.

Miljanovic, B., et al. "Relation Between Dietary n-3 and n-6 Fatty Acids and Clinically Diagnosed Eye Syndrome in Women." *American Journal of Clinical Nutrition* 82 (2005): 887–93.

Noci, F., et al. "The Fatty Acid Composition of Muscle Fat and Subcutaneous Adipose Tissue of Pasture-Fed Beef Heifers: Influence of the Duration of Grazing." *Journal of Animal Science* 83 (2005): 1167–78.

Oddy, W. H., et al. "Ratio of Omega-6 to Omega-3 Fatty Acids and Childhood Asthma." *Journal of Asthma* 41(3) (2004): 319–26.

Okuyama, H., et al. "Cancers Common in the USA Are Stimulated by 6 Fatty Acids and Large Amounts of Animal Fats, but Suppressed by 3 Fatty Acids and Cholesterol." *World Review of Nutrition and Dietetics* 96 (2007): 143–49.

Okuyama, H., et al. "Dietary Fatty Acids: The n-6/n-3 Balance and Chronic Elderly Diseases, Excess Linoleic Acid and Relative n-3 Deficiency Syndrome in Japan." *Progress in Lipid Research* 35(4) (1997): 409–57.

Okuyama, H., et al. "Omega-3 Fatty Acids Effectively Prevent Coronary Heart Disease and Other Late-Onset Diseases—The Excessive Linoleic Acid Syndrome." *World Review of Nutrition and Dietitics* 96 (2007): 83–103.

Pearce, M. L., et al. "Incidence of Cancer in Men on a Diet High in Polyunsaturated Fat." *Lancet* 1(7,697) (1971): 464–67.

Pella, D., et al. "Effects of an Indo-Mediterranean Diet on the Omega-6/Omega-3 Ratio in Patients at High Risk of Coronary Artery Disease: The Indian Paradox." *World Review of Nutrition and Dietetics* 92 (2003): 74–80.

Rule, D. C., et al. "Comparison of Muscle Fatty Acid Profiles and Cholesterol Concentrations of Bison, Beef Cattle, Elk, and Chicken." *Journal of Animal Science* 80 (2002): 1202–11.

Simopoulos, A. P. "Evolutionary Aspects of Omega-3 Fatty Acids in the Food Supply." *Prostaglandins, Leukotrienes and Essential Fatty Acids* 60 (1999): 421–29.

Simopoulos, A. P., et al. "Workshop Statement on the Essentiality of and Recommended Dietary Intakes for Omega-6 and Omega-3 Fatty Acids." *Prostaglandins, Leukotrienes and Essential Fatty Acids* 63(3) (2000): 119–21.

Simopoulos and Cleland (eds.) "Omega-6/Omega-3 Essential Fatty Acid Ratio: The Scientific Evidence." *World Review of Nutrition and Dietetics* 92 (2003):

Stockhausen, C. J., ed. "About 1% Linolenic Soybean Oil." Healthier Soybean Oil Web page, Iowa State University (2003–5). Retrieved December 20, 2005, www.notrans.iastate.edu /about.html.

USDA. "Nutrient Content of US Food Supply, 1909–2000." *Home Economics Research Report* no. 56, November 2004.

Weiss, L. A., et al. "Ratio of n-6 to n-3 Fatty Acids and Bone Mineral Density in Older Adults: The Rancho Bernardo Study." *American Journal of Clinical Nutrition* 81 (2005): 934–38.

Yehuda, S. "Omega-6/Omega-3 Ratio and Brain-Related Functions." *World Review of Nutrition and Dietetics* 92 (2003): 37–56.

Chapter 4, Dousing Inflammation

Calder, P. C. "Polyunsaturated Fatty Acids and Inflammation." *Inflammation and Haemostasis* 33 (pt. 2) (2005): 423–27.

Cleland, L. G. "Fish Oil: What the Prescriber Needs to Know." *Arthritis Research and Therapy* 8 (2006): 202 (doi:10.1186/ar1876).

Cleland, L. G., et al. "Fish Oil and Rheumatoid Arthritis: Antiinflammatory and Collateral Health Benefits." *Journal of Rheumatology* 27(10) (2000): 2305–7.

De Caterina, R., et al. "From Asthma to Atherosclerosis: 5-Lipoxygenase, Leukotrienes, and Inflammation." *New England Journal of Medicine* 350(1) (2004): 4–7.

De Caterina, R., et al. "Omega-3 Fatty Acids and the Regulation of Expression of Endothelial Pro-Atherogenic and Pro-Inflammatory Genes." *Journal of Membrane Biology* 206 (2005): 103–16.

DuBois, R. N. "Leukotriene Signaling, Inflammation, and Cancer." *Journal of the National Cancer Institute* 95(14) (2003): 1028–29.

Ferrucci, L., et al. "Relationship of Plasma Polyunsaturated Fatty Acids to Circulating Inflammatory Markers." *Journal of Clinical Endocrinology and Metabolism* 91(2) (2006): 439–46.

Fosslien, E. "Review: Cardiovascular Complications of Non-Seroidal Anti-Inflammatory Drugs." *Annals of Clinical and Laboratory Science* 35(4) (2005): 347–85.

Hansson, G. K. "Inflammation, Atherosclerosis, and Coronary Artery Disease." *New England Journal of Medicine* 352(16) (2005): 1685–95.

Harbige, L. S. "Fatty Acids, the Immune Response, and Autoimmunity: A Question of n-6 Essentiality and the Balance Between n-6 and n-3." *Lipids* 38 (2003): 323–41.

Kelley, D. S., et al. "Regulation of Human Immune and Inflammatory Responses by Dietary Fatty Acids." *Advances in Food and Nutrition Research* 50 (2005): 101–38.

Koch, T., et al. "Benefits of ω-3 Fatty Acids in Parenteral Nutrition." *Clinical Nutrition Supplements* 1 (2005): 17–24.

Lukiw, W. J., et al. "A Role for Docosahexaenoic Acid–Derived Neuroprotectin D1 in Neural Cell Survival and Alzheimer Disease." *Journal of Clinical Investigation* 115(10) (2005): 2774–83.

MacLean, C. H., et al. "Systematic Review of the Effects of n-3 Fatty Acids in Inflammatory Bowel Disease." *American Journal of Clinical Nutrition* 82 (2005): 611–19.

Matsuyama, W., et al. "Effects of Omega-3 Polyunsaturated Fatty Acids on Inflammatory Markers in COPD." *Chest* 128 (2005): 3817–27.

McKeever, T. M., et al. "Diet and Asthma." *American Journal of Respiratory and Critical Care Medicine* 170 (2004): 725–29.

Mickleborough, T. D., et al. "Fish Oil Supplementation Reduces Severity of Exercise-Induced Bronchorestriction in Elite Athletes." *American Journal of Respiratory and Critical Care Medicine* 168 (2003): 1181–89.

Mickleborough, T. D., et al. "Protective Effect of Fish Oil Supplementation on Exercise-Induced Bronchoconstriction in Asthma." *Chest* 129 (2006): 39–49.

Oddy, W. H., et al. "Atopy, Eczema and Breast Milk Fatty Acids in a High-Risk Cohort of Children Followed from Birth to 5 yr." *Pediatric Allergy and Immunology* 17 (2006): 4–10.

Peat, J. K., et al. "Three-Year Outcomes of Dietary Fatty Acid Modification and House Dust Mite Reduction in the Childhood Asthma Prevention Study." *Journal of Allergy and Clinical Immunology* 114 (2004): 807–13.

Raisz, L. G. "Pathogenesis of Osteoporosis: Concepts, Conflicts, and Prospects." *Journal of Clinical Investigation* 115(12) (2005): 3318–25.

Rigas, B., et al. "Cancer Prevention: A New Era Beyond Cyclooxygenase-2." *Journal of Pharmacology and Experimental Therapeutics* 314 (2005): 1–8.

Romano, C., et al. "Usefulness of ω-3 Fatty Acid Supplementation in Addition to Mesalazine in Maintaining Remission in Pediatric Crohn's Disease: A Double-Blind, Randomized, Placebo-Controlled Study." *World Journal of Gastroenterology* 11(45) (2005): 7118–21.

Schottenfeld, D., et al. "Chronic Inflammation: A Common and Important Factor in the Pathogenesis of Neoplasia." *CA: A Cancer Journal for Clinicians* 56 (2006): 69–83.

Serhan, C. N., et al. "Resolvins, Docosatrienes, and Neuroprotectins, Novel Omega-3-Derived Mediators, and Their Aspirin-Triggered Endogenous Epimers: An Overview of Their Protective Roles." *Prostaglandins and Other Lipid Mediators* 73 (2004): 155–72.

Serhan, C. N., et al. "Resolution of Inflammation: The Beginning Programs the End." *Nature Immunology* 6(12) (2005): 1191–97.

Spector, S. L., et al. "Diet and Asthma: Has the Role of Dietary Lipids Been Overlooked in the Management of Asthma?" *Annals of Allergy, Asthma and Immunology* 90 (2003): 371–77.

Trak-Fellermeier, M. A., et al. "Food and Fatty Acid Intake and Atopic Disease in Adults." *European Respiratory Journal* 23 (2004): 575–82.

Wang, D., et al. "Prostaglandins and Cancer." *Gut* 55 (2006): 115–22.

Wong, K. W. "Clinical Efficacy of n-3 Fatty Acid Supplementation in Patients with Asthma." *Journal of the American Dietetic Association* 105 (2005): 98–105.

Chapter 5, Heart Health

Albert, C. "Fish Oil: An Appetizing Alternative to Anti-Arrhythmic Drugs?" *Lancet* 363 (2004): 1412–13.

Albert, C. M., et al. "Blood Levels of Long-Chain n-3 Fatty Acids and the Risk of Sudden Death." *New England Journal of Medicine* 346(15) (2002): 1113–18.

Armstrong, E. J., et al. "Inflammatory Biomarkers in Acute Coronary Syndromes: Part III, Biomarkers of Oxidative Stress and Angiogenic Growth Factors." *Circulation* 113 (2006): e289–e292.

Balsinde, J., et al. "Phospholipase A2 Regulation of Arachidonic Acid Mobilization." *Federation of European Biochemical Societies* 531 (2002): 2–6.

Baylin, A., et al. "Arachidonic Acid in Adipose Tissue Is Associated with Nonfatal Acute Myocardial Infarction in the Central Valley of Costa Rica." *Journal of Nutrition* 134 (2004): 3095–99.

Berliner, J. A. and A. D. Watson. "A Role for Oxidized Phospholipids in Atherosclerosis." *New England Journal of Medicine* 353(1) (2005): 9–12.

Calo, L., et al. "N-3 Fatty Acids for the Prevention of Atrial Fibrillation After Coronary Artery Bypass Surgery." *Journal of the American College of Cardiology* 45(10) (2005): 1723–28.

Christensen, J. H., et al. "Heart Rate Variability and Fatty Acid Content of Blood Cell Membranes: A Dose-Response Study with n-3 Fatty Acids." *American Journal of Clinical Nutrition* 70 (1999): 331–37.

Christensen, J. H., et al. "N-3 Fatty Acids and Ventricular Arrhythmias in Patients with Ischaemic Heart Disease and Implantable Cardioverter Defibrillators." *Europace* 7 (2005): 338–44.

De Lorgeril, M., et al. "Mediterranean Diet, Traditional Risk Factors, and the Rate of Cardiovascular Complications After Myocardial Infarction: Final Report of the Lyon Diet Heart Study." *Circulation* 99 (1999): 779–85.

De Lorgeril, M., et al. "Use and Misuse of Dietary Fatty Acids for the Prevention and Treatment of Coronary Heart Disease." *Reproduction, Nutrition, Development* 44 (2004): 283–88.

De Lorgeril, M., et al. "The Mediterranean-Style Diet for the Prevention of Cardiovascular Diseases." *Public Health Nutrition* 9(1A) (2006): 118–23.

Dwyer, J. H., et al. "Arachidonate 5-Lipoxygenase Promoter Genotype, Dietary Arachidonic Acid, and Atherosclerosis." *New England Journal of Medicine* 350(1) (2004): 29–37.

Esposito, K., et al. "Diet and Inflammation: A Link to Metabolic and Cardiovascular Diseases." *European Heart Journal* 27 (2006): 15–20.

Funk, C. D. "Leukotriene Modifiers as Potential Therapeutics for Cardiovascular Disease." *Nature* 4(8) (2005): 664–72.

Harris, W. S., et al. "The Omega-3 Index: A New Predictor for Cardiac Mortality?" *ISSFAL Newsletter* (International Society for the Study of Fatty Acids and Lipids) 11(2) (2004): 6–11.

Kang, J. X., et al. "Prevention of Fatal Cardiac Arrhythmias by Polyunsaturated Fatty Acids." *American Journal of Clinical Nutrition* 71 (supp.) (2000): 202S–207S.

Kark, J. D., et al. "Adipose Tissue n-6 Fatty Acids and Acute Myocardial Infarction in a Population Consuming a Diet High in Polyunsaturated Fatty Acids." *American Journal of Clinical Nutrition* 77 (2003): 796–802.

Kris-Etherton, P. M., et al. "Omega-3 Fatty Acids and Cardiovascular Disease: New Recommendations from the American Heart Association." *Arteriosclerosis, Thrombosis and Vascular Biology* 23 (2003): 151–52.

Lands, W. E. M. "Primary Prevention in Cardiovascular Disease: Moving out of the Shadows of the Truth About Death." *Nutrition, Metabolism, and Cardiovascular Diseases* 13 (2003): 154–64.

Lands, W. E. M. "Learning How Membrane Fatty Acids Affect Cardiovascular Integrity." *Journal of Membrane Biology* 206 (2005): 75–83.

Leaf, A. "On the Reanalysis of the GISSI-Prevenzione." *Circulation* 105 (2002): 1874–75.

Leaf, A., et al. "Clinical Prevention of Sudden Cardiac Death by n-3 Polyunsaturated Fatty Acids and Mechanism of Prevention of Arrhythmias by n-3 Fish Oils." *Circulation* 107 (2003): 2646–52.

Leaf, A., et al. "Prevention of Fatal Arrhythmias in High-Risk Subjects by Fish Oil n-3 Fatty Acid Intake." *Circulation* 112 (2005): 2762–68.

Mozaffarian, D., et al. "Effect of Fish Oil on Heart Rate in Humans: A Meta-Analysis of Randomized Controlled Trials." *Circulation* 112 (2005): 1945–52.

Nestel, P., et al. "The n-3 Fatty Acids Eicosapentaenoic Acid and Docosahexaenoic Acid Increase Systemic Arterial Compliance in Humans." *American Journal of Clinical Nutrition* 76 (2002): 326–30.

Okuyama, H., ed. "Prevention of Coronary Heart Disease from the Cholesterol Hypothesis to Omega-6/Omega-3 Balance." *World Review of Nutrition and Dietetics* 96 (2007): 1–168.

Sudhir, K. "Clinical Review: Lipoprotein-Associated Phospholipase A2, a Novel Inflammatory Biomarker and Independent Risk Predictor for Cardiovascular Disease." *Journal of Clinical Epidemiology and Metabolism* 90(5) (2005): 3100–5.

Tedgui, A., and Z. Mallat. "Cytokines in Atherosclerosis: Pathogenic and Regulatory Pathways." *Physiological Reviews* 86 (2006): 515–81.

Yang, E. H., et al. "Lipoprotein-Associated Phospholipase A2 Is an Independent Marker for Coronary Endothelial Dysfunction in Humans." *Arteriosclerosis, Thrombosis, and Vascular Biology* 26 (2006): 106–11.

Chapter 6, The Developing Brain

Agostoni, C., et al. "DHA in Pregnancy Benefits Child Development." *Pediatric Research* 54 (2003): 292–93.

American Academy of Pediatrics. "Policy Statement: Breastfeeding and the Use of Human Milk." *Pediatrics* 115(2) (2005): 496–506.

Auestad, N., et al. "Visual, Cognitive, and Language Assessments at 39 Months: A Follow-Up Study of Children Fed Formulas Containing Long-Chain Polyunsaturated Fatty Acids to 1 Year of Age." *Pediatrics* 112(3) (2003): e177–e183.

Birch, E. E., et al. "Visual Maturation of Term Infants Fed Long-Chain Polyunsaturated Fatty Acid–Supplemented or Control Formula for 12 Months." *American Journal of Clinical Nutrition* 81 (2005): 871–79.

Bouwstra, H., et al. "Long-Chain Polyunsaturated Fatty Acids Have a Positive Effect on the Quality of General Movements of Healthy Term Infants." *American Journal of Clinical Nutrition* 78 (2003): 313–18.

Cheruku, S. R., et al. "Higher Maternal Plasma Docosahexaenoic Acid During Pregnancy Is Associated with More Mature Neonatal Sleep-State Patterning." *American Journal of Clinical Nutrition* 76(3) (2002): 608–13.

Decsi, T., et al. "N-3 Fatty Acids and Pregnancy Outcomes." *Current Opinion in Clinical Nutrition and Metabolic Care* 8 (2005): 161–66.

Forsyth, J. S., et al. "Long Chain Polyunsaturated Fatty Acid Supplementation in Infant Formula and Blood Pressure in Later Childhood: Follow Up of a Randomized Controlled Trial." *British Medical Journal* 326 (2003): 953–57.

Francois, C. A. "Supplementing Lactating Women with Flaxseed Oil Does Not Increase Docosahexaenoic Acid in Their Milk." *American Journal of Clinical Nutrition* 77(1) (2003): 226–33.

Helland, I. B., et al. "Maternal Supplementation with Very-Long-Chain n-3 Fatty Acids During Pregnancy and Lactation Augments Children's IQ at 4 Years of Age." *Pediatrics* 111 (2003): e39–e44.

Innis, S. M. "Perinatal Biochemistry and Physiology of Long-Chain Polyunsaturated Fatty Acids." *Journal of Pediatrics* 143 (2003): S1–S8.

Kitajka, K., et al. "Effects of Dietary Omega-3 Polyunsaturated Fatty Acids on Brain Gene Expression." *Proceedings of the National Academy of Sciences* 101 (2004): 10931–36.

Larque, E., et al. "Perinatal Supply and Metabolism of Long-Chain Polyunsaturated Fatty Acids: Importance for the Early Development of the Nervous System." *Annals of the New York Academy of Sciences* 967 (2002): 299–310.

Olsen, S. F., et al. "Low Consumption of Seafood in Early Pregnancy as a Risk Factor for Preterm Delivery: Prospective Cohort Study." *British Medical Journal* 324 (2002): 1–5.

Stene, L. C., et al. "Use of Cod Liver Oil During the First Year of Life Is Associated with Lower Risk of Childhood-Onset Type 1 Diabetes: A Large, Population-Based, Case-Control Study." *American Journal of Clinical Nutrition* 78 (2003): 1128–34.

Weisinger, H. S., et al. "Perinatal Omega-3 Fatty Acid Deficiency Affects Blood Pressure Later in Life." *Nature Medicine* 7(3) (2001): 258–59.

Chapter 7, Why It's Good to Have a Fat Head

Adams, P. B., et al. "Arachidonic Acid to Eicosapentaenoic Acid Ratio in Blood Correlates Positively with Clinical Symptoms of Depression." *Lipids* 31 (1996): S157–S161.

Bazinet, R. P., et al. "Valproic Acid Selectively Inhibits Conversion of Arachidonic Acid to Arachidonoyl-CoA by Brain Microsomal Long-Chain Fatty Acyl-CoA Synthetases: Relevance to Bipolar Disorder." *Psychopharmacology* 184 (2006): 122–29.

Das, U. N. "Can Perinatal Supplementation of Long-Chain Polyunsaturated Fatty Acids Prevent Schizophrenia in Adult Life?" *Medical Science Monitor* 10(12) (2004): HY33–37.

Freeman, et al. "Omega-3 Fatty Acids: Evidence Basis for Treatment and Future Research in Psychiatry." *Journal of Clinical Psychiatry* 67 (2006): 1954–67.

Hakkarainen, R., et al. "Is Low Dietary Intake of Omega-3 Fatty Acids Associated with Depression?" *American Journal of Psychiatry* 161 (2004): 567–69.

Hallahan, B., et al. "Essential Fatty Acids and Mental Health." *British Journal of Psychiatry* 186 (2005): 275–77.

Hibbeln, J. R. "Fish Consumption and Major Depression." *Lancet* 351 (9,110) (1998): 1213.

Logan, A. C. "Omega-3 Fatty Acids and Major Depression: A Primer for the Mental Health Professional." *Lipids in Health and Disease* 3 (2004): 25.

McIntosh, A., et al. "Cross-National Differences in Diet, the Outcome of Schizophrenia and the Prevalence of Depression: You Are (Associated with) What You Eat." *British Journal of Psychiatry* 184 (2004): 381–82.

Naliwaiko, K., et al. "Effects of Fish Oil on the Central Nervous System: A New Potential Antidepressant?" *Nutritional Neuroscience* 7(2) (2004): 91–99.

Nemets, H., et al. "Omega-3 Treatment of Childhood Depression: A Controlled, Double-Blind Pilot Study." *American Journal of Psychiatry* 163(6) (2006): 1098–1100.

Noaghiul, S., et al. "Cross-National Comparisons of Seafood Consumption and Rates of Bipolar Disorders." *American Journal of Psychiatry* 160 (2003): 2222–27.

Peet, M. "A Dose-Ranging Study of the Effects of Ethyl-Eicosapentaenoate in Patients with Ongoing Depression Despite Apparently Adequate Treatment with Standard Drugs." *Archives of General Psychiatry* 59 (2002): 913–19.

Rapoport, S. I., et al. "Do Lithium and Anticonvulsants Target the Brain Arachidonic Acid Cascade in Bipolar Disorder?" *Archives of General Psychiatry* 59 (2002): 592–96.

Silvers, K. M., et al. "Randomised Double-Blind Placebo-Controlled Trial of Fish Oil in the Treatment of Depression." *Prostaglandins, Leukotrienes and Essential Fatty Acids* 72 (2005): 211–18.

Stoll, A. L., et al. "Omega-3 Fatty Acids in Bipolar Disorder." *Archives of General Psychiatry* 56 (1999): 407–12.

Zanarini, M. C., et al. "Omega-3 Fatty Acid Treatment of Women with Borderline Personality Disorder: A Double-Blind, Placebo-Controlled Pilot Study." *American Journal of Psychiatry* 160 (2003): 167–69.

Chapter 8, The Ultimate Chill Pill

Burgess, J. R., et al. "Long-Chain Polyunsaturated Fatty Acids in Children with Attention-Deficit Hyperactivity Disorder." *American Journal of Clinical Nutrition* 71 (supp.) (2000): 327S–330S.

Hallahan, B., et al. "Essential Fatty Acids and Their Role in the Treatment of Impulsivity Disorders." *Prostaglandins, Leukotrienes and Essential Fatty Acids* 71 (2004): 211–16.

Hamazaki, K., et al. "Effect of ω-3 Fatty Acid-Containing Phospholipids on Blood Catecholamine Concentrations in Healthy Volunteers: A Randomized, Placebo-Controlled, Double-Blind Trial." *Nutrition* 21 (2005): 705–10.

Hamazaki, T., et al. "The Effect of Docosahexaenoic Acid on Aggression in Young Adults." *Journal of Clinical Investigation* 97(4) (1996): 1129–34.

Hamazaki, T., et al. "Letter: The Effect of Docosahexaenoic Acid–Containing Food Administration on Symptoms of Attention-Deficit/Hyperactivity Disorder: A Placebo-Controlled Double-Blind Study." *European Journal of Clinical Nutrition* 58 (2004): 838.

Hirayama, S., et al. "Effect of Docosahexaenoic Acid–Containing Food Administration on Symptoms of Attention-Deficit/Hyperactivity Disorder: A Placebo-Controlled Double-Blind Study." *European Journal of Clinical Nutrition* 58 (2004): 467–73.

Iribarren, I., et al. "Dietary Intake of n-3, n-6 Fatty Acids and Fish: Relationship with Hostility in Young Adults—the CARDIA Study." *European Journal of Clinical Nutrition* 58 (2004): 24–31.

Itomura, M., et al. "The Effect of Fish Oil on Physical Aggression in Schoolchildren: A Randomized, Double-Blind, Placebo-Controlled Trial." *Journal of Nutritional Biochemistry* 16 (2005): 163–71.

Johnson, S. M., et al. "Evidence That Eicosapentaenoic Acid Is Effective in Treating Autism." *Journal of Clinical Psychiatry* 64(7) (2003): 848–49.

MacLean, C. H., et al. "Effects of Omega-3 Fatty Acids on Cognitive Function with Aging, Dementia, and Neurological Diseases." Evidence Report/Technology Assessment No. 114 (prepared by the Southern California Evidence-Based Practice Center, under Contract No. 290-02-0003), AHRQ Publication No. 05-E011-2. Rockville, MD: Agency for Healthcare Research and Quality, February 2005.

Richardson, A. J., et al. "Fatty Acid Deficiency Signs Predict the Severity of Reading and Related Difficulties in Dyslexic Children." *Prostaglandins, Leukotrienes and Essential Fatty Acids* 63(1/2) (2000): 69–74.

Richardson, A. J., et al. "A Randomized Double-Blind, Placebo-Controlled Study of the Effects of Supplementation with Highly Unsaturated Fatty Acids on ADHD-Related Symptoms in Children with Specific Learning Difficulties." *Progress in Neuro-Psychopharmacology and Biological Psychiatry* 26 (2002): 233–39.

Richardson, A. J., et al. "Clinical Trials of Fatty Acid Treatment in ADHD, Dyslexia, Dyspraxia and the Autistic Spectrum." *Prostaglandins, Leukotrienes and Essential Fatty Acids* 70 (2004): 383–90.

Richardson, A. J., et al. "The Oxford-Durham Study: A Randomized, Controlled Trial of Dietary Supplementation with Fatty Acids in Children with Developmental Coordination Disorder." *Pediatrics* 115 (2005): 1360–66.

Solfrizzi, V., et al. "Dietary Fatty Acids Intake: Possible Role in Cognitive Decline and Dementia." *Experimental Gerontology* 40 (2005): 257–70.

Song, C., et al. "Effects of Dietary n-3 or n-6 Fatty Acids on Interleukin-1B-Induced Anxiety, Stress, and Inflammatory Responses in Rats." *Journal of Lipid Research* 44 (2003): 1984–91.

Takeuchi, T., et al. "Possible Regulatory Mechanism of DHA-Induced Anti-Stress Reaction in Rats." *Brain Research* 964 (2003): 136–43.

Yehuda, S., et al. "The Role of Polyunsaturated Fatty Acids in Restoring the Aging Neuronal Membrane." *Neurobiology of Aging* 23 (2002): 843–53.

Young, G. S., et al. "Blood Phospholipid Fatty Acid Analysis of Adults with and Without Attention Deficit/Hyperactivity Disorder." *Lipids* 39 (2004): 117–23.

Zimmer, L., et al. "The Dopamine Mesocorticolimbic Pathway Is Affected by Deficiency in n-3 Polyunsaturated Fatty Acids." *American Journal of Clinical Nutrition* 75 (2002): 662–67.

Chapter 9, On the Horizon

Ailhaud, G., et al. "Temporal Changes in Dietary Fats: Role of *n*-6 Polyunsaturated Fatty Acids in Excessive Adipose Tissue Development and Relationship to Obesity." *Progress in Lipid Research* (2006) [Epub ahead of print].

Berson, E. L., et al. "Further Evaluation of Docosahexaenoic Acid in Patients with Retinitis Pigmentosa Receiving Vitamin A Treatment: Subgroup Analyses." *Archives of Ophthalmology* 122 (2004): 1306–14.

Bougnoux, P., et al. "Diet, Cancer, and the Lipidome." *Cancer Epidemiology, Biomarkers and Prevention* 15(3) (2006): 416–21.

Cordain, L. "Implications for the Role of Diet in Acne." *Seminars in Cutaneous Medicine and Surgery* 24 (2005): 84–91.

Cordain, L., et al. "Acne Vulgaris: A Disease of Western Civilization." *Archives of Dermatology* 138 (2002): 1584–90.

Couer, C., et al. "Effect of Dietary Fish Oil on Body Fat Mass and Basal Fat Oxidation in Healthy Adults." *International Journal of Obesity* 21 (1997): 637–43.

Ebbesson, S. O., et al. "Diabetes Is Related to Fatty Acid Metabolism Imbalance in Eskimos." *International Journal of Circumpolar Health* 58(2) (1999): 108–19.

Ebbesson, S. O., et al. "A Successful Diabetes Prevention Study in Eskimos: The Alaska Siberia Project." *International Journal of Circumpolar Health* 64(4) (2005): 409–24.

French, L. "Dysmenorrhea." *American Family Physician* 71(2) (2005): 285–92.

Haag, M., et al. "Dietary Fats, Fatty Acids and Insulin Resistance: Short Review of a Multifaceted Connection." *Medical Science Monitor* 11(12) (2005): RA359–367.

Hardman, W. E. "Omega-3 Fatty Acids to Augment Cancer Therapy." *Journal of Nutrition* 132 (2002): 3508S–3512S.

Harel, Z., et al. "Supplementation with Omega-3 Polyunsaturated Fatty Acids in the Management of Dysmenorrhea in Adolescents." *American Journal of Obstetrics and Gynecology* 174 (1996): 1335–38.

Larsson, S. C., et al. "Dietary Long-Chain n-3 Fatty Acids for the Prevention of Cancer: A Review of Potential Mechanisms." *American Journal of Clinical Nutrition* 79 (2004): 935–45.

Lu, M., et al. "Prospective Study of Dietary Fat and Risk of Cataract Extraction Among U.S. Women." *American Journal of Epidemiology* 161(10) (2005): 948–59.

Massiera, F., et al. "Arachidonic Acid and Prostacyclin Signaling Promote Adipose Tissue Development: A Human Health Concern?" *Journal of Lipid Research* 44 (2003): 271–79.

Nettleton, J. A., et al. "N-3 Long-Chain Polyunsaturated Fatty Acids in Type 2 Diabetes: A Review." *Journal of the American Dietetic Association* 105 (2005): 428–40.

"Nutrition Recommendations and Interventions for Diabetes: A Position Statement of the American Diabetes Association." *Diabetes Care* 30 (2007): S48–S65.

Pellizzon, M., et al. "Effects of Dietary Fatty Acids and Exercise on Body-Weight Regulation and Metabolism in Rats." *Obesity Research* 10(9) (2002): 947–55.

Ruzickova, J., et al. "Omega-3 PUFA of Marine Origin Limit Diet-Induced Obesity in Mice by Reducing Cellularity of Adipose Tissue." *Lipids* 39(12) (2004): 1177–85.

Seddon, J. M., et al. "Dietary Fat and Risk for Advanced Age-Related Macular Degeneration." *Archives of Ophthalmology* 119 (2001): 1191–99.

Chapter 10, Get Enough Short-Chain Omega-3 Fats

James, M. J., et al. "Metabolism of Stearidonic Acid in Human Subjects: Comparison with the Metabolism of Other n-3 Fatty Acids." *American Journal of Clinical Nutrition* 77 (2003): 1140–45.

Okuyama, H., et al. "Dietary Fatty Acids—the n-6/n-3 Balance and Chronic Elderly Diseases, Excess Linoleic Acid and Relative n-3 Deficiency Syndrome See in Japan." *Progress in Lipid Research* 35(4) (1997): 409–57.

Parker, T. D., et al. "Fatty Acid Composition and Oxidative Stability of Cold-Pressed Edible Seed Oils." *Journal of Food Science* 68(4) (2003): 1240–43.

Parry, J., et al. "Fatty Acid Composition and Antioxidant Properties of Cold-Pressed Marionberry, Boysenberry, Red Raspberry, and Blueberry Seed Oils." *Journal of Agricultural and Food Chemistry* 53 (2005): 566–73.

Parry, J., et al. "Fatty Acid Content and Antioxidant Properties of Cold-Pressed Black Raspberry Seed Oil and Meal." *Journal of Food Science* 69(3) (2004): 189–93.

Simpopoulos, A. P. "Omega-3 Fatty Acids and Antioxidants in Edible Wild Plants." *Biological Research* 37(2) (2004): 263–77.

USDA Nutrient Database. http://www.nal.usda.gov/fnic/foodcomp/search.

Chapter 11, Get Enough Long-Chain Omega-3 Fats

Crawford, M. A., et al. "Polyunsaturated Fatty Acids in Free-Living and Domesticated Animals." *Biochemical Society Transactions* 8(3) (1980): 294.

Food and Drug Administration (FDA). "FDA Announces Qualified Health Claims for Omega-3 Fatty Acids." News release, September 8, 2004.

Food and Drug Administration (FDA). 2004N-0217: Nutrient Content Claims: DHA, EPA, and ALA (omega-3 fatty acids). Dockets Management pages of FDA website, http://www.fda.gov/ohrms/dockets/dockets/04n0217/04n0217.htm (last updated January 3, 2005).

Food and Drug Administration (FDA). 2005P-0189: Nutrient Content Claims: ALA and DHA Omega-3 Fatty Acids. Dockets Management pages of the FDA website: http://www.fda.gov/ohrms/dockets/dockets/05p0189/05p0189.htm (last updated May 23, 2005).

Food and Drug Administration (FDA), Center for Food Safety and Applied Nutrition. Letter Responding to Health Claim Petition Dated November 3, 2003 (Martek petition): Omega-3 fatty acids and reduced risk of coronary heart disease (Docket No. 2003Q-0401), http://www.cfsan.fda.gov/~dms/ds-ltr37.html (September 8, 2004).

Food and Drug Administration (FDA), Center for Food Safety and Applied Nutrition. Letter Responding to Health Claim Petition Dated June 23, 2003 (Wellness petition): Omega-3 Fatty Acids and Reduced Risk of Coronary Heart Disease (Docket No. 2003Q-0401), http://www.cfsan.fda.gov/~dms/ds-ltr38.html (September 8, 2004).

Foran, J. A., et al. "Quantitative Analysis of the Benefits and Risks of Consuming Farmed and Wild Salmon." *Journal of Nutrition* 135 (2005): 2639–43.

Foran, J. A., et al. "Risk-Based Consumption Advice for Farmed Atlantic and Wild Pacific Salmon Contaminated with Dioxins and Dioxin-Like Compounds." *Environmental Health Perspectives* 113(5) (2005): 552–55.

Gochfield, M., et al. "Good Fish/Bad Fish: A Composite Benefit-Risk by Dose Curve." *Neurotoxicology* 26 (2005): 511–20.

Hamilton, M. C., et al. "Lipid Composition and Contaminants in Farmed and Wild Salmon." *Environmental Science and Technology* 39(22) (2005): 8622–29.

Hites, R. A., et al. "Global Assessment of Organic Contaminants in Farmed Salmon." *Science* 303 (2004): 226–29.

Salem, N. Jr., et al. "Alpha-Linolenic Conversion Revisited." *PUFA Newsletter* 7(4) (2003): 3–4.

Sinclair, A. J., et al. "Influence of Grazing or Short-Term Grain Feeding on Polyunsaturated Fatty Acid Concentrations of Australian Beef." *Proceedings of the Nutrition Society of Australia* 26 (2002): S255.

Chapter 12, Consider Taking an Omega-3 Supplement

Buckley, M. S., et al. "Fish Oil Interaction with Warfarin." *Annals of Pharmacotherapy* 38 (2004): 50–53.

DeFilippis, A. P., et al. "Understanding Omega-3s." *American Heart Journal* 151 (2006): 564–70.

Environmental Defense. "Fish Oil Supplements: Is the Brand You're Taking Safe?" Eat Smart pages of Oceans Alive website, www.oceansalive.org/eat.cfm?subnav=fishoil&sort=Company.

Geppert, J., et al. "Docahexaenoic Acid Supplementation in Vegetarians Effectively Increases Omega-3 Index: A Randomized Trial." *Lipids* 8 (2005): 807–14.

Harris, W. S. "Fish Oil Supplementation: Evidence for Health Benefits." *Cleveland Clinic Journal of Medicine* 71(3) (2004): 208–18.

"Omega-3 Oil: Fish or Pills." Consumer Reports website, www.consumerreports.org:80/cro /health-fitness/drugs-supplements/fishoil-pills-703/overview/index.htm.

Chapter 13, Nix the Six

Adam, O., et al. "Anti-Inflammatory Effects of a Low Arachidonic Acid Diet and Fish Oil in Patients with Rheumatoid Arthritis." *Rheumatology International* 23 (2003): 27–36.

Berry, E. M. "Who's Afraid of n-6 Polyunsaturated Fatty Acids? Methodological Considerations for Assessing Whether They Are Harmful." *Nutrition, Metabolism and Cardiovascular Diseases* 11 (2001): 181–88.

Cleland, L. G., et al. "Linoleate Inhibits EPA Incorporation from Dietary Fish-Oil Supplements in Human Subjects." *American Journal of Clinical Nutrition* 55 (1992): 395–99.

Cunnane, S. C. "Problems with Essential Fatty Acids: Time for a New Paradigm?" *Progress in Lipid Research* 42 (2003): 544–68.

De Lorgeril, M., et al. "Dietary Prevention of Coronary Heart Disease: The Lyon Diet Heart Study and After." *World Review of Nutrition and Dietetics* 95 (2005): 103–14.

Dubnov, G., et al. "Omega-6 Fatty Acids and Coronary Artery Disease: The Pros and Cons." *Current Atherosclerosis Reports* 6 (2004): 441–46.

Hamazaki, T., et al. "The Japan Society for Lipid Nutrition Recommends to Reduce the Intake of Linoleic Acid: A Review and Critique of the Scientific Evidence." *World Review of Nutrition and Dietetics* 92 (2003): 109–32.

Komprda, T., et al. "Arachidonic Acid and Long-Chain n-3 Polyunsaturated Fatty Acid Contents in Meat of Selected Poultry and Fish Species in Relation to Dietary Fat Sources." *Journal of Agricultural and Food Chemistry* 53 (2005): 6804–12.

Meyer, B. J., et al. "Dietary Intakes and Food Sources of Omega-6 and Omega-3 Polyunsaturated Fatty Acids." *Lipids* 38(4) (2003): 391–98.

Taber, L., et al. "Assessment of the Arachidonic Acid Content in Foods Commonly Consumed in the American Diet." *Lipids* 33(12) (1998): 1151–57.

Index

Entries in italics refer to recipes. Page numbers followed by f or t refer to figures or tables respectively.